Forensic Medical Investigation of Motor Vehicle Incidents

Forensic Medical Investigation of Motor Vehicle Incidents

Michael P. Burke

Taylor & Francis
Taylor & Francis Group
Boca Raton   London   New York

CRC is an imprint of the Taylor & Francis Group,
an informa business

CRC Press
Taylor & Francis Group
6000 Broken Sound Parkway NW, Suite 300
Boca Raton, FL 33487-2742

© 2007 by Taylor & Francis Group, LLC
CRC Press is an imprint of Taylor & Francis Group, an Informa business

No claim to original U.S. Government works
Printed in the United States of America on acid-free paper
10 9 8 7 6 5 4 3 2 1

International Standard Book Number-10: 0-8493-7859-1 (Hardcover)
International Standard Book Number-13: 978-0-8493-7859-1 (Hardcover)

This book contains information obtained from authentic and highly regarded sources. Reprinted material is quoted with permission, and sources are indicated. A wide variety of references are listed. Reasonable efforts have been made to publish reliable data and information, but the author and the publisher cannot assume responsibility for the validity of all materials or for the consequences of their use.

Library of Congress Cataloging-in-Publication Data

Burke, Michael P.
    Forensic medical investigation of motor vehicle incidents / Michael P. Burke.
       p. cm.
    Includes bibliographical references and index.
    ISBN 0-8493-7859-1 -- ISBN 0-8493-7860-5
    1. Traffic accident investigation. 2. Medical jurisprudence. I. Title.

HV8079.55.B87 2006
614'.1--dc22
                                       2006048507

Visit the Taylor & Francis Web site at
http://www.taylorandfrancis.com

and the CRC Press Web site at
http://www.crcpress.com

Table of Contents

5 Injuries Sustained by Motor Vehicle Occupants 61

Preface

The most favorable outcome of any forensic case is best served by open discussion between the forensic pathologist, investigating police officers, and other relevant members of the investigation.

In ideal circumstances, in which the pathologist's routine work load permits attendance at the scene of a motor vehicle incident coupled with expert examination of a motor vehicle's exterior and interior damage, a more reasoned analysis of a crash victim's injuries can be made. When conditions dictate that the pathologist cannot attend the scene, the investigators (and courts) will still usually derive sufficient information from the postmortem report, providing accurate documentation of injuries has been performed and important concerns regarding the case have been communicated by the investigating team.

The autopsy examination of a victim of a motor vehicle incident needs to address a number of issues that may be of interest to a variety of different groups. A fundamental purpose of the postmortem examination is to provide a reasonable cause of death. A further important function of the pathologist is to detail the extent of internal injury in those who initially survive the trauma arising from the vehicle impact to allow objective audit for those involved in trauma care. Other interested parties may include researchers and engineers who wish to correlate impact points to motor vehicles and the associated injuries to occupants and pedestrians.

This book is written as a preliminary resource for those interested in the investigation of motor vehicle incidents and it is hoped the reader is stimulated to further study and productive associations with his or her colleagues in related fields of study.

Acknowledgments

The author wishes to acknowledge the Victorian Institute of Forensic Medicine, the Major Collision Investigation Group of the Victoria Police Force, Mary Reddan, Kerry Johannes, Caroline Rosenberg, and BMW Australia.

Author

Michael Philip Burke is a senior pathologist at the Victorian Institute of Forensic Medicine, Victoria, Australia. He completed a bachelor of science in 1980 and bachelor of medicine and surgery in 1984. He obtained the postgraduate qualification of Fellow of the Royal College of Pathologists of Australasia by examination in anatomic pathology in 1993 and completed a diploma in forensic pathology of the Royal College of Pathologists of Australasia in 1994.

He was a member of the multidisciplinary team in the forensic investigation of a mass murder committed at the Port Arthur penal colony site, Tasmania, Australia, in 1996.

In 1999, he was part of the British Forensic Investigating Team in Kosovo. Over the past decade, he has developed an interest in the problems associated with the postmortem interpretation of injuries sustained in motor vehicle incidents.

Dr. Burke has published articles in the *American Journal of Forensic Medicine and Pathology, Journal of Clinical Neuroscience, Emergency Medicine, Australian and New Zealand Journal of Medicine, Medicine, Science and the Law, Epilepsia,* and *Pathology.*

Motor Vehicle Design and Causation of Injuries

1

Overview

Motor vehicle collisions are the major cause of death in the 15- to 30-year age group, the major cause of injury leading to death in the 5- to 15-year age group, and the source of enormous financial and social cost to the community as a whole.

In developed countries, a large proportion of deaths arising from motor vehicle incidents occur on roads with higher speed limits (i.e., faster than 100 km/hr). On Australian roads, approximately 32% of deaths occur in 100 km/hr zones, 12% occur in 110 km/hr zones, and 21% happen in 60 km/hr zones. Most crashes involving loss of life occur during daytime (56.9%) and the great majority of crashes occur in fine weather (72.3%).[1]

For any given collision, it has been shown that the size of the motor vehicles involved is a significant factor in the outcome of a crash. Occupants of a larger vehicle by size and mass have a more favourable outcome than those in a smaller vehicle.[2] This "vehicle mismatch" is of particular concern in side impact collisions.

Collisions between traditional passenger vehicles and four-wheel drive (4WD) and sports utility vehicles (SUV) lead to more significant injuries to the occupants of the passenger vehicle.[3]

The increase in injury also occurs when the passenger vehicle has a larger mass than the 4WD vehicle.[4] The relative and absolute numbers of 4WD vehicles and SUVs on the roads are increasing and the "aggressive" nature of these vehicles in crashes is an important issue for research into vehicle safety design.

It has been estimated that sitting in the rear seat of a passenger vehicle may reduce the risk of death in a motor vehicle collision by approximately 39% and reduce the risk of serious injury by a similar amount.[5] An earlier study by Brown showed that injured motor vehicle occupants presenting to a hospital emergency department also showed the protective effect of rear seat occupancy.[6]

Introduction

Modern motor vehicles have numerous safety features for drivers and passengers including seat belts with pretensioners, front, side and curtain airbags, collapsible steering columns and pedals, and frontal crush zones.

The dashboard fascia has a moulded, curved configuration with padding to cushion impact from the knees and lower legs. The dashboard padding must be of sufficient thickness and compressibility to cushion impact to the knees in a frontal collision, yet firm enough to prevent forceful contact of the knee into underlying hard materials. The most efficient type and thickness of interior padding has utilised information derived from research on the biomechanics of injury causation.[7] It has been shown from computer simulation that increasing the thickness of the roof side rail padding to 5 cm reduced the peak acceleration to the head during a motor vehicle collision, with a subsequent 85% reduction in the head injury score.[8]

Research in exterior vehicle designs progresses for strategies to minimise fatalities and long-term physical effects to pedestrians injured in crashes.

Important motor vehicle design features discussed in this chapter include:

- Crashworthiness
- Seat belts
- Airbags
- Antilock braking systems
- Electronic stability control
- Event data recorders
- Pedestrian friendly motor vehicles
- Intelligent vehicle systems
- Improvements in lighting

Crashworthiness

Crashworthiness is the measure of how well a vehicle provides protection to its occupants during a collision. An analysis of British data between 1980 and 1998 on improvements in the crashworthiness of motor vehicles has estimated a reduction in the number of drivers killed or seriously injured to be at least 19.7%.[9] Government-regulated tests and a number of private organisations provide objective measures of a vehicle's performance in a number of simulated crash tests. Typically frontal, offset frontal, side impact, rear impact, and rollover tests are employed in various combinations.

The vehicle must impart sufficient stiffness in the body shell to prevent cabin intrusion yet provide frontal crush zones to dissipate kinetic energy and decrease the risk of deceleration injury (Figure 1.1). Deforming elements in the front and rear of modern vehicles include engine support arms, radiator assemblies and longitudinal support arms (Figure 1.2). Cross-bars in the front of a vehicle allow some energy to be absorbed by the "nonaffected" side in an offset frontal collision.

Protection in side impact collisions is afforded by a rigid passenger cell with cross-bars, side impact protectors, and structural designs to absorb energy to the frame and offside of the vehicle. Steering columns and foot pedals are engineered to collapse away from the driver to reduce the probability of significant direct blunt force injury to the chest and feet/ankles.

Vehicles such as trucks, vans, 4WD, and SUV, which have a relatively high center of gravity, have a higher incidence of rollover events. In these vehicles, it is important for manufacturers to address excessive roof crush if identified in controlled rollover tests or real life situations.

Figure 1.1 Frontal crash test showing frontal "crush" zones. (Photo courtesy of BMW.)

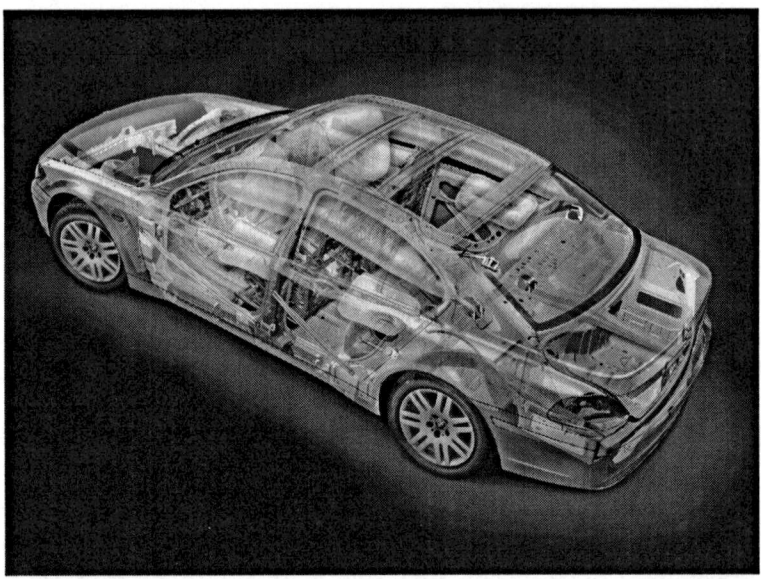

Figure 1.2 Longitudinal and transverse components of body shell. (Drawing courtesy of BMW.)

Figure 1.3 Frontal collision of passenger sedan and four-wheel drive vehicle showing override.

SUVs are an increasingly popular choice of vehicle for motorists. Collisions involving SUVs and conventional passenger cars tend to lead to proportionally greater injuries the occupants of the conventional vehicle. In a frontal collision, the SUV may override the bumper and hood of the passenger vehicle, causing intrusion of the steering column and dashboard in the passenger car. If override occurs, the relatively stiff nature of the SUV front end can lead to marked floor pan intrusion into a conventional vehicle (Figure 1.3). In side impact collisions, some SUVs may override the passenger car door, resulting in significant cabin intrusion.

Seat Belts

The legislative requirement to wear seat belts resulted in a marked decline in the incidence of injury and death associated with motor vehicle collisions in the State of Victoria, Australia. Seat belt use led to reduced deaths from head injury, chest injury, and the effects of rapid deceleration. Seat belts are designed principally for frontal crashes and the protective effect is primarily for these types of collisions. Wearing a seat belt also reduces the incidence of occupant ejection. The use of seat belts has not resulted in a similar reduction in injuries for nearside side impact motor vehicle occupants in which head injury is caused by impact with the adjacent cabin interior and vehicle intrusion.

More recent developments in seat belt design include pretensioners and energy management systems (Figure 1.4). Seat belt pretensioners virtually instantaneously retract excess slack in the seat belt, resulting in better approximation between the occupant and the seat and hence improving the individual's deceleration profile during the collision. The better approximation between the occupant and seat also minimises "out of position" events in which injuries from airbag deployment are more likely to arise. The closer fit between the occupant and seat also decreases the probability of submarining injuries.

Figure 1.4 Seat belt assembly with pretensioner. (Drawing courtesy of BMW.)

Energy management systems are features that allow seat belts to yield during a collision to decrease the forces that are concentrated on the chest by the seat belt. The most common types of energy management systems are load limiters, which are typically present within the seat belt retractor.

Other features include "tear stitching" in the belt webbing, which allows the belt to gradually stretch during a crash. Walz has reported significant reductions in head injury criteria scores and chest acceleration and deflection in anthropomorphic dummies in frontal collisions in vehicles fitted with seatbelt pretensioners.[10] Energy management systems led to significant decreases in chest acceleration and deflection. While further research is warranted to confirm these findings, it would seem reasonable to suggest that seat belt pretensioners and load limiters will provide further protection to occupants in crashes.

Pediatric restraint systems have been demonstrated to protect babies and infants, toddlers, and children. Baby capsules and forward-facing child restraint systems are highly effective in preventing serious injury and death in motor vehicle collisions. A recent study showed a 78% reduction in serious injury for children in forward-facing child restraint systems compared with seat belts.[11]

Airbags

Introduction

The introduction of frontal airbags in otherwise unrestrained vehicle occupants resulted in a reduction in the incidence of injury and deaths in frontal impacts. The National Highway Traffic Safety Administration, a division of the U.S. Department of Transportation, reported that the risk of fatal injury to car drivers in frontal crashes was reduced by 31% through the use of airbags alone. The protective effect that frontal airbags give to front seat occupants when used alone is considerably less than the protection afforded to occupants who also use a seat belt. Airbags should be viewed as a supplementary restraint system. Side airbags have been shown to decrease the incidence of significant head and chest injury in side impact collisions.

The airbag was introduced as a passive safety restraint system requiring no active input from the vehicle occupants. In countries with a low rate of seat belt use, the driver and passenger frontal airbags in a frontal collision provide significant protection from impact with the steering wheel assembly, dashboard, windshield, and surrounds.

Airbag deployment must occur rapidly as most vehicle collisions are over in about 100 msec.

The impact force of the expelled plastic module cover and expanding airbag, and physicochemical effects of the chemicals and gases produced in the deployment have been shown to cause injuries to vehicle occupants. Most injuries are relatively minor abrasions and bruises. Fractures of the face and extremities are well described. Upper limb fractures to children are common when in close proximity to the airbag when it is deployed.[12]

Airbag deployment may also cause lethal injury. The great majority of these cases involve children and adults of small stature who are "out of position" (i.e., not in a normal driving position relative to the airbag when deployment occurs). Risk reduction is attained by keeping children younger than 12 years of age in the rear seat of a motor vehicle, or, if circumstances are such that they must travel in the front passenger seat, by pushing the seat back as far as possible and correctly fastening the seatbelt. Small adults should also push the seat back at least 10 in from the module cover. In some jurisdictions on/off switches can be installed to deactivate the airbag.

Design

The driver airbag is located within the steering wheel hub and the front passenger airbag is located above or adjacent to the glove box. Depending on the design of the particular manufacturer, the side airbag may be located in the seat, roof, or pillars (Figure 1.5).

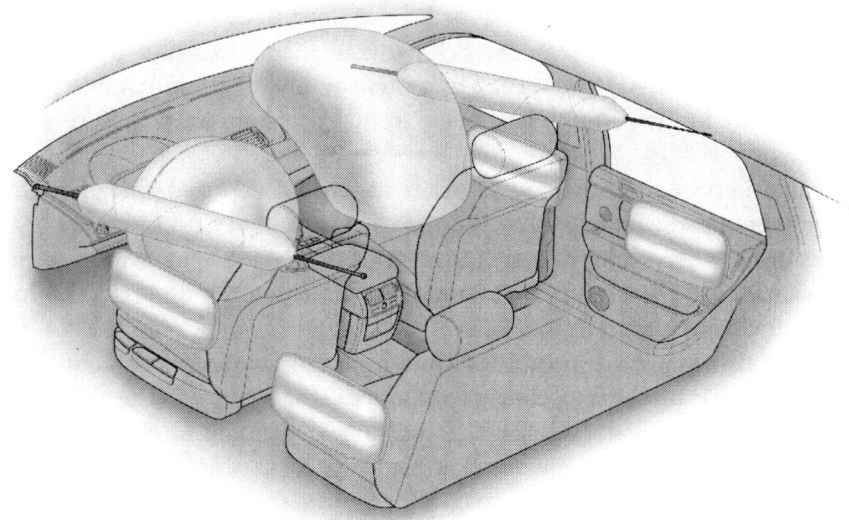

Figure 1.5 Typical driver and passenger airbag locations. (Drawing courtesy of BMW.)

The driver and front passenger front airbags are deployed after the detection of an impact by sensors usually present in the front bumper and engine bay. The change in velocity (delta V) required for deployment is usually of the order of 15 to 20 km/hr, but may be increased if the system allows detection of the occupant wearing a seat belt.

When the control module detects a deployment signal, a charge ignites the sodium azide propellant within the airbag. The subsequent explosion results in the rapid generation of nitrogen gas with smaller amounts of nitrogen oxide, carbon monoxide, ammonia, and numerous hydrocarbon compounds, which rapidly inflate the nylon fabric airbag.[13] The airbag accelerates from 225 to 325 km/hr in 25 to 30 msec. The airbag rapidly deflates by gas escaping through vents.

Early generation airbags utilised a large amount of energy in deployment. A serious consequence of this energy was airbag-related injury and deaths. The introduction of depowered airbags led to a reduction in airbag deployment injury. Depowered airbags had less vigorous inflation characteristics and used an increased number and size of vents to allow escape of gases. Further improvements in design led to dual-stage, multistage, and variable output airbags. Dual and multistage airbags utilise inflators that fire in steps to alter the inflation, depending on the severity of the frontal collision. Variable output airbags can decrease the output of a single inflation. In severe frontal collisions, each type of system utilises a rapid, full-energy deployment.

Advanced frontal airbags have been introduced to some motor vehicles and will inevitably become standard equipment. Advanced frontal systems have various detectors in the seat or vehicle floor to detect the weight of an object (occupant) in the seat, seat belt use, and position sensors to determine occupant position (Figure 1.6). The system resolves how much energy the airbags should utilise for a particular frontal collision given the prevailing occupant variables.

Side impact collisions are associated with an increased risk of serious injury compared with frontal collisions. The major injury risks in side impact collisions are head injury from contact with the B-pillar, side windows, and surrounds, and chest injury from contact with the interior aspect of the door and vehicle intrusion (Figure 1.7).

Side airbags provide protection from injury by forming energy absorbing barriers between vehicle occupants and the side of the cabin. The side airbag will deploy following a side impact collision, depending on the severity of the crash, the site, and angle of the impact. Side airbags are generally smaller in size compared with frontal airbags. There are various combinations of side airbags to protect the head or thorax that deploy from seat mouldings, doors, and roof in the front and rear compartments.

Difficulties for designers and manufacturers include ergonomic considerations such as the physical size of the driver and passenger and engineering

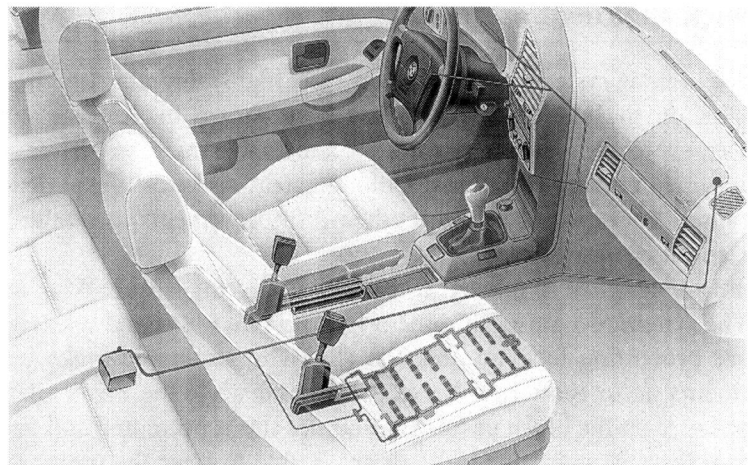

Figure 1.6 Schematic diagram of front passenger airbag with occupancy detector. (Drawing courtesy of BMW.)

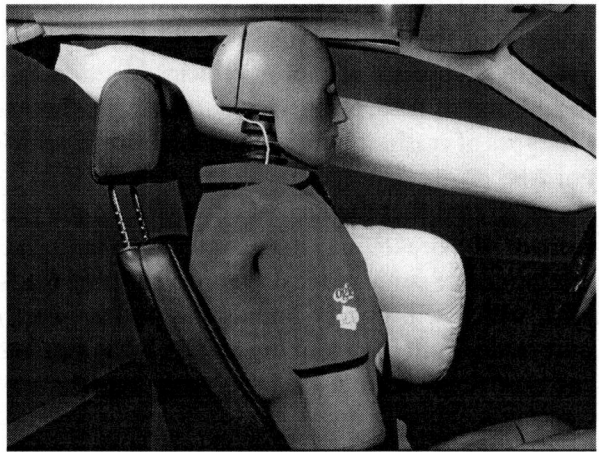

Figure 1.7 Side airbags for head and neck protection. (Drawing courtesy of BMW.)

problems such as available space for the devices and obstructing elements such as the seats and seat belts. Because of the lack of a frontal crush zone, side airbags need to deploy more rapidly than frontal airbags. Deployment must occur within approximately 4 to 8 msec of impact. Thorax side airbags take approximately 10 msec to fully inflate and curtain airbags approximately 25 msec to inflate.

Early studies have suggested a reduction in deaths of drivers with side airbags designed for head protection in driver side collisions.[14]

Antilock Braking Systems

Antilock braking systems (ABS) demonstrate highly desirable braking characteristics on the test track.[15] ABS has been shown to decrease stopping distances, especially on slippery surfaces, and enable increased driver control in emergency braking situations. Unfortunately, real-world experience has not realised the expected across-the-board improvements in crashes, morbidity, and mortality rates.[16]

ABS are designed to prevent wheel lock up during hard braking maneuvers. The system recognises imminent lock up of a wheel and releases brake pressure preventing lock up and tire slip. The automatic brake pressure adjustments occur numerous times per second while the driver maintains firm pressure on the brake pedal. Because tire slip is prevented and tire/road frictional force is maintained, the driver is able to steer the motor vehicle. The frictional force between a dry road surface and locked wheels is similar to the braking efficiency of a vehicle fitted with ABS. It is on slippery surfaces, where the coefficient of friction is very low, that ABS is clearly superior to conventional brakes in test conditions.[17]

Studies addressing the performance of ABS have examined accident and fatality rates in occupants of motor vehicles identical in every aspect except for the addition of ABS. Somewhat surprisingly, there has not been a decrease in all types of crashes, injuries, and fatalities in vehicles following the addition of ABS.

It has been suggested that the lack of education of the general driving public on the use of ABS brakes may have contributed to the lack of benefit. The braking technique of some older drivers on slippery roads is to pump the brake pedal, which will clearly impair the performance of ABS and may significantly reduce effective braking ability. It has also been suggested that drivers of cars fitted with ABS drive more aggressively than other drivers.

Deaths from collisions with pedestrians and cyclists have been shown to decrease after the introduction of ABS. The driver's ability to steer the motor vehicle during emergency braking is the likely cause. A study on ABS showed an increase in deaths in rollover and single vehicles running off the road collisions in ABS-equipped vehicles.[18] The ability to steer the ABS-fitted motor vehicle during an emergency may paradoxically increase the risk for running off the road and subsequent rollover incidents. The inexpert driver who panics while braking and turns the steering wheel sharply may run off the road or overcorrect and drive into oncoming traffic.

Electronic Stability Control

Electronic stability control is a technology to assist drivers in maintaining safe handling of the motor vehicle and decrease the incidence of run off the road incidents and rollover. The system automatically adjusts the throttle and braking of the vehicle if oversteer or understeer is detected.[19] The system monitors the vehicle's speed, yaw, and lateral acceleration and adjusts the throttle and individual wheel brakes accordingly.

Other systems in development monitor the rapidity and force that a driver uses on the brake and, if the situation is deemed critical yet the driver has applied insufficient force to the pedal, the system applies maximum force to minimize the stopping distance.

Event Data Recorders

Event data recorders (EDR) have been present in selected motor vehicle incidents since the 1990s.

EDRs are analogous to the "black box" cockpit recorders within aircraft and similar systems present for some time in ships, trains, trucks, and buses. EDRs evolved with electronic systems in motor vehicles and especially with the introduction and evolution of airbag technology. The control unit is usually positioned beneath the driver's seat or dashboard.

The EDR stores information derived immediately before a collision and information on the severity of the collision. The type and format of information recorded in the system varies with different manufacturers but can include precrash throttle position and brake operation, restraint use, crash characteristics, and can potentially relay postcrash data to an automatic collision notification system.[20] Depending on the particular system of the manufacturer, the EDR can store up to two different deployment events, stored in near-deployment and deployment files. A near-deployment event can be overwritten by a deployment event, but a deployment event cannot be cleared from the system. There is a need for standardisation in data retrieved from different systems.

With the availability of satellite positioning, the EDR can relay information regarding a collision to appropriate emergency personnel and provide the exact location of the crash. The system can provide the delta V as an objective measure of crash severity, which has been shown to be superior in triage and the perception of crash severity than assessment by medical and paramedical personnel.

The information recorded in EDR systems has obvious benefit to collision reconstructionists, motor vehicle safety designers, and road safety engineers.[21] The National Highway Traffic Safety Administration has sponsored Rohan University in the United States to develop a database of EDR data from real-world crashes.[22] More accurate information regarding velocity changes during collisions and the performance of restraint systems has potential benefits for the development and introduction of future safety systems.

EDRs have limitations. In studies of controlled collisions, the measured delta V was found to be slightly higher than true delta V because of restitution during the incident. Side impact and rollover events require appropriate detection systems that are not readily available in most models. Rear end collisions are not recorded in the target vehicle. Multiple events may not be captured as two deployment and near-deployment events are recorded. A complex multiple incident collision may mean that the most important and most severe impact is not recorded.

Information may be lost if the vehicle's electrical system is damaged during the collision. If there is severe deformation from the collision, the control module may not be physically accessible. Recent technology with wireless probes is being developed so that investigators can still download information from the unit at the scene or via a direct telecommunication link to a central data location.[22]

Privacy is an issue with EDR data. Accurate information regarding a motor vehicle incident is obviously of interest to law enforcement personnel, lawyers and the courts, and insurance companies. The information within EDR systems can provide an objective measure of a vehicle's history. Depending on the local jurisdiction, the information may be ordered by a coroner, be obtained as evidence through a search warrant, or be considered the property of the vehicle's owner.

Design Features to Protect Pedestrians

Pedestrian collisions result in significant mortality and morbidity in both developing and Western societies. Education programs, measures to decrease vehicle speed, and engineering measures to separate pedestrians from vehicles have been introduced to address pedestrian collisions, injuries, and deaths.

Depending upon the relative configurations of the motor vehicle and stature of the pedestrian, there are differences in the types and distribution of injuries sustained by the pedestrian. In the usual case of an adult pedestrian and conventional passenger sedan with a defined hood, primary impact occurs to the driver's pelvis and lower limbs, after which the victim is scooped up onto the hood and head impact occurs from contact with the windshield and windshield surrounds. Death or significant brain injury is a common outcome. In those trauma victims who survive the crash, impact to the pelvis and lower limbs can cause major bone and joint disruption requiring operative fixation, joint reconstruction, and often residual reduction in mobility and subsequent osteoarthritis.

Research and development is assessing the options to site airbags beneath the windshield with appropriate sensors in the bumper to detect impact with a pedestrian. The deployed airbag could protect the pedestrian's head from blunt force injury from the windshield and surrounds. Collapsing segments to windshield surrounds require more wide-ranging engineering input. Increasing the space between the yielding sheet metal of the hood and the metallic components of the engine would also reduce significant injuries and requires engineers to redesign engine components such that solid metallic objects are sited away from the hood region.

Motor vehicle engineers have reviewed safety issues relating to the front of motor vehicles in which the majority of pedestrian incidents occur to make cars more "pedestrian friendly." Bumper impact in the vicinity of the knee is associated with serious knee injuries. Injuries to the lower limbs may be decreased by a lower profile to the front of the motor vehicle so that pedestrians are "scooped" up onto the hood to prevent differential movement of the thigh and lower leg region. A bumper lead angle below 60 degrees will reduced injury severity to the lower extremity in car-pedestrian accidents.[23]

Improvements in Lighting

Enhanced Rear Lighting

Enhanced rear lighting and signalling systems have been proposed to address the problem of rear end collisions. Centre high-mounted stop lights were introduced to alert following drivers of the lead vehicle's deceleration. The introduction of the centre light system was estimated to result in a 4% reduction in rear end crashes.[24] Another focus of research into early warning mechanisms has suggested more rapid illumination of the brake light using circuits from accelerator pedal release.

Adaptive Headlighting

Several approaches have been employed to improve the performance of vehicle headlights.[25] These include:

- Raising the beam of light with increasing speed
- Releveling the beam of light under different load distributions
- Adjusting lights in the event of adverse weather conditions (e.g., fog)
- Rotating the beam of light when cornering.

A study by Sullivan demonstrated that pedestrian deaths on rural roads were related to the amount of ambient light.[26] Depending on a vehicle's speed when a pedestrian is encountered on a rural road, the vehicle lights may not provide early enough illumination and warning to prevent a collision. Adaptive head lights that raise the level of the beam of light with increasing speed may reduce such collisions.

Pedestrian incidents leading to injury and death at intersections may be addressed by adaptive head lights that rotate the beam of light when the car turns through the intersection. Another approach utilises side lights that are activated with the turn signal.

In addition to possible reductions in pedestrian injuries and deaths, the introduction of adaptive head lights has the potential to decrease headlight glare for motorists and reduce driver fatigue and stress.[26]

Intelligent Vehicle Systems

It is generally accepted that most motor vehicle collisions are caused by driver behaviour or error.

Driver errors may occur from an inability to perceive a potential hazard or the failure to react quickly and appropriately. Information technology has the potential to aid drivers' tasks to provide early warning of hazardous situations and, in some instances, arrest control of the vehicle for some time in an avoidance effort. Smart technologies in current top-of-the-line motor vehicles include adaptive cruise control which incorporates a warning system when the vehicle is approaching the lead vehicle and alters speed to avoid a collision.

Intelligent vehicle systems include warning systems and collision avoidance systems. Intelligent vehicle systems that provide warning of rear end collisions have been available in buses and heavy vehicles for some time.

Other warning systems in development are designed to avoid running off the road, warn drivers of hazards when changing lanes, and improve driver decisions when approaching hazardous situations.

These systems use electronic sensors, infrared and radar technology, global positioning systems, in-vehicle cameras and computer systems, and driver-vehicle interface using audio and visual warnings.

Intelligent vehicle systems have to be compatible with current technology, driver ergonomics, and human behaviours and expectations.[27] False warnings may lead to drivers ignoring positive warnings. A preliminary study on the effect of false forward collision warnings showed that nondistracted drivers stopped responding to false warnings after only a few exposures. Interestingly and importantly, distracted drivers still responded to a false warning regardless of prior false warning exposures.[28]

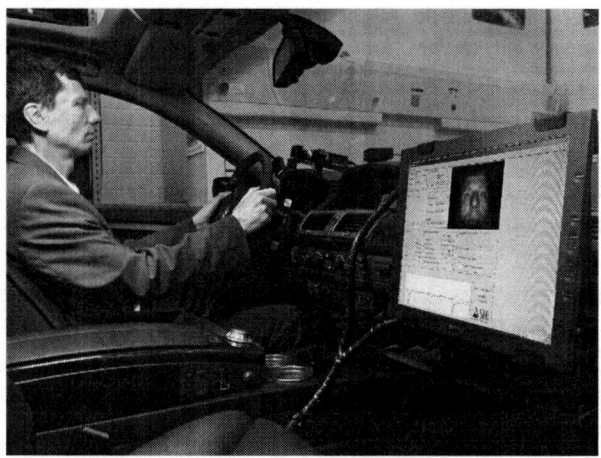

Figure 1.8 Intelligent vehicle system addressing drowsy driving. (Photo courtesy of BMW.)

Head-up displays of dashboard and other information can decrease the time a driver has to take his or her eyes off the road to gather pertinent information.[29] This may be especially helpful for elderly drivers. Head-up display could provide appropriate and relevant information with depth characteristics that are readily understandable to the driver. Enhanced visual displays for night time and poor visibility driving are in research and development.

Evolving technology that uses infrared cameras to determine the opening angle of the driver's eyes and rapidity and frequency of blinking is being assessed as an early warning device to alert drowsy drivers (Figure 1.8).

Collision avoidance systems use more sophisticated sensors and computer technology than warning systems. Collision avoidance systems identify an imminent collision such as a run-off-the-road event, side swipe crash or head-on collision, and arrest control of the vehicle's steering, clutch, or braking from the driver and initiate a collision avoidance manoeuver. Although these concepts appeared futuristic in the not too distant past, the technologies required for the successful implementation of such systems are evolving rapidly.

References

1. Fildes B, Logan D, Fitzharris M, Scully J, Burton D. ANCIS—the first three years. Monash University Accident Research Centre; Report No. 207.

2. Wood DP, Simms CK. Car size and injury risk: a model for injury risk in frontal collisions. *Accident Analysis and Prevention* 2002; 34:93–99.

3. Broyles RW, Clark SR, Warine L, Baker DR. Factors contributing to the amount of vehicular damage resulting from collisions between four-wheel drive vehicles and passenger cars. *Accident Analysis and Prevention* 2001; 33(5):673–678.

4. Mayrose J, Jehle DV. Vehicle weight and fatality risk for sport utility vehicles-versus-passenger car crashes. *Journal of Trauma* 2001; 53(4):751–753.

5. Smith KM, Cummings P. Passenger seating position and the risk of passenger death in traffic crashes. *Accident Analysis and Prevention* 2004; 36(2): 257–260.

6. Brown CK, Cline DM. Factors affecting injury severity to rear-seated occupants in rural motor crashes. *American Journal of Emergency Medicine* 2001; 19(2):93–98.

7. King AI, Yang KH. Research in biomechanics of occupants protection. *The Journal of Trauma* 1995; 38:570–576.

8. Nirula A, Kaufman R, Tencer A. Traumatic brain injury and automotive design: making motor vehicles safer. *The Journal of Trauma* 2003; 55(5):844–848.

9. Broughton J. The benefits of improved car secondary safety. *Accident Analysis and Prevention* 2003; 35:527–555.

10. Walz M. NCAP test improvements with pretensioners and load limiters. *Traffic Injury Prevention* 2004; 5:18–25.

11. Arbogast KB, Durbin DR, Cornejo RA, Kallan MJ, Winston FK. An evaluation of the effectiveness of forward facing child restraint systems. *Accident Analysis and Prevention* 2004; 36:585–589.

12. Durbin DR, Kallan M, Cornejo RA, Arbogast KB, Winston FK. Risk of injury to restrained children from passenger airbags. *Traffic Injury Prevention* 2003; 4:58–63.

13. Schreck RM, Rouhana SW, Santrock J, D'Arcy JB, Wooley RG, Bender H, Terzo TS, De Saele KH, Webb SR, Salva DB et al. Physical and chemical characterization of airbag effluents. *Journal of Trauma* 1995; 38(4):528–532.

14. Braver ER, Kyrychenko SY. Efficacy of side airbags in reducing driver deaths in driver-side collisions. Insurance Institute for Highway Safety. ID 00964774; 2003.

15. Williams A, Wells J. Driver experience with antilock brake systems. *Accident Analysis and Prevention* 1994; 26:807–811.

16. Farmer CM. New evidence concerning fatal crashes of passenger vehicles before and after adding antilock braking systems. *Accident Analysis and Prevention* 2001; 33:361–369

17. Hitner E, Arehart C, Radlinski R. Light vehicle ABS performance evaluation DOT-HS-807–813). Washington DC: National Highway Traffic Safety Administration, 1991.

18. Evans L. ABS and relative crash risk under different roadway, weather and other conditions (SAE 950353). Warrendale, PA: Society of Automotive Engineers.

19. Lie A, Tingvall C, Krafft M, Kullgren A. The effectiveness of ESP (Electronic Stability Program) in reducing real life accidents. *Traffic Injury Prevention* 2004; 5:37–41.

20. Department of Transportation. National Highway Traffic Safety Administration, 2002, Docket No. NHTSA-02-13546; Notice 1 RIN 2127-A172. Event data recorders.

21. German A, Comeau J-L, Monk B, McClafferty KJ, Tiessen PF, Chan J. The use of event data recorders in the analysis of real-world crashes. *Proceedings of the Canadian Multidisciplinary Road Safety Conference XII,* 2001.

22. Gabler HC, Hampton C, Roston T. Estimating crash severity: can event data recorders replace crash reconstruction? National Highway Traffic Safety Administration, 2003, Paper No. 490.

23. Bunketorp O, Aldman B, Thorngren L, Romanus B. Clinical and experimental studies on leg injuries, in Backaitis S, editor. *Car-Pedestrian Accidents. In Biomechanics of Impact Injury and Injury Tolerances of the Extremities.* Warrendale: Society of Automotive Engineers and Stanley H. Backaitis, 1995.

24. Lee SE, Wierwille WW, Klauer SG. Enhanced rear lighting and signalling systems: literature review and analysis of alternative system concepts 2002 NHTSA, Report No: HS-809-425.

25. Kobayashi S, Takahashi K, Yagi S., in *Development of New Forward Lightning Systems with Controllable Beams.* Warrendale: Society of Automotive Engineers, 1997, no. 970646.

26. Sullivan JM, Flannagan MJ. The role of ambient light level in fatal crashes: inferences from day light saving time transitions. *Accident Analysis and Prevention* 2002; 34:487–498.

27. Vahidi A, Eskandarian A. Research advances in intelligent collision avoidance and adaptive cruise control. *IEE Transactions on Intelligent Transportation Systems* 2003; 4:143–153.

28. Gish KW, Mercadante M, Perel M, Barickman F. The effect of false forward collision warnings on driver responses. Transportation Research Board 2002 Report No. 00922111.

29. Tufano D. Automotive HUDs: the overlooked safety issues. *Human Factors* 1997; 39:303–311.

Additional Reading

Broughton J, Baughan C. The effectiveness of antilock braking systems in reducing accidents in Great Britain. *Accident Analysis and Prevention* 2002; 34:347–355.

Crandall JR, Bhalla KS, Madeley J. Designing road vehicles for pedestrian protection. *British Medical Journal* 2002; 324:1145–1148.

Evans L, Gerrish P. Antilock brakes and risk of front and rear impact in two-vehicle crashes. *Accident Analysis and Prevention* 1996; 28:315–323.

Farmer CM, Lund AY, Tremple RE, Braver ER. Fatal crashes of passenger vehicles before and after adding antilock braking systems. *Accident Analysis and Prevention* 1997; 27:745–757.

Noland RB, Oh L. The effect of infrastructure and demographic change on traffic-related fatalities and crashes: a case study of Illinois County-level data. *Accident Analysis and Prevention* 2004; 36:525–532.

Olsen PL, Sivak M. Comparisons of headlamp visibility distance and stopping distance. *Perceptual and Motor Skills* 1983; 57:117–1178.

Behavioural Factors in Motor Vehicle Incidents

2

Introduction

Behavioural factors and associated decision-making processes are generally accepted to be the main underlying cause of most motor vehicle collisions, injuries, and fatalities.

Behaviours that contribute significantly to motor vehicle incidents, injury, and death include:

- Driving at an excessive speed for the prevailing conditions
- Driving whilst intoxicated with alcohol
- Driving under the influence of drugs that adversely affect the ability to drive
- Driving whilst fatigued or drowsy
- Inattention and distraction from the task of driving
- Behaviour associated with a history of traffic law violations
- Aggressive driving behaviour
- Noncompliance with seat belts
- Age-related issues (inexperience)
- Driver decision errors

Driving at an Excessive Speed

The use of excessive speed for the prevailing conditions is the most significant factor in most motor vehicle collisions, injuries, and fatalities. The average travelling speed for motor vehicles has increased significantly. This change has occurred mainly from infrastructure and design improvements to the road network, leading to higher speeds travelled on major roads and freeways. Various traffic engineering methods discourage or prevent vehicles from using small neighbourhood roads and divert the traffic to larger arterial roads.

Driving at speeds over the legal limit is a common behaviour of many drivers. One speed survey showed that just over half of drivers stayed below the designated 60 km/hr speed limit. The speed limit was exceeded by over 10 km/hr in 8.1% of cases, by at least 20 km/hr in 1% of cases and by at least 30 km/hr in 0.18% of cases. Speeding was much more common in the early morning, with 75% of vehicles exceeding the 60 km/hr limit between 1:00 and 5:00 a.m. on weekdays.

The odds ratio for a motor vehicle collision increases 40 times when travelling in excess of 84 km/hr as opposed to less than 60 km/hr.[1] At an excessive speed for the prevailing road conditions, there is less time and available roadway for the vehicle to stop safely. The prevailing conditions may refer to inclement weather such as heavy rain, fog, or snow.

Occupant injury and death is directly related to the change in velocity (delta V) that occurs during a motor vehicle collision. A Canadian study showed the odds of a fatality in a collision occurring in a 70 to 90 km/hr zone was almost six times that of crashes in areas with lower speed limits.[2] Furthermore, it has been estimated that the odds of a fatality occurring when travelling at a speed of 112 km/hr is increased 164% over the odds of a fatality occurring with speeds lower than 56 km/hr.[3]

Speed Cameras

The introduction of fixed and mobile speed cameras has been shown to result in significant decreases in crashes causing injury in both day and night time, and on roads with speed limits varying from 60 to 110 km/hr. The reduction in crashes is related to incidents involving pedestrians, motorcyclists, and motorists.[4] A trial in New Zealand using hidden speed cameras in conjunction with a publicity campaign resulted in a more general reduction in speed on all roads.[5]

Studies performed by the Monash University Accident Research Centre have addressed the effectiveness of overt and covert speed enforcement through fixed and mobile speed enforcement devices in Victoria, Australia.[6,7] It was initially found that the introduction of the speed camera program did not lead to a reduction in motor vehicle collision frequency. The results of the program suggested the presence of cameras and the receipt of an infringe-ment notice did not have a general overall effect in slowing motorists. How-ever, a later study showed a 4-day residual effect on crashes causing injury following mobile radar operations in rural Victoria. The change was most effective when associated with campaigns to heighten public awareness.

More recent studies in Victoria have shown that speed cameras were effective in reducing crashes causing injury on arterial roads in metropolitan Melbourne and country towns and rural highways. The use of mobile radar devices reduced casualty rates in rural areas on undivided roads with 100 km/hr speed limits. Hand-held laser devices decreased crash frequency, but not severity on arterial roads. Overt speed cameras reduced speeds within the immediate vicinity of the camera. Covert operations with a subsequent infringement notice resulted in a reduction in crash frequency for approximately 2 weeks after the notice was received.

Particular sites with a high accident risk may be targeted using speed cameras, and an associated publicity campaign until definitive engineering solutions can be implemented. It appears that a general reduction in speed is best achieved by educating drivers and the general community, a program of overt and covert speed cameras, roadside signs to reinforce the possibility of apprehension, and appropriate speeding fines.

Driving whilst Intoxicated with Alcohol

The presence of alcohol within the blood of a driver causes an increase in the risk of collision, injury, and death. The different blood alcohol limits for drivers imposed by different jurisdictions are purely arbitrary and are influenced by factors other than road safety. The risk of a collision is exacerbated by other issues such as a driver's inexperience. Alcohol-related motor vehicle incidents tend to occur at greater speeds, involve more vehicles, and are associated with an increased incidence of rear end, sideswipe, and rollover incidents.

Numerous studies have demonstrated a direct relationship between blood alcohol concentration (BAC) and impairment of motor coordination and cognitive performance, including the skilled performance required to operate a motor vehicle. There is a logarithmic relationship between impairment and BAC with concentrations in excess of 0.02%. The risk of a collision with a BAC of 0.05% is double that of a sober individual. Alcohol has been shown to adversely affect tasks such as tracking, perception of distance and speed, and reaction times to respond to changes in road conditions. Furthermore, the disinhibition effects of alcohol on the cerebral cortex of the brain can reveal aggressive and risk taking behaviour in some individuals.

A study on drunk drivers in Illinois in the United States showed that following the reduction of the legal BAC from 0.10 to 0.08 g/100 mL, there was a corresponding increase in driving under the influence arrests, convictions, and sentences from the courts, but, more important, there was an estimated 14% reduction in deaths associated with drunk driving.[8]

Driving under the Influence of Drugs

The use of illicit and therapeutic drugs by a driver may be associated with an increased risk of a motor vehicle collision and is an important issue for health care professionals and road and traffic authorities. Individuals who use illicit drugs cannot be certain of the concentration and purity of the drugs they use, and hence the pharmacologic effects on their bodies.

The effect of therapeutic drugs on an individual's driving ability is becoming an increasingly important issue for many Western countries with aging populations. A significant proportion of older individuals have complex medical problems that can require a number of diverse medications. Therapeutic drugs in normal doses may lead to impairment of skills important to driving in some individuals. The presence of multiple different medications can result in complex drug interactions.

A common example of the problem associated with driving and the use of therapeutic drugs is illustrated by the benzodiazepine group of drugs. Benzodiazepines are used in the treatment of anxiety disorders and alcohol withdrawal. They may interact with alcohol, other central nervous system depressants, anticholinergic drugs, and anticonvulsants. Use of benzodiazepines may result in the inability to operate machinery, including motor vehicles the day following use of the drug.

Many other therapeutic drugs have the potential to cause a reduction in driving ability and especially in elevated or toxic levels. For example, elevated blood levels of phenytoin, a drug used in the treatment of epilepsy, can result in disturbance of vision and incoordination. A thorough drug history may be crucial in understanding the complete circumstances of a given motor vehicle collision.

Driving whilst Fatigued or Drowsy

Driver fatigue and drowsy driving covers a spectrum ranging from driving while clearly tired, up to episodes of "microsleeping," and finally to falling asleep at the wheel. Risk factors include lack of sleep, driving while intoxicated with alcohol or other drugs, long periods of driving without rest, sleep apnea, and other medical disorders. The problem is common and widespread. It has been estimated that more than one-third of the driving population admits to have "nodded off" for at least a moment while driving. The problem is almost twice as common in males, with almost half admitting to transient episodes of being asleep at the wheel.

Fifty-eight percent of individuals with a recent drowsy episode reported that it had occurred on an open highway. Most instances tend to occur late at night, with only 9% happening between 6:00 and 11:00 a.m., whereas 28% of instances occurred from midnight to 6:00 a.m. On average, most drivers report having been on the road for a few hours before the drowsy driving episode. A population-based, case-control study on crashes in North Carolina showed that drivers identified by police as asleep or fatigued at the time of the collision averaged fewer hours of sleep per night, had poor quality sleep, were sleepier during the day, drove more at night, and reported prior episodes of driving whilst drowsy.[9] Reported outcomes of a drowsy driving episode include becoming suddenly startled and awake (92%), running off the road (10%), crossing over the center line (90%), and wandering into adjacent lanes or onto the shoulder of the road (33%). Being involved in a collision was reported as being relatively uncommon (2%).

Most drivers were aware of the potential dangers of driving when tired or fatigued. However, although 95% of drivers stated that being sleepy or drowsy while driving was a major threat to the safety of themselves, family, and other road users, there were marked differences between drivers in what further action was taken. The actions included pulling of the road to take a nap (43%), having a cup of coffee or other drink (17%), getting out of the car to stretch/exercise (9%), or to change drivers (6%). Of some concern are the actions taken by a significant percentage of drivers who would either open a window (26%) or turn the radio on loud (14%).

Inattention and Distraction from the Task of Driving

In the process of driving a motor vehicle, the driver must select, analyse, and act on various stimuli from the roadway and the vehicle. An experienced driver is able to perform complex tasks with little "conscious thought" because learned techniques enable sizeable portions of the driving process to become virtually automatic. At other times, and often without warning, a dangerous situation arises that demands rapid processing of a large amount of information so that the driver may avoid a collision.

It has been estimated that approximately 25% of all crashes in the United States result from driver inattention or distraction.[10] The presence of passengers within a motor vehicle can result in driver distraction. Older drivers are less likely to engage in conversations than younger drivers.

Psychologic research has shown that some individuals voluntarily add tasks to the work of driving. Additional tasks are often a consequence of an interaction with technology. These technology-based distractions including mobile phones, e-mail and the Internet, radio, CD and DVD players, and route guidance systems and all may have a detrimental effect on driver performance.[10] Distractions may also arise from personal grooming, using the rear view mirror, or reading maps, newspapers, or other material. Different drivers have varying perceptions of the danger associated with such behaviour. For example, most drivers regard reading a map significantly more dangerous than behaviour such as eating or drinking in the car.

The use of mobile phones is recognized as a major cause of driver distraction. A study from the United States investigated mobile phone use on a major highway and found 1.5% of drivers were using mobile phones during the designated study period. The rate of mobile phone use decreased on weekends and at night time, when the driver was exceeding the speed limit and when passengers were in the motor vehicle.[11] The adjusted relative risk of a collision for heavy use of mobile telephones while driving is at least 2 compared with those making minimal use of the telephone.[12]

It has been shown that using a personal hands-free mobile telephone was associated with a significantly lower additional work load than a hand-held mobile telephone or hands-free speaker mobile telephone while driving on a highway.[13] The study found that subjective physical demand was low for the hand-held telephone during highway driving. The results suggested that driver inattention is the predominant contributor to vehicle collisions attributed to phone use rather than the physical demand of using the telephone.

A laboratory study demonstrated that brake reaction simulation times were increased when the driver had a conversation with either a passenger or via a mobile phone.[14] A study by Patten and colleagues compared the effects of conversation type (simple versus complex) and telephone mode (hands-free vs. hand-held) to baseline conditions and found that the more difficult and complex the situation, the greater the possible negative effect of driver distraction.[15] The experiment suggested that the content of the conversation was more important in causing driver distraction than the particular type of telephone.

Looked-but-Failed-to-See Errors

A specific type of motor vehicle incident related to driver inattention is the "looked-but-failed-to-see" collision. In these incidents, the motor vehicle driver states that they looked in the direction of the vehicles, but failed to see them.[16] The problem was investigated by examining the incidence of these errors in collisions between motor vehicles and cyclists at roundabouts. Surprisingly, the study showed that these errors were more common in experienced drivers. It was suggested that inexperienced and experienced drivers may have different mechanisms for visual search scanning. Experienced drivers tend to scan the road further than do inexperienced drivers, furthermore, experienced drivers search specifically for oncoming dangers such as other motor vehicles. The look-but-to-fail-to-see phenomenon may reflect experienced drivers unconsciously scanning the road for other motor vehicles rather than cyclists or pedestrians.[17]

Behaviour Associated with a History of Traffic Law Violations

The violation of traffic laws, including laws other than speeding and driving under the influence of alcohol or other drugs, are associated with an increased risk of motor vehicle collisions, injury, and death.

Significant issues which are commonly associated with a motor vehicle incident include:

Running Red Lights

A study by Retting estimated that there are just over a quarter of a million red light running crashes each year in the United States of America that result in about 750 deaths.[18] Most collisions associated with running red lights are side-on collisions. The majority of red light running incidents are perpetrated by young males. The probability of a driver running a red light is increased by the presence of alcohol in the driver's blood, a history of other traffic violations, and speeding. More red light running incidents occur during the early evening and night time.

The introduction of red light cameras has led to a decrease in collisions causing injury and death.

Red light cameras employ an under-road detector linked to fixed cameras. A photograph is taken to confirm the vehicle in question passed through the intersection and did not suddenly brake and stop. The photographs are designed to identify the vehicle registration number plate.

The installation of red light cameras is associated with an increased incidence of rear end collisions.

This is related to drivers becoming suddenly aware of the presence of the cameras, abruptly braking, and the following vehicle is then unable to stop in time. Despite the increase in rear end collisions, there is an overall reduction in crashes, and most important, in side-on crashes. Unintentional red light running incidents have been shown to occur when traffic signal sequences have a short yellow signal.

Ignoring Traffic Signals

Ignoring traffic intersection signs is a common cause of motor vehicle collisions leading to property damage and injury. Stop sign violations accounted for about 70% of such crashes.[19] Depending on other engineering factors, the installation of four-way stop signs can lead to lower vehicle speeds and hence lower impact velocities and injury. The installation of roundabouts has also been shown to decrease crash rates while maintaining traffic flow.

Aggressive Driving Behaviour

Aggressive driving behaviour can be difficult to define. When described by numerous and rapid lane changes, hard braking, and rapid acceleration, the behaviour is relatively common in an urban environment. Martinez defined aggressive driving as that which "endangers or is likely to endanger people or property."[20] Aggressive behaviour arising from conflict on the roads may escalate to verbal and physical assaults that have been termed "road rage." It has been shown that motorists who frequently make indecent gestures to other drivers, and particularly those who engage in arguments with other motorists, also tend to violate traffic laws and are poor drivers.[21] Other relatively mild expressions of annoyance including the "flashing" of headlights, the use of the car horn, and unobtrusive verbal expressions have not been shown to be associated with an increased crash risk.[22]

Close following or "tail gating" is commonly seen on both metropolitan and country roads. Drivers may use close following in an attempt to prevent others from merging in front of them, whereas other drivers proceed closely behind the leading vehicle to "force" the vehicle to move out of a particular lane.[23] On two-lane roads, close following may be related to variations in vehicle speeds, with the associated requirement for more overtaking maneuvers. Overtaking lanes on two lane highways has been shown to be an inexpensive solution to this overtaking problem.[24]

Close following behaviour is more likely in young male drivers and those who have incurred more traffic offenses than other drivers.[25] There is evidence to suggest that this driving behaviour may become routine for the offending driver and may also be associated with speeding. It would seem reasonable to assume that close following behaviour is associated with an increased risk of a rear end motor vehicle collision, because there is less time for emergency braking if a sudden incident occurred further up the road. However, close following behaviour and increased accident involvement has not been conclusively demonstrated. It does not necessarily follow that a driver who leaves a longer distance between his or her vehicle and the forward vehicle is a safer driver. There is some evidence to suggest that closer following drivers are more alert than other drivers and with more experience negotiating slower vehicles.

Noncompliance with Seat Belts

It has been conclusively shown that correctly wearing a seat belt provides protection to all vehicle occupants in motor vehicle crashes and especially in frontal collisions and in preventing occupant ejection. The use of seat belts is mandatory in Victoria, Australia, and compliance is generally good. However, in 2003 in Victoria, Australia, 22% of vehicle occupants killed in crashes were not wearing seat belts. Of the drivers who were killed while not wearing a seat belt, 38% had a BAC of equal or greater than 0.05 g/100 mL.

A study by Monash University Accident Research Centre evaluated a range of safety issues on metropolitan roads in Melbourne, Victoria, in 2001. Observational data were obtained on 4665 motor vehicles. It was found that seat belts were worn correctly in 91% of cases. The most common causes of incorrect use were a loose or twisted belt or having the belt in contact with the neck. Nonwearing rates for drivers were 2.6% for males and 1.9% for females. The proportion of adult passengers not wearing a belt was 7.7% for males and 3.5% for females.

The seat belt wearing rate for children was 70.5%; 10.7% of children in the age group 8 to 13 years did not wear a belt, and in 25.3% of those between 4 and 7 years the belt was not worn correctly.

Age-Related Issues

Most elderly drivers are safe and responsible drivers. The ability to drive their cars has an important function in maintaining independence in the community and for preserving social interactions.

With advancing age, there is a decline in perception, psychomotor and cognitive skills in some drivers.

In the majority of older drivers, the acquisition of years of experience on the road, coupled with a voluntary limitation in certain driving tasks such as driving at night time, during peak traffic periods, and on freeways with higher travelling speeds, more than compensates for the negative affects of their age.

Older drivers who voluntarily give up driving usually do so because of declining health, though it is uncommon for a driver to be counselled in this regard by his or her health practitioner.[26]

A driver simulator study that examined perception–reaction times and brake movement times showed significant age-related deficits in perception reaction time in older drivers. No significant differences in brake movement times were observed.[27] The deficit in perception–reaction time may affect the ability to judge distances and react quickly with respect to oncoming vehicles.

An additional age-related issue is the increased risk of serious injury and death in older drivers and passengers for a given collision. It is intuitively obvious that a 70-year-old man of average health is at greater risk than a 20-year-old man of average health in a motor vehicle crash that results in identical trauma to each. The increased risk was quantified by

Evans, who showed that "after the age of 20, the risk of death from the same severity blunt trauma impact increases by: −2.52 ± 0.08% per year for males and 2.16 ± 1.0% per year for females." In simple terms, a population of 70-year-old males subjected to identical trauma as a population of 20-year-old males will result in 250% more fatalities.[28]

Individuals with dementia and other major consequences of old age that dramatically reduce their ability to safety drive a motor vehicle, and who lack insight into their advanced state of decline, pose a significant risk to themselves and others on the road. Furthermore, the presence of certain diseases and disabilities can adversely affect the process of driving a motor vehicle. These specific issues are addressed in Chapter 3.

Inexperienced Drivers

Motor vehicle collisions leading to injury and death are common in the younger age groups.[29]

Younger drivers are more likely to drive at excessive speed. They also have an increased incidence of following too closely to a leading vehicle, disobeying traffic signs and signals, overtaking in a risky manner, not allowing enough time to merge with traffic, and failing to yield to pedestrians.[30]

Of these driving characteristics, speeding is the major factor in motor vehicle collisions involving young and inexperienced individuals. Fatalities that occur in collisions involving young drivers have a higher incidence during the night time, and when multiple young passengers are present within the vehicle.[31] Research has shown that the presence in the vehicle of an individual older than the driver is associated with a decreased risk of a crash.

The greatest risk of motor vehicle collision for young drivers is in the first month of driving.[32] There is a dramatic decrease in crash rate during the following 6 months of driving. Certain types of crashes (e.g., running off the road or single vehicle, night and weekend crashes) show rapid improvement.[33] Analysis of these types of crashes involving inexperienced drivers led to the introduction of graduated licensing programs.

Graduated license programs provide a way of managing an inexperienced driver's real-life driving by beginning to drive in low-risk situations and avoiding circumstances that have been demonstrated to be associated with an increased crash risk.[32] The restrictions of graduated licencing programs must be weighed against the individual's rights, social interaction and mobility, sporting and work activities, and other personal issues.

Different jurisdictions have various restrictions for graduated license programs. Learner periods requiring the presence of a fully licenced driver, optional or mandatory completion of learner log books, and restrictions on night time driving and the number of passengers the probationary driver is able to lawfully transport are common features of graduated programs.

Driver Decision Errors

A driver decision error may be viewed as an umbrella term for a situation in which a motor vehicle collision is caused by the action or inaction of a driver. This conclusion may not necessarily be correct because a driver's actions may have resulted from inattention to some important aspect of the driving task, a looked-for-but failed-to-see error, and ignoring environmental factors such as sun glare, obscured signs, or view of the roadway from parked vehicles.

Decision errors may be catastrophic if the situation involves driving across roads with high traffic volumes and speeds. Elderly drivers are particularly at risk because of their decreased reaction times and potential problems with depth perception.

A recent approach to the issue of human error is to view such errors as a symptom of system failure, and the premise that systems are not inherently safe.[34] In this approach, one endeavours not to use hindsight to identify critical moments in which alternate action would have produced a different (and safer) result, but to attempt to address the fundamental issue of "why was this particular course of action taken by that particular individual at that point in time."[35] This approach to road safety endeavors to shift blame from the individual driver and instead attempts to improve the overall safety of the road system.

References

1. Moore VM, Dolinis J, Woodward AJ. Vehicle speed and risk of a severe crash. *Epidemiology* 1995; 6:258–262.

2. Zhang J, Lindsay J, Clarke K, Robbins G, Mao Y. Factors affecting the severity of motor vehicle crashes involving elderly drivers in Ontario. *Accident Analysis and Prevention* 2000; 32:117–125.

3. Bedard M, Guyatt GH, Stones MJ, Hirdes JP. The independent contribution of driver, crash, and vehicle characteristics to driver fatalities. *Accident Analysis and Prevention* 2002; 34:717–727.

4. Christie SM, Lyons RA, Dunstan FD, Jones SJ. Are mobile speed cameras effective? A controlled before and after study. *Injury Prevention* 2003; 9:302–306.

5. Keall MD, Povey LJ, Frith WJ. The relative effectiveness of a hidden versus visible speed camera program. *Accident Analysis and Prevention* 2001; 33:277–284.

6. Diamantopoulou K, Cameron M. An evaluation of the effectiveness of overt and covert speed enforcement achieved through mobile radar operations. Report No. 187. Victoria, Australia: Monash University Accident Research Centre, 2003.

7. Delaney A, Diamantopoulou K, Cameron M. *MUARC's Speed Enforcement Research: Principals Learnt and Implications for Practice 2003*. Victoria, Australia: Monash University, Report No. 200.

8. Voas RB, Tippetts AS, Taylor EP. The Illinois .08 law. An evaluation. *Journal of Safety Research* 2002; 33:73–80.

9. Stutts JC, Wilkins JW, Osberg JS, Vaughan BV. Driver risk factors for sleep-related crashes. *Accident Analysis and Prevention* 2003; 35:321–331.

10. Young K, Regan M, Hammer N. Driver distraction: a review of the literature. Victoria, Australia: Monash University Accident Research Centre, Report No 206.

11. Johnson MB, Voas, RB, Lacey JH, McKnight AS, Lange JE. Living dangerously: driver distraction at high speed. *Traffic Injury Prevention* 2004; 5:1–7.

12. Laberge-Nadeau C, Magg U, Bellavance F, Lapierre SD, Desjardins D, Messier R, Saidi A. Wireless telephones and the risk of road crashes. *Accident Analysis and Prevention* 2003; 35:649–660.

13. Matthews R, Legg S, Charlton S. The effect of cellphone type on drivers subjective workload during concurrent driving and conversing. *Accident Analysis and Prevention* 2003; 35:451–457.

14. Consiglio W, Driscoll P, Witte M, Berg WP. Effect of cellular telephone conversations and other potential interference on reaction time in a braking response. *Accident Analysis and Prevention* 2003; 35:495–500.

15. Patten CJD, Kircher A, Ostlund J, Nilsson L. Using mobile telephones: cognitive work load and attention resource allocation. *Accident Analysis and Prevention* 2004; 36:341–350.

16. Herslund MB, Jorgensen NO. Looked-but-failed-to-see-errors in traffic. *Accident Analysis and Prevention* 2003; 35:885–891.

17. Langham M, Hole G, Land M. Looking and failing to see error. The cost of experience? School of Cognitive and Computing Sciences. Sussex Centre for Neuroscience, University of Sussex, Brighton; 1998.

18. Retting RA, Ulmer RG, Williams AF. Prevalence and characteristics of red light running crashes in the United States. *Accident Analysis and Prevention* 1999; 31:687–694.

19. Retting RA, Weinstein HB, Solomon MG. Analysis of motor-vehicle crashes at stop signs in four U.S. cities. *Journal of Safety Research* 2003; 34:485–489.

20. Martinez R. Testimony to House Transportation and Infrastructure Committee. Surface Transportation Subcommittee; July 17, 1997.

21. Hemmingway D, Solnick SJ. Fuzzy dice, dream cars, and indecent gestures: correlates of driver behaviour? *Accident Analysis and Prevention* 1993; 25:161–170.

22. Wells-Parker E, Ceminsky J, Hallberg V, Snow RW, Dunaway G, Guiling S, Williams M, Anderson B. An exploratory study of the relationship between road rage and crash experience in a representative sample of US drivers. *Accident Analysis and Prevention* 2002; 34:271–278.

23. Colbourn CJ, Brown ID, Copeman AK. Drivers judgements of safe distances in vehicle following. *Human Factors* 1978; 20:1–11.

24. Harwood DW, Hoban CJ. Low cost methods for improving traffic operations on two lane roads. Washington DC: Federal Highway Administration; 1987.

25. Rajalin S, Hassel SO, Summala H. Close-following drivers on two-lane highways. *Accident Analysis and Prevention* 1997; 29:723–729.

26. Hakamies-Blomqvist L, Wahlstrom B. Why do older drivers give up driving? *Accident Analysis and Prevention* 1998; 30:305–312.

27. Warshawsky-Levne L, Shinar D. Effects of uncertainty, transmission type, driver age and gender on brake reaction and movement time. *Journal of Safety Research* 2002; 33(1):117-128.

28. Evans L. Age and fatality risk from similar severity impacts. *Journal of Traffic Medicine* 2001; 29:10–19.

29. Ballesteros MF, Dischinger PC. Characteristics of traffic crashes in Maryland (1996–1999): differences among the youngest drivers. *Accident Analysis and Prevention* 2002; 34:279–284.

30. Williams AF, Ferguson SA. Rationale for graduated licensing and the risks it should address. *Injury Prevention* 2002; 8:ii9–ii16.

31. Chen LH, Baker SP, Braver ER, Li G. Carrying passengers as a risk factor for crashes fatal to 16 and 17 year old drivers. *Journal of the American Medical Association* 2000; 283:1578–1582.

32. Williams AF. The compelling case for graduated licencing. *Journal of Safety Research* 2003; 34:3–4.

33. Mayhew DR, Simpson HM, Pak A. Changes in collision rates amongst novice drivers during the first month of driving. *Accident Analysis and Prevention* 2003; 35:683–691.

34. Hoffman RR, Woods DD. Studying cognitive systems in context. *Human Factors* 2002; 42:1–7.

35. Dekker SWA. Reconstructing human contributions to accidents: the new view on error and performance. *Journal of Safety Research* 2002; 33:371–385.

Additional Reading

Brown ID. Driver fatigue. *Human Factors* 1994; 36:298–314.

Evans L The dominant role of driver behaviour in traffic safety. *American Journal of Public Health* 1996; 86:784–786.

Hedlund J, Compton R. Graduated driver licensing research in 2003 and beyond. *Journal of Safety Research* 2004; 35:5–11.

Hilakivi I, Veilahti J, Asplund P, Sinivuo J, Laitinen L, Koskenvuo K. A 16-factor personality test for predicting automobile accidents of young drivers. *Accident Analysis and Prevention* 1990; 21:413–418.

Horne JA, Rayner LA. Sleep related vehicle accidents. *British Medical Journal* 1995; 310:565–567.

Katila A, Keskinen E, Hatakka N, Laapotti S. Does increased confidence among novice drivers imply a decrease in safety? The effects of skid training on slippery road accidents. *Accident and Analysis Prevention* 2004; 36:543–550.

Kweon Y-J, Kockelman KM. Overall injury risk to different drivers: combining exposure, frequency and severity models. *Accident Analysis and Prevention* 2003; 35:441–450.

McKnight AJ, McKnight AS. Young novice drivers: careless or clueless? *Accident Analysis and Prevention* 2003; 35:921–925.

Morrow PC, Crum MR. Antecedents of fatigue, close calls, and crashes among commercial motor-vehicle drivers. *Journal of Safety Research* 2004; 35:59–69.

Petridou E, Moustaki M. Human factors in the causation of road traffic crashes. *European Journal of Epidemiology* 2000; 16:819–826.

Porter BE, England KJ. Predicting red-light running behaviour: a traffic study in three urban settings. Journal of Safety Research 2000; 31:1–8.

Retting RA, Ferguson SA, Hakkert AS. Effects of red light cameras on violations and crashes: a review of the international literature. *Traffic Injury Prevention* 2003; 4:17–23.

Shinar D, Compton R. Aggressive driving: an observational study of driver, vehicle, and situational variables. *Accident Analysis and Prevention* 2004; 36:429–437.

Siegal JH, Ho SM, Qufera JA. The effect of change in velocity on the development of medical complications in patients with multisystem trauma sustained in vehicular crashes. *Accident Analysis and Prevention* 1998; 30:831–837.

Whelan M, Diamantopoulou K, Senserrick T, Cameron M. Establishing a benchmark of safety on Melbourne roads during 2001. Victoria, Australia: Monash University Accident Research Centre, 2003, Report No 198.

Medical Factors in Motor Vehicle Incidents

3

Introduction

Motor vehicle collisions caused by an underlying medical condition are uncommon compared with the usual causes of crashes (i.e., excessive speed for the prevailing conditions and driving while under the influence of alcohol). A study in Arizona identified 614,000 collisions over a 6-year period of which 859 were related to all medical conditions.[1] Furthermore, Gresset found that a group of older drivers with chronic disease showed no evidence of an increased odds ratio for crashes from illness.[2]

Although it is uncommon, various disease processes do have the potential to cause a driver to lose control of a motor vehicle. The circumstances and witness accounts may support the premise of driver incapacitation prior to a collision. The driver may have been seen to slump in the seat prior to the collision or the motor vehicle may have veered off the roadway onto the curb or into another motor vehicle with no attempt to correct the path or speed of the car.

In cases in which a driver survives the motor vehicle collision and the overall circumstances suggest the possibility of underlying natural disease contributing to the incident, medical investigations performed in the hospital can document the presence of relevant natural disease. In cases in which the driver dies following the motor vehicle incident, a postmortem examination will document the presence and severity of the underlying natural disease. The absence of any significant injury that would reasonably lead to death may enable the forensic pathologist to conclude the death occurred as a consequence of natural disease. In most cases, the presence of natural disease is coincidental to the cause of the motor vehicle incident.

Legislation

In Australia, the Driver Licencing Authority (DLA) is responsible by law for making decisions concerning private and commercial vehicle licences. In 2003, the Authority published the booklet *Assessing Fitness to Drive for Commercial and Private Vehicle Drivers 2003.*[3] The document was produced by the National Road Transport Commission and Austroads in consultation with a variety of experts in various medical disciplines and the transportation industry. The booklet serves as a guide for health professionals who provide medical support and opinions on drivers referred by the DLA.

The guidelines for commercial vehicles are more stringent than for private drivers, reflecting their increased time on the road carrying large numbers of passengers, and controlling large and potentially dangerous vehicles.

In Australia, health professionals should be aware of privacy legislation applicable in their jurisdiction. Indemnity under transport law is provided for general practitioners who notify the DLA of patients with serious illnesses who have ignored repeated advice to stop driving because of serious illness and are a significant hazard to other road users.[4] The DLA may grant a conditional commercial or private licence following a medical assessment, neuropsychiatric tests, a report of a driver assessor, or consequent to corrective treatment or appropriate modification to the vehicle.

The regulatory requirement for driver testing varies between the various states and territories in Australia. For example, in the State of Victoria, there is no requirement for medical assessment for a prescribed age, whereas in the State of Tasmania a medical assessment is required yearly from 75 years of age. In the State of New South Wales, a medical assessment is required at 80 years of age and annually thereafter.

Medical Conditions

A comprehensive literature review on the influence of chronic disease on crash involvement of motor vehicle drivers was recently published by the Monash University Accident Research Centre.[5] In some of the studies methodologic problems were identified, such as selection of appropriate controls, ambiguous diagnostic criteria, and lack of comparison to driving exposure. The Monash University Accident Research Centre review identified eight medical issues that were deemed high risk for a motor vehicle collision: alcohol abuse and dependence, dementia, epilepsy, multiple sclerosis, psychiatric disorders, sleep apnea and cataracts.

The following review of medical conditions will address medical diseases that can result in sudden incapacitation of a driver at the wheel of a motor vehicle.

Cardiovascular System

A reduction in blood pressure leading to inadequate brain perfusion is manifested clinically as a "faint," and is the common final pathway by which cardiac disorders can cause a motor vehicle collision. Low blood pressure is most commonly caused by an abnormality in heart rhythm, which in turn has a number of underlying causes. There is evidence to suggest that in most cases of "heart attack" while driving, most drivers have sufficient warning to slow or stop the vehicle before a crash can occur.

Common Cardiac Conditions

Ischaemic Heart Disease (Coronary Artery Atherosclerosis). Ischaemic heart disease is the most common cause of death in developed countries (Figure 3.1). Ischaemic heart disease refers to a relative deficiency of blood flow to the myocardium from stenosis of one or more coronary arteries. Coronary artery atherosclerosis is primarily a disease of older individuals, but is not uncommon in males in their third and fourth decades and may occasionally be seen in younger individuals with underlying disorders such as familial hypercholesterolaemia. One requires a stenosis of greater than 75% for the coronary plaque to be deemed a reasonable cause of death at postmortem (Figure 3.2).

An acute complication of a coronary artery plaque such as coronary thrombosis or haemorrhage into the plaque may be associated with the sudden development of an abnormality in cardiac rhythm resulting in sudden collapse. Furthermore, the presence of myocardial fibrosis is associated with cardiac arrhythmias. Medications to treat ischaemic chest pain, especially in the early stages of the commencement of therapy, can also result in an abrupt fall in blood pressure.

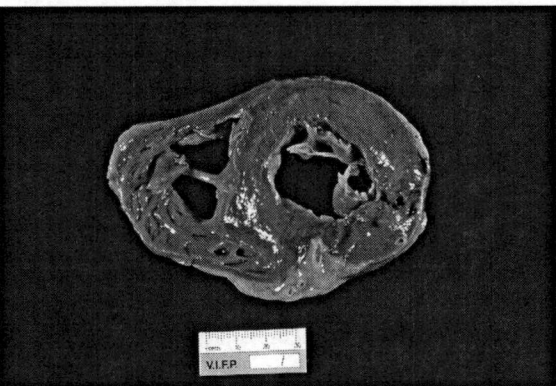

Figure 3.1   Cross-section of heart showing acute infarction and rupture (3 o'clock).

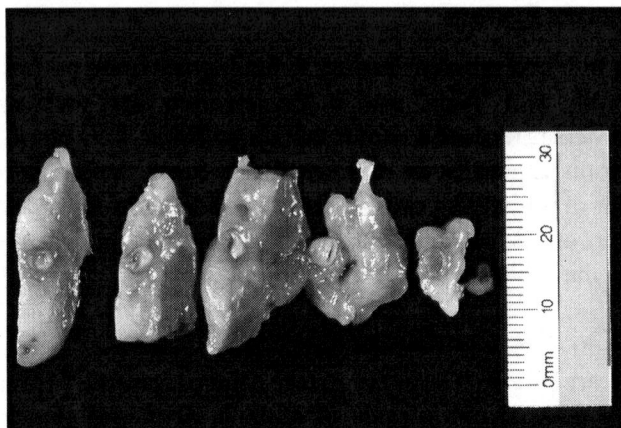

Figure 3.2   Transverse sections of coronary artery showing up to at least 90% stenosis.

In drivers who survive a motor vehicle collision and in whom there is suspicion of an acute ischaemic episode contributing to the collision, the clinical investigations including serum troponin levels and serial electrocardiographs may suggest a cardiac event around the time of the incident. However, blood loss or hypoxia arising from injuries sustained in the collision could precipitate a heart attack at the scene or shortly thereafter. The treating physician may be able to arrive at a reasonable conclusion as to the probability of the heart attack occurring before or after the collision, although in some instances no determination is possible.

In Australia, it is recommended that the minimum nondriving period for private vehicle drivers following an established acute myocardial infarction is 2 weeks. The recommended minimum nondriving period for commercial vehicle drivers is 3 months.

It is important to note that the presence of cardiac disease does not usually necessitate a reduction or cessation of driving. A population of 97 patients with severe coronary artery disease who underwent cardiac surgery was investigated with respect to their driving habits before and after the procedure. Before the operation, 78% of the patients were active drivers. After the operation, 64% continued to drive. Only 13% reduced their driving activity and this was largely as a result of decreased cognitive ability following the procedure.[6]

Hypertensive Heart Disease.   Hypertensive heart disease is manifested as left ventricular hypertrophy in individuals with arterial hypertension.[7] Hypertensive heart disease is associated with an increased risk of myocardial infarction, cerebrovascular accidents, ventricular arrhythmias, and sudden cardiac death.

Other Cardiovascular Conditions

Myocarditis.   Myocarditis is defined as inflammation of the heart muscle. In rare cases, an individual with myocarditis will suffer a sudden cardiac arrhythmia secondary to the electrical instability in the heart caused by the inflammatory process.

Myocarditis is typically caused by a primary viral infection, or secondary to an autoimmune disease process. The autoimmune disease may be viral induced or part of a systemic autoimmune disease process. Rarely myocardial inflammation may occur in drug-induced eosinophillic myocarditis, and in conditions of uncertain aetiology such as giant cell myocarditis and sarcoidosis.

Aortic Dissection.   Aortic dissection may rupture into the chest cavity, resulting in rapid exsanguination or dissect back to the pericardial sac causing cardiac tamponade.

Risk factors for aortic dissection include hypertension and Marfan's syndrome. Marfan's syndrome is a multisystem disorder with cardiovascular, skeletal, and ocular manifestations. The typical case has aortic root dilatation, heart valve abnormalities and dysfunction, disproportionate growth of long bones, and lens dislocation.[8]

Cardiomyopathy.   A cardiomyopathy is a disease of the myocardium that may be inherited, postinflammatory (myocarditis), or secondary to an identifiable factor such as long-term alcohol abuse. Cardiomyopathies may cause sudden collapse or death as a result of a cardiac arrhythmia (Figure 3.3).

Well recognised and described cardiomyopathies include hypertrophic cardiomyopathy, dilated cardiomyopathy, and arrhythmogenic right ventricular dysplasia.[9,10] Research into the molecular genetics of inherited

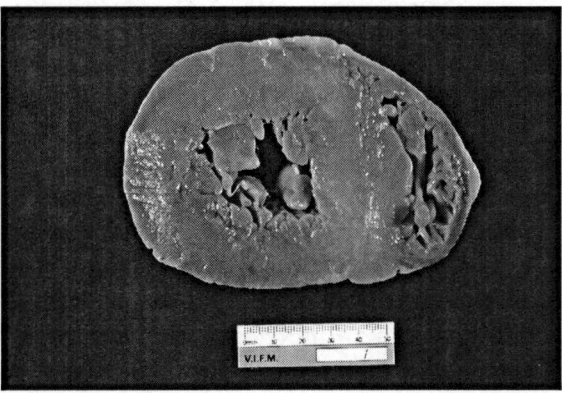

Figure 3.3   Enlarged heart of young male with hypertrophic cardiomyopathy. Microscopic examination showed classical branching of myofibres.

cardiomyopathies has revealed that these disorders can be classified with respect to sarcomere diseases (e.g., hypertrophic cardiomyopathy), cytoskeleton diseases (e.g., dilated cardiomyopathies), cell junction diseases (e.g., arrhythmogenic right ventricular dysplasia), and ion channel disease (conduction abnormalities).[11]

Conduction system disorders include short and long QT syndrome and Brugada syndrome.[12–14]

Abnormal Cardiac Valves.   Severe aortic stenosis that causes a significant pressure gradient across the valve is associated with a small risk of syncope and sudden death. Mitral valve prolapse is relatively common in the community and is usually asymptomatic. It may rarely be associated with sudden cardiac arrhythmias.[15]

Coronary Artery Abnormalities.   Coronary artery abnormalities affect approximately 1% of the population. Symptomatic coronary artery abnormalities are rare.[16] Relatively common incidental coronary artery abnormalities identified at autopsy and angiography include "high take off" of an artery at the aortic root and coronary artery bridging. Coronary artery bridging may cause a variety of clinical problems including angina pectoris, acute myocardial infarction, and life-threatening cardiac arrhythmias and sudden death.[17]

Relatively rare coronary artery abnormalities include anomolous origin of the artery from other than the aortic root.

Nervous System

Disease processes affecting the central nervous system can lead to sudden and severe clinical symptoms or rapid death.

Epilepsy

Epilepsy is a medical condition characterised by seizures. The seizures may range from subtle change in conscious state up to easily recognised local or generalised tonic/clonic rhythmical muscle contractions.

Epilepsy is usually idiopathic but may be caused by pathologic processes associated with gliosis of the cerebral cortex. Secondary epilepsy may result from old head trauma, remote central nervous system infection, haemorrhage from vascular malformations, prior stroke, or tumours (Figure 3.4). Examination of the brain in an individual with epilepsy is usually unremarkable. Mesial temporal sclerosis, a gliotic thickening, or scarring of the hippocampus results from the effects of epileptiform seizures rather than being the underlying cause.

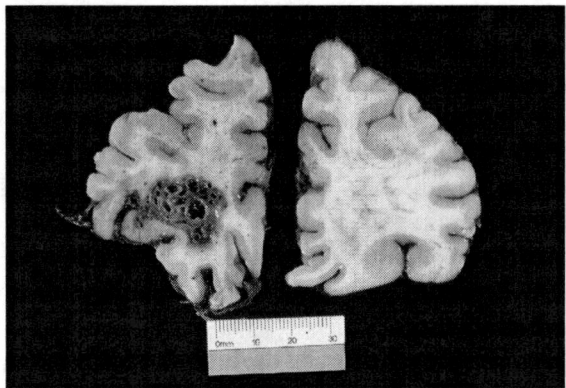

Figure 3.4   Arteriovenous malformation within frontal lobe as a cause of seizures.

The diagnosis of epilepsy results in restriction of driving based on medical fitness to drive. Granting of a licence generally requires a seizure free interval, the duration of which varies in different jurisdictions. In the State of Victoria, Australia, a seizure-free interval of 3 to 6 months is required. In Canada in 1998 an invitational symposium comprising various medical experts recommended a seizure free interval of 6 to 12 months before driving was resumed.[18]

A study from Arizona investigated the incidence of seizure-related motor vehicle collisions for a duration of 3 years, both prior to and following the alteration of the specified seizure-free interval decreasing from 18 months down to 3 months.[1] The study demonstrated no change in the incidence of seizure-related collisions. Furthermore, other studies of drivers with epilepsy have documented important individual features such as the type of seizure activity, consistent presence of an aura and the medical management of the disorder.[19, 20]

Individuals with epilepsy who consistently have a premonition or aura before the onset of seizure activity may be able to avoid potentially dangerous situations before other clinical symptoms appear.

A case-by-case approach is indicated with a review process combining both forensic and neurologic opinions.

Stroke

A cerebrovascular accident (stroke) most commonly occurs as a complication of hypertension, cerebrovascular disease, or rupture of a berry aneurysm. The clinical manifestations of the stroke are determined by the site of the central nervous system involved, the underlying pathology, and the severity of the insult.

Intracranial Haemorrhage.   Intracranial haemorrhage classically leads to the sudden onset of symptoms ranging in severity from headache up to immediate collapse. Intracranial haemorrhage occurs most commonly as a complication of hypertension or rupture of a berry aneurysm, and rarely from bleeding vascular lesions, tumours and coagulation disorders.

Hypertensive intracerebral haemorrhage typically involves the basal ganglia and thalamus within the cerebral hemispheres, the pons, and the cerebellar hemispheres (Figure 3.5). Because the precise anatomic location of pathology within the brain is associated with specific neurologic deficits, one can predict the clinical consequences of haemorrhage into a particular region of the brain. The degree of neurologic deficit also depends on the size and rapidity of the haemorrhage.

Haemorrhage overlying the base of the brain is usually the result of rupture of a berry aneurysm within the circle of Willis (Figure 3.6). A berry aneurysm results from a congenital weakness within the wall of the artery, which occurs

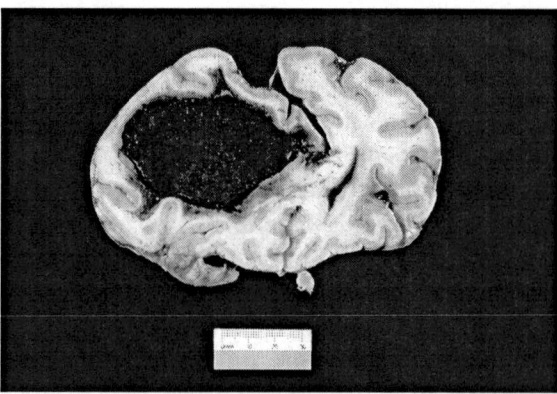

Figure 3.5 Hypertensive intracerebral haemorrhage arising from the basal ganglia.

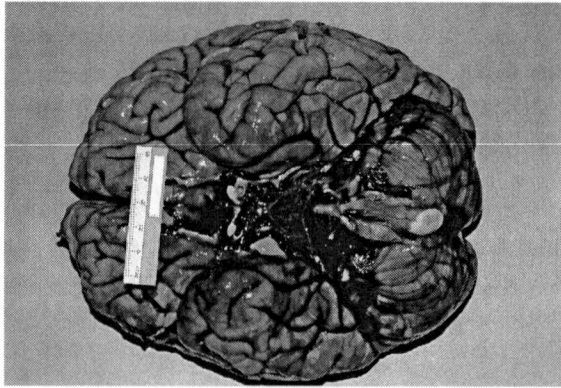

Figure 3.6 Subarachnoid haemorrhage overlying the base of the brain arising from a berry aneurysm.

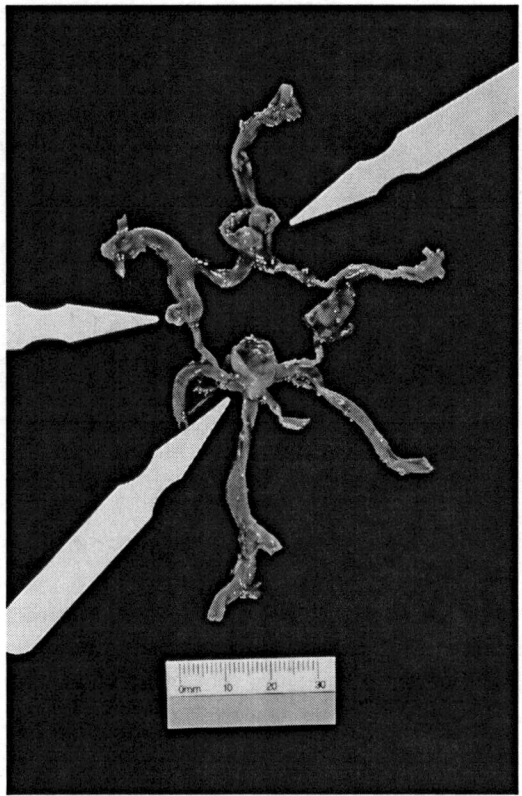

Figure 3.7 Major arteries at base of brain (circle of Willis) showing three berry aneurysms.

at branching points (Figure 3.7). Rupture of the aneurysm causes a large amount of bleeding around the brain within the subarachnoid space and sometimes into the ventricular system. This characteristically causes sudden onset of severe headache and may also cause rapid change in conscious state.

Investigations in Intracranial Haemorrhage. A trauma victim who presents to hospital with central nervous system pathology will undergo diagnostic procedures, which may include multislice computed tomography scanning, magnetic resonance imaging, and angiography. The postmortem examination on an individual who dies as a consequence of a motor vehicle incident and who has underlying central nervous system pathology will have the pathologic processes identified and documented by neuropathologic examination.

The pathologist, neurologist, or neurosurgeon is often able to provide an opinion on the likelihood of the central nervous system haemorrhage being of natural or traumatic origin and the probability of the stroke contributing to the motor vehicle incident.

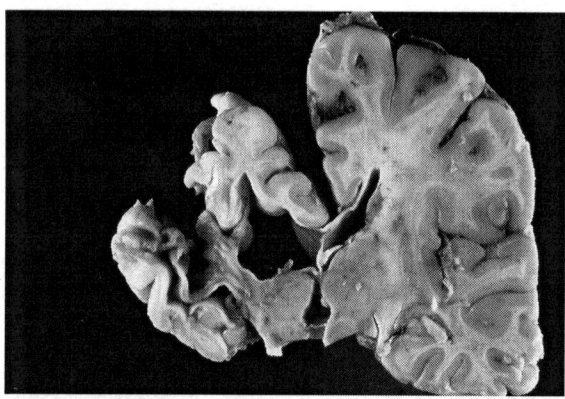

Figure 3.8   Coronal section of brain showing old cerebral infarction. Whilst the anatomic location may provide information on the likely neurologic deficit, clinical evaluation provides more reliable information on functional abilities.

Driving After Stroke.   Depending on the particular jurisdiction, it has been recommended that an individual who has suffered a stroke should not drive for at least 1 month after the event and 3 months after a subarachnoid haemorrhage. Review by an appropriate specialist with regard to problems of visual field deficits, hemiplegia, and sensory neglect is important (Figure 3.8). The Stroke Drivers Screening Assessment used in Great Britain is based on three tests, Dot Cancellation, Square Matrices and Road Sign Recognition, and is believed to predict whether a stroke patient is safe to resume driving.[21]

Old Age and Dementia

In Western societies, the proportion of elderly drivers is increasing. Elderly drivers have an increased risk of being involved in a motor vehicle incident with respect to all age groups except for men younger than 25 years of age. However, it is important to recognize that most older drivers are safe on road. The ability to drive a motor vehicle affords important mobility and independence for older members of the community.[22] Many elderly drivers recognise their decreased driving abilities and compensate by driving at slower speeds, not driving at night, and avoiding peak hour traffic and other difficult driving situations.[23]

Analysis of motor vehicle incidents leading to injury and death shows that the characteristics of motor vehicle incidents involving elderly drivers tend to be different from those involving younger drivers. Elderly drivers are more likely to be involved in a collision at an intersection and to be involved in multiple vehicle incidents. Elderly drivers are involved in collisions causing greater injury even after correcting for their less robust physical condition.[24]

Driving a motor vehicle is a complex task requiring sensory input, cognitive function, and motor output. A decrease in all three functions occurs with age.[25–27] Cognitive impairment was associated with an increased risk of collision in the older population.[28] Cognitive impairment has been shown to affect more than 20% of those older than 85 years of age in a retirement village community.[29] The most common cause of cognitive impairment in our community is Alzheimer's disease. Laboratory tests have showed that individuals with Alzheimer's disease perform poorly on psychometric tests, with visual search studies predictive of driving impairment.[30] A proportion of individuals with dementia lack insight and continue to drive when clearly impaired.[31,32]

A study by Johanssen and colleagues examined the incidence of cognitive impairment in drivers older than 65 years who had had their driving licences suspended because of traffic offences including collisions, speeding, and signal violations, and compared them with a group of matched control subjects.[33] The groups underwent a standard medical examination that did not identify any difference in crash risk between the subjects. However, a specific assessment of cognitive abilities identified those with an increased incidence of traffic violations.

Driver simulator studies can measure cognitive and perception deficiencies. A PC-based interactive driving simulator study by Lee and colleagues showed that individuals at increased risk of crashes could be identified using the driving simulator.[34] The inability to make rapid decisions, impaired memory, and lack of confidence while driving at highway speeds were associated with crash events.[34]

On-road driving assessments can provide a sensitive and reliable indicator of a particular individual's ability to safety drive a motor vehicle. In the State of Victoria, Australia, there is no compulsory system for testing older drivers. An individual may be reported to the appropriate authority by a concerned party, usually a police officer or medical practitioner. A specialist medical assessment or driving review test may be required by the DLA. The latter test entails a "real-life" demonstration of the driver's driving skill in his or her usual driving environment.[35]

Head Injury

Motor vehicle collisions are the principle cause of closed head injury (CHI) in Western societies.

Because victims of CHI are often young individuals, it is important that they are able to regain mobility and independence as soon as is practical. Those with mild or moderate degrees of CHI usually resume driving without much difficulty. Severely head-injured patients can have significant issues that impair their ability to drive, including decreased perception and cognition, and motor and behavioural problems including aggression.

A review by Brouwer showed that 50% of very severely affected CHI patients can regain their license after rehabilitation.[36] The impairments leading to failure to acquire a license were usually issues of perception and judgement.

Psychiatric Disorders

The major psychiatric disorders of interest with respect to motor vehicle collisions are schizophrenia, depressive illness, and anxiety disorders. Psychiatric disorders are common in Western societies.

Approximately one-quarter of all adult individuals will suffer a psychiatric illness during their lifetime.

Schizophrenia is a condition characterised by thought disorder, delusions, and hallucinations. The condition commonly affects relatively young men and women, and despite the use of psychotropic medications and support services, many affected individuals are marginalised in the community. Acute psychotic episodes with severe abnormalities in thought processes can lead to bizarre behaviour.

Depressive illness is a mood disorder characterised by marked decrease in mood and affect, feelings of hopelessness, disturbance of sleep, and suicidal ideation. Depressive illness may also be associated with psychotic episodes. Anxiety disorders are a varied group of psychiatric disorders characterised by excessive, inappropriate, and irrational anxiety that may be directed to specific situations.

Chronic psychiatric disorders have potential detrimental affects on the process of driving because of problems with concentration, information processing, aggressive driving behaviour, and suicidal thoughts. A study by Vernon and colleagues showed that drivers with psychiatric disorders have significantly higher rates of at fault crashes compared with controls.[37] An increased risk of crashes in individuals with schizophrenia has been reported.[38] However, other studies did not find a positive correlation between various types of psychiatric disorders and risk of road crashes.

Suicide by motor vehicle undoubtedly occurs but can be difficult to prove. A series of patients undergoing psychiatric assessment expressed the desire to use a motor vehicle to commit suicide.[39]

Endocrine System (Diabetes Mellitus)

Insulin-dependent diabetes mellitus has been associated with impaired driving performance.[40] The potential for hypoglycaemia is allied with the therapeutic use of insulin.[41] Diabetic patients may also have visual problems from diabetic retinopathy. A literature review did not support the suggestion that insulin-dependent diabetic drivers have an increased risk of traffic collisions over nondiabetic drivers.[42]

Studies have shown that young insulin-dependent diabetic women who maintain good control of their blood glucose levels and have good awareness of hypoglycaemia are able to recognize their cognitive impairment and inability to drive when hypoglycaemic. On the other hand, older insulin-dependent drivers showed impaired judgement of hypoglycaemia.[43]

Visual Problems

Cataract is the most common cause of visual impairment in developed societies and effects about 50% of those age 65 years and older. The Impact of Cataract on Mobility project showed that those patients who underwent cataract surgery and intraocular lens implantation had half the rate of collision involvement compared with matched controls.[44] Other factors that effect vision and may contribute to a collision include visual field loss, night vision impairment, and contrast sensitivity deficits.[45,46]

Sleep Apnea

Drowsy driving can be associated with the use of prescription and illicit drugs, any cause of lack of sleep including depressive illness and work-related issues, sleep apnea, and related disorders.[47,48]

Typical motor vehicle incidents that are caused by drowsy driving are single-vehicle run-off-the-road crashes and rear-end collisions.

Sleep apnea is a disorder characterised by multiple episodes of upper airway obstruction during sleep that leads to a cessation of breathing for about 10 or more seconds. The disorder is particularly common in obese, middle-age males. The disturbed sleep pattern may be associated with sleepiness during the daytime with short episodes of daytime sleep. Studies have shown an increased risk of crashes in individuals diagnosed with sleep apnea.[49,50]

References

1. Drazkowski JF, Fisher RS, Sirven JI, Demaerschalk BM, Uber-Zak L, Hentz JL, Labiner D. Seizure-related motor vehicle crashes in Arizona before and after reducing the driving restriction from 12 to 3 months. *Mayo Clinic Proceedings* 2003; 78:819–825.

2. Gresset J, Meyer F. Risk of automotive accidents amongst elderly drivers with impairments or chronic diseases. *Canadian Journal of Public Health* 1994; 85:282–285.

3. Austroads. Assessing fitness to drive for commercial and private vehicle drivers. Vermont South: Austroads, 2003. Article available at www.austroads.com.au

4. Hocking B, Landgren F. New medical standards for drivers. *Australian Family Physician* 2003; 32:732–737.

5. Charlton J, Koppel S, O'Hare M, Andrea D, Smith G, Khodr B, Langford J, Odell M, Fildes B. *Influence of Chronic Illness on Crash Involvement of Motor Vehicle Drivers.* Victoria, Australia: Monash University Accident Research Centre 2004; Report No. 213.

6. Ahlgren E, Rutberg H. Patients with coronary artery disease are active car drivers both before and soon after heart surgery. *Traffic Injury Prevention* 2002; 3:205–208.

7. Diamond JA, Phillips RA. Hypertensive heart disease. *Hypertension Research* 2005; 28:191–202.

8. Judge DP, Dietz HC. Marfan's syndrome. *The Lancet* 2005; 366:1965–1976.

9. Maron BJ. Hypertrophic cardiomyopathy: a systematic review. *The Journal of the American Medical Association* 2002; 287:1308–1320.

10. Sen-Chowdhry S, Lowe MD, Sporton SC, McKenna WJ. Arrhythmogenic right ventricular cardiomyopathy: clinical presentation, diagnosis, and management. *American Journal of Medicine* 2004; 117:685–695.

11. Thiene G, Basso C, Calabrese F, Angelini A, Valente M. Twenty years of progress and beckoning frontiers in cardiovascular pathology. Cardiomyopathies. *Cardiovascular Pathology* 2005; 14:165–169.

12. Bjerregaard P, Gussak I. Sort QT syndrome. *Annals of Noninvasive Electrocardiology* 2005; 10:436–440.

13. Roberts R. Genomics and cardiac arrhythmias. *Journal of the American College of Cardiologists* 2006; 47:9–21.

14. Corrado D, Buja G, Basso C, Nava A, Thiene G. What is the Brugada syndrome? *Cardiology in Review* 1999; 7:191–195.

15. Hayek E, Gring CN, Griffin BP. Mitral valve prolapse. *Lancet* 2005; 365:507–518.

16. Baltaxe HA, Wixson D. The incidence of congenital abnormalities of the coronary arteries in the adult population. *Radiology* 1977; 122:47–52.

17. Bourassa MG, Butnaru A, Lesperance J, Tardif J-C. Symptomatic myocardial bridges: overview of ischemic mechanisms and current diagnostic and treatment strategies. *Journal of the American College of Cardiologists* 2003; 41:351–359.

18. Remillard GM, Zifkin BG, Andermann F. Epilepsy and motor vehicle driving—a symposium held in Quebec City, November 1998. *Canadian Journal of Neurological Sciences* 2002; 29:315–325.

19. Taylor JF, editor. *Medical Aspects of Fitness to Drive. A Guide for Medical Practitioners.* 5th ed. London: Medical Commission on Accident Prevention, 1995.

20. Gastaut H, Zifkin BG. The risk of automobile accidents with seizures occurring while driving: relation to seizure type. *Neurology* 1987; 37:1613–1616.

21. Radford KA, Lincoln NB. Concurrent validity of the stroke driver's screening assessment. *Archive of Physical Medicine and Rehabilitation* 2004; 85:324–328.

22. Evans L. Risk older drivers face themselves and threats they pose to other road users. *Internal Journal of Epidemiology* 2000; 29:315–322.

23. Hakamies-Blomqvist L. Aging and fatal accidents in male and female drivers. *Journal of Gerontology* 1994; 49:S286–S290.

24. Hakamies-Blomqvist L, Wahlstrom B. Why do older drivers give up driving? *Accident Analysis and Prevention* 1998; 30:305–312.

25. Friedland RP, Koss E, Kumar A. Motor vehicle crashes in dementia of the Alzheimer's type. *Annals of Neurology* 1988; 24:782–6.

26. Halpern D. Age differences in response time to vehicle traffic signs. *Experimental Aging Research* 1984; 10:201–204.

27. Larsson L. Aging in mammalian skeletal muscle. In Mortimer JA, Pirrozolo FJ, Maletta GJ, editors. *The Aging Motor System.* New York: Praeger, 1982; pp 60–97.

28. Drachman DA, Swearer JM. Driving and Alzheimer's disease: the risk of crashes. *Neurology* 1993; 43:2448–2456.

29. Pheiffer RI, Afifi AA, Chance JM. Prevalence of Alzheimer's disease in a retirement community. *American Journal of Epidemiology* 1987; 125:420–436.

30. Duchek JM, Hunt L, Ball K, Buckles V, Morris JC. Attention and driving performance in Alzheimer's disease. *Journal of Gerontology: Psychological Sciences* 1998; 53:130–141.

31. Couper PJ, Tallman K, Tuokko H, Beattie BL. Vehicle crash involvement and cognitive deficit in older drivers. *Journal of Safety Research* 1993; 24:9–17.

32. Retchin SM, Cox J, Fox M, Irwin L. Performance based measurements among elderly drivers and non-drivers. *Journal of the American Geriatrics Society* 1988; 36:813–819.

33. Johansson K, Bronge L, Lundberg C, Persson A, Seideman M, Viitanen M. Can a physician recognize an older driver with increased crash risk potential? *Journal of the American Geriatrics Society* 1996; 44:1198–1204.

34. Lee HC, Lee AH, Cameron D, Li-Tsang C. Using a driver simulator to identify older drivers at inflated risk of motor vehicle crashes. *Journal of Safety Research* 2003; 34:453–459.

35. Di Stefano M, Macdonald W. Assessment of older drivers; relationships among on-road errors, medical conditions and test outcome. *Journal of Safety Research* 2003; 34:415–429

36. Brouwer WH, Withaar FK. Fitness to drive after traumatic brain injury. *Neuropsychological Rehabilitation* 1997; 7:177–193.

37. Vernon DD, Diller EM, Cook LT, Reading JL, Suruda AJ, Deane JM. Evaluating the crash and citation rates of Utah drivers licensed with medical conditions, 1992–1996. *Accident Analysis and Prevention* 2002; 34:237–246.

38. Edlund MJ, Conrad C, Morris P. Crashes among schizophrenic outpatients. *Comprehensive Psychiatry* 1989; 30:522–526.

39. Hamburger E. "Vehicular Suicidal Ideation." *Military Medicine* 1969; 134:441–445.

40. Taylor J, Chadwick D, Johnston T. Risk of accidents in drivers with epilepsy. *Journal of Neurology, Neurosurgery and Psychiatry* 1996; 60:621–627.

41. Gill G, Durston J, Johnston R, Macleod K, Watkins P. Insulin-treated diabetes and driving in the UK. *Diabetic Medicine* 2002; 19:435–441.

42. MacLeod KM. Diabetes and driving: towards equitable, evidence-based decision-making. *Diabetic Medicine* 1999; 16(4):282-290.

43. Weinger K, Kinsely BT, Levy CJ, Bajaj M, Simonson DC, Cox DJ, et al. The perception of safe driving ability during hypoglycemia in patients with type 1 diabetes mellitus. *American Journal of Medicine* 1999; 107:246–253.

44. Owsley C, McGwin G Jr., Sloane M, Wells J, et al. Impact of cataract surgery on motor vehicle crash involvement by older adults. *Journal of the American Medical Association* 2002; 288:841–850.

45. Owsley C, Ball K, Sloane ME, Roenker DL, Bruni JR. Visual/cognitive collaterals of vehicle accidents in older drivers. *Psychology of Aging* 1991; 6:430–414.

46. Ball K, Owsley C, Ball K, Sloane ME, Roenker DL, Bruni JR. Visual attention problems as a predictor of vehicle crashes in older drivers. *Investigative Ophthalmology and Visual Science* 1993; 34:3110–3123.

47. Stutts JC, Wilkins JW, Osberg JS, Vaughn BV. Driver risk factors for sleep-related crashes. *Accident Analysis and Prevention* 2003; 35(3):321–331.

48. Findley LJ, Fabrizo MJ, Thommi G, Suratt PM. Severity of sleep apnea and automobile crashes (correspondence). *New England Journal of Medicine* 1989; 320:68–69.

49. Horstman S, Hess CW, Basetti C, Gugger M, Mathis J. Sleepiness-related accidents in sleep apnea patients. *Sleep* 2000; 23:1–7.

50. Barbe F, Pericas J, Munoz A, Findley L, Anto JM, Agusti AGN, De Lluc JM. Automobile accidents in patients with sleep apnea syndrome: an epidemiological and mechanistic study. *American Journal of Respiratory Critical Care Medicine* 1998; 158:18–22.

Forensic Classification of Injuries

4

Classification

The forensic classification of injuries may be separated into the following categories:

- Abrasions
- Lacerations
- Bruises
- Incised and stab injuries
- Fractures and ligamentous injuries
- Burns

Abrasions

Definition and Overview

An abrasion may be defined as an injury resulting from blunt force that removes the surface epidermal layer of the skin.

The position of an abrasion on the skin surface indicates a site of the application of blunt force. The characteristics of the injury may provide information with respect to the direction of the impact force and occasionally information regarding the shape and nature of the object that caused the injury.

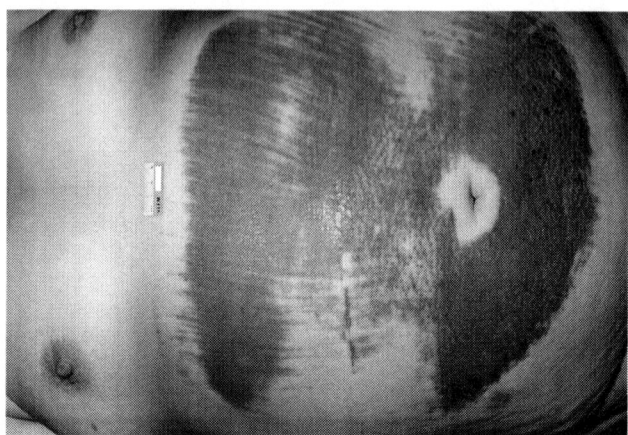

Figure 4.1   A large parchment-like abraded injury to the abdomen with longitudinal linear components typically seen with movement of the body along a roadway or similar surface.

Following death from a traumatic event that resulted in abraded injuries, it is not uncommon for the affected skin surface to develop a tan-coloured leathery appearance (Figure 4.1). This parchment effect is due to drying of the tissues and does not indicate the injuries were sustained postmortem. Subcutaneous dissection may demonstrate the presence of bruising, which confirms the injuries were sustained during life, although some parchment-like abraded injuries that had clearly occurred in life do not show subcutaneous bruising.

Direction of Impact

Skin tags can indicate the relative movement of an object and the skin. Skin tags are small, raised pieces of skin produced when an object moves across the skin surface and point toward differential blunt force contact. Thus if a broad metallic object impacted the lower limbs at the knee joint and travelled down the leg toward the foot, the skin tags produced from contact with the skin would tend to be located at the distal aspect of the abraded injuries. It is important to note that such injuries do not indicate which object was moving and which was stationary.

Surface and Nature of the Object

Examination of an abrasion can provide information regarding the surface of the object that impacted with the skin surface. Scratches or linear abrasions are injuries to the skin that occur from contact with a fine point. Broad abraded injuries result from contact with a relatively wide surface. It is not uncommon for large abrasions to have areas of uninvolved intact skin that correspond to recessed regions of the body that are protected from the impacting object.

Depending upon the nature of the object that abrades the skin, there may be foreign material derived from the object embedded or adherent to the surface of the skin. The most common materials associated with the skin of the pedestrian victim of a collision are flecks of paint, fine particles of glass, and grease.

Shape of the Object

Examination of the abrasion may provide information regarding the shape of the object that impacted with the skin surface. The majority of abraded injuries to the skin are nonspecific; however, some have distinct shapes called patterned, abraded injuries (Figure 4.2). An analogy is a stamp producing its image on a sheet of white paper. If the process is repeated with the paper placed on a firm and irregular surface, only portions of the stamp surface might be seen on the paper. Because the human body has numerous curves, is covered with various layers of clothing, and may come into contact with a small portion of a larger object, patterned injuries usually do not reproduce the complete mirror image of the object. There may even be disagreement between observers as to whether an injury is patterned and whether a given patterned abraded is significant.

The classic patterned abraded injury is the seat belt abrasion (Figure 4.3). Patterned abrasions are also caused from contact with objects within the vehicle cabin in occupants of motor vehicles. Peculiar shapes and patterns are becoming less common with improved restraint systems and vehicle designers producing rounded edges to instrument and door panels.

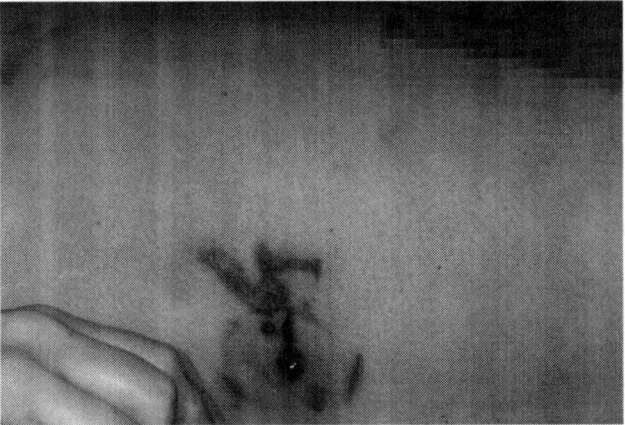

Figure 4.2   Patterned abraded injury to the right hip of motor vehicle occupant reflecting forceful contact from a window wiper handle on older style car.

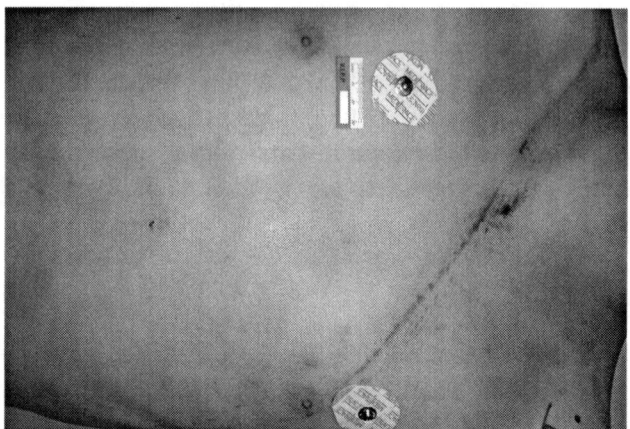

Figure 4.3   Classical patterned abrasion from a seat belt.

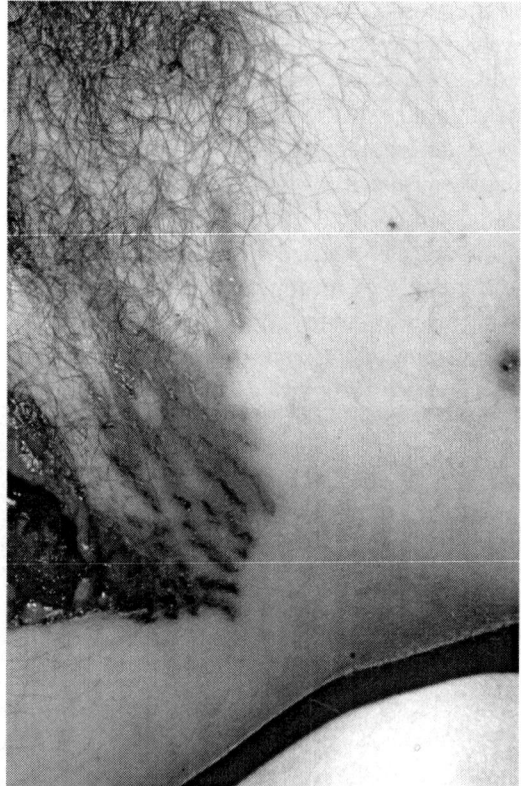

Figure 4.4   Creases to inguinal skin from stretching associated with an open-book fracture of the pelvis.

Pedestrians may suffer patterned, abraded injuries from contact with various external regions of a motor vehicle. These include grill components, headlight and windshield surrounds and wiper assemblies, and wheels. The identification of a patterned, abraded injury in a pedestrian may aid in determining the pedestrian's position at impact.

Abrasions from Indirect Forces

Incidents involving extreme forces that cause marked deformation to the body may result in superficial stretch marks to the skin. These marks may develop anywhere in the body, but tend to occur in natural creases such as the groin and axillae. A common setting in which this injury is seen is in cases in which the torso is run over by a motor vehicle resulting in a fractured pelvis with wide separation of the pubic rami. Stretch-type injuries may then be seen in the inguinal creases (Figure 4.4).

Lacerations

Definition

A laceration may be defined as an injury resulting from blunt force that results in tearing of the skin.

A laceration usually has irregular margins with so-called skin bridges within the depths of the wound. Skin bridges are connective tissues, nerves, and blood vessels beneath the skin in subcutaneous tissue that extend across the opposing edges of the laceration (Figure 4.5). Because lacerations are due

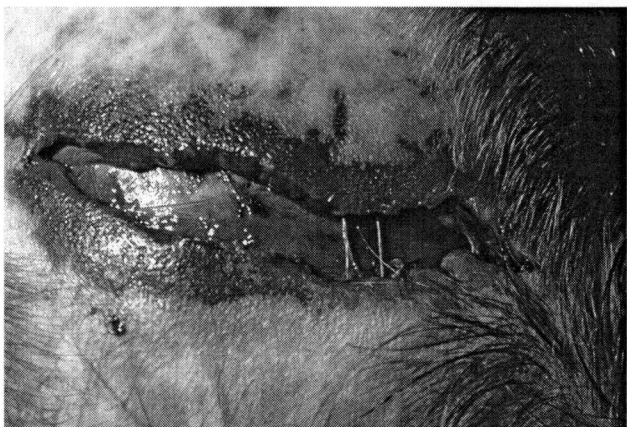

Figure 4.5 Lacerated injury to the scalp showing surrounding abrasion and connective tissues forming "skin bridges" within the depths of the wound.

to the application of blunt force, there is usually an associated abraded injury surrounding the laceration.

Direction and Nature of the Impact

A laceration indicates a site of the application of blunt force. A tangential impact can result in undermining of the laceration in the direction of the force. Degloving-type lacerated injuries refer to extreme undermining with separation of the skin from the underlying deeper tissues. These injuries are especially prominent in runover incidents from the action of a rotating tire, but may also be seen in tangential impacts involving considerable force.

Bruises

Definition

A bruise may be defined as the extravasation of blood from the blood vessels into surrounding tissues. A bruise results from the application of blunt force. The haemorrhage may involve subcutaneous fat or deep soft tissues including muscle.

Point of Impact

The site of bruising to the skin surface does not always correlate with the point of impact. A fractured base of skull may lead to bruising behind the ears or bilateral periorbital hematomas. These bruises result from blood tracking between tissue planes from a distant point to the surface of the skin.

Examination of a bruise to the surface of the skin does not allow a determination of the direction of the impact. In a postmortem examination, subcutaneous and deeper dissection may reveal varied degrees of bruising in sequentially deeper tissues with a directional component. In these circumstances, one may provide a guarded opinion as to the direction of force.

Macroscopic and microscopic examination of fatty tissue may shed light on the origin of a bruise. Bruising that occurs from blood tracking from a distant site will travel along tissue planes. Direct trauma of a mild degree results in perilobular haemorrhage. As the degree of force increases, there is additional intralobular haemorrhage and then rupture and destruction of supporting connective tissues, ultimately leading to a fluid-filled cavity.

Surface and Shape of the Object

Because bruising is caused by haemorrhage from blood vessels into the soft tissues, there is a tendency for the bruise to be larger than the object that impacted the skin. For the same reason, the shape of the bruise is usually not well defined. Intradermal bruises may be viewed as analogous to a patterned abrasion, and the production of such patterned injuries is often due to a combination of abrasion of the skin and localised haemorrhage into the dermis (Figure 4.6).

Degree of Bruising

The amount of bruising that occurs from impact by a particular object with a certain degree of force can vary considerably between different individuals. The bruising produced does not necessarily reflect the degree of force in a particular incident. Bruising varies with extremes of age, the site of injury, and the presence of underlying medical conditions. Regions of the body with a rich vascular supply or abundant subcutaneous fatty tissue tend to develop a greater amount of bruising. Facial trauma will tend to develop a greater degree of bruising than a chest injury of identical force. Disease processes such as bleeding disorders and severe chronic liver and kidney disease are examples of the many conditions that can lead to excess bruising. Several medical therapies, such as anticoagulant medications and corticosteroids, are associated with a bleeding tendency.

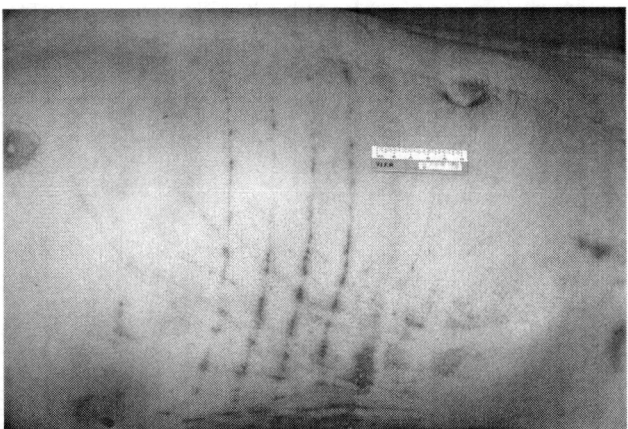

Figure 4.6 A patterned intradermal bruise from contact from a tire of a motor vehicle.

Petechial Haemorrhages

Petechial haemorrhages may be defined as small extravasations of blood from capillaries and venules resulting in minute, pinpoint haemorrhage. Petechial haemorrhages are most commonly seen on skin and mucous membranes. On the skin, they often involve periorbital and retroauricular skin. The mucosal surfaces often affected include the conjunctivae, sclera, and buccal mucosa. During an autopsy examination, petechiae may be visible over many organs.

Petechial haemorrhages are nonspecific but classically seen in asphyxial deaths. Deaths from mechanical asphyxia usually have widespread and often confluent petechiae.

Incised and Stab Injuries

Definition

Incised and stab injuries may be defined as injuries that result from the application of sharp force. An incised injury is wider than it is deep whereas a stab injury is deeper than it is wide.

Sharp force injuries differ from lacerations in that the edges are clean and well defined with no surrounding abrasions unless there is an associated blunt force injury. Compared with lacerations, there are no skin bridges as the sharp implement also divides the deeper connective tissues. In motor vehicle incidents, sharp-force injuries may result from contact with glass and metal edges (Figure 4.7). Contact from broken tempered glass from windows typically causes punctate, dicing, incised injuries.

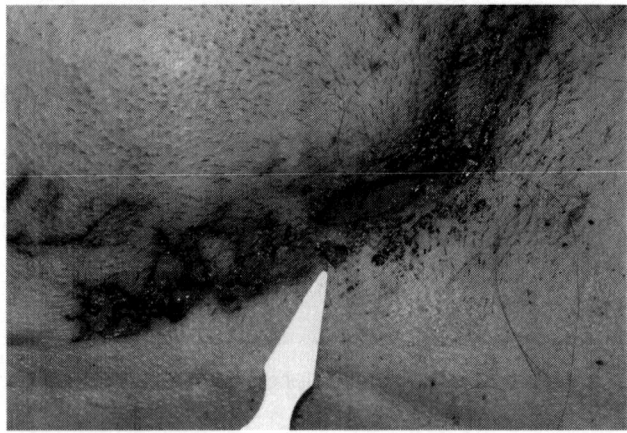

Figure 4.7 Incised injury from partial penetration of the windshield with surrounding abraded injuries.

Fractures and Ligament Injuries

Definition

A fracture is a disruption of bone that occurs from the application of direct or transmitted force. Ligaments are connective tissues that maintain the structural integrity of joints. A ligamentous tear may be partial or complete and lead to varying laxity of the joint.

Fractures

Bone is a highly specialised connective tissue that generally has an inner spongy trabecular region surrounded by dense cortical bone. Long bones are composed of a central portion called the diaphysis, which expands toward its opposing ends at the metaphysis, and two opposing cartilage capped ends adjacent to joints called the epiphyses. Fractures may occur at any of these points. A fracture may extend transversely across the bone, spiral around the bone, or shatter into numerous fragments in comminuted fractures (Figure 4.8). A fracture may be closed or compound. Different mechanisms of injury tend to result in certain types of fracture. Rotational forces tend to cause spiral fractures, axial loads tend to cause compression fractures, and direct perpendicular forces tend to cause transverse fractures.

Bone is stronger in compression than it is in tension. Thus when one considers an upright pedestrian in which a force is applied to the anterior aspect of the tibia, the fracture begins at the posterior aspect of the bone where the tensile forces are acting. The fracture then extends to the anterior part of the bone that is under compression force.

Ligament Injury

Joints are complex structures that in varying degrees depend on ligaments and muscles to maintain anatomic and functional integrity. The importance

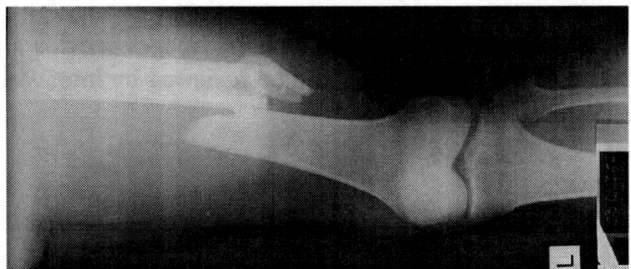

Figure 4.8 Radiograph showing fracture to left femur. Angulation of distal fractured portion of femur with displacement of bone fragment suggests impact from medial aspect of thigh.

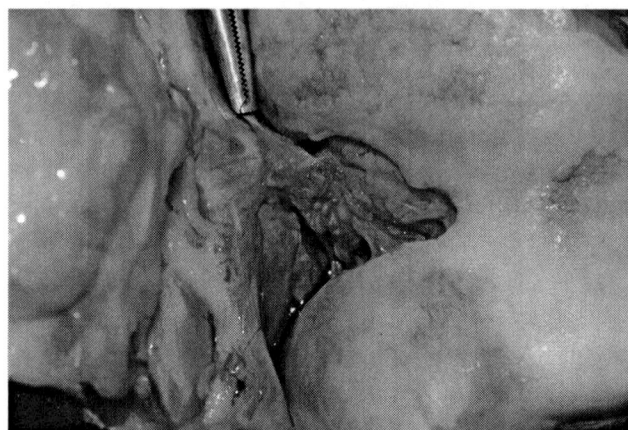

Figure 4.9 Knee joint opened anteriorly to demonstrate the femoral condyles and show ruptured anterior cruciate ligament.

of different ligaments to joint stability varies with the particular type and position of the joint. The ball-and-socket joint of the hip has far greater stability from its bony configuration than the rolling type joint of the knee.

Each different ligament around a particular joint prevents excessive movement in a particular direction. The lateral collateral ligament of the knee resists adduction of the joint. Severe force that leads to excessive adduction of the knee may result in a partial or complete tear of the lateral collateral ligament or avulsion of the ligament's attachment to bone (Figure 4.9). Identification of ligament injuries may thus provide information regarding the direction of the application of force.

Demonstration of Fractures and Ligament Injuries

In the clinical setting and at postmortem radiographs, computed tomography scans and magnetic resonance imaging can demonstrate fractures and soft-tissue injury.

At the postmortem examination, conventional radiographs, computed tomography, and magnetic resonance imaging images provide a permanent objective record of the fracture that can be reviewed by interested parties at a later date (Figures 4.8 and 4.9).

Burns

Burns in motor vehicle incidents occur most commonly when a fire results from a collision and an occupant is unable to extricate himself or herself from the vehicle. This may be due to injuries sustained in the incident, from the effects of natural disease, or from being trapped by parts of the vehicle.

Definition

A burn may occur from contact with chemicals, electricity, or friction; however, in the context of a motor vehicle collision, radiant heat and direct contact with flames are the two important causes. Burns may be superficial or full thickness and involve the skin, soft tissues, bone, or airway. Occasionally, ejected occupants of a motor vehicle and motorcycle riders may suffer contact burns from hot segments of the vehicle's exhaust system.

Injuries Sustained by Motor Vehicle Occupants

5

Introduction

The severity and distribution of injuries sustained in a motor vehicle collision depends on a number of factors, including the site of impact to the particular vehicle, the speeds and mass of the vehicles involved, and the use of restraint systems. In addition, the seating position of a vehicle occupant determines his or her risk of injury. It has been shown that the rear seat position, and in children the centre rear seat position, carries a lower risk of injury and death compared with the front seat in motor vehicle crashes. It has been estimated that sitting in the rear seat results in a 39% reduction in the risk of death.[1]

For a collision with a change in velocity (delta V) of 60 Kph (30 mph), the risk of a serious injury (MAIS 3+) for frontal, side impact near side, side impact far side, and rear impact collisions are 38.9%, 83.8%, 47.8%, and 19.9%, respectively.[2]

The major types of vehicle collisions may be classified as:

- Frontal collisions
- Side impact collisions
- Rear impact collisions
- Rollover incidents

Frontal Collision

The impact that results from two cars that had been travelling in opposite directions is often severe (Figure 5.1). Head on collisions may be offset, with

Figure 5.1   Lateral photograph showing the degree of front end damage. Note the integrity of the vehicle cabin and deployed airbags.

a metre or less of vehicle width coming into contact. The design of vehicle safety features, in particular restraint systems and frontal crush zones, were largely developed to address the forces involved in frontal impacts.

Frontal collisions are common in rural locations. Driver drowsiness and inattention on two-lane highways may be a contributing factor when cars drift onto the wrong side of the road. Overtaking maneuvers are a further important issue in some cases of frontal collisions. Less commonly, an incident that occurred in the correct lane leads to the vehicle crossing onto the wrong side of the road, resulting in a frontal collision.

Oblique Frontal Collisions

Oblique frontal collisions (OFCs) are defined as collisions involving the left or right front quarters of a motor vehicle in which the impact is angled. OFCs cause approximately 6% of all road crashes that lead to injury. OFCs are more common in elderly drivers.

OFCs occur most commonly when a vehicle is turning at an intersection and moves into the path of an oncoming vehicle. OFCs have a higher incidence of significant injury and death compared with true frontal collisions of a given severity and is partly related to increased cabin intrusion.

Unrestrained Occupant

Newton's First Law of Motion states that an object will continue at its velocity unless acted on by another force. The practical consequence of the Law for the occupant of a motor vehicle is that following a frontal collision, the occupant will continue to move rapidly in his or her preimpact direction until acted upon by some other force. If one ignores the minor frictional forces that are present between the occupant and seat and floor, the major force that will alter the occupant's velocity is contact with interior components of the vehicle cabin.[3]

Contact with the interior of the vehicle cabin introduces consequences of Newton's Second Law of Motion. The Second Law states that force is equal to the mass of a body multiplied by its acceleration. From this equation, it is clear that the abrupt deceleration that occurs from the occupant's body impacting with the vehicle interior following a high-speed crash will lead to the application of considerable force. The seat belt prevents rapid deceleration against the interior components of the vehicle cabin.

Unrestrained drivers in frontal crashes impact with the steering wheel and assembly, the windshield and surrounds, instrument panel, and floor pan (Figure 5.2). The major injury associated with direct impact is head injury.[4] Unrestrained rear seat passengers have been shown to pose a significant threat to drivers and front seat passengers in frontal collisions.[5]

The passenger does not have the steering column directly in front, so initial contact is with the windshield and dashboard. Head impact tends to be frontal, leading to forced hyperextension of the upper cervical spine, and fracture dislocation of the atlanto-occipital joint is a common injury and cause of death (Figure 5.3). Subsequent blunt force trauma leads to further chest, abdominal, pelvic, and upper and lower leg injuries.

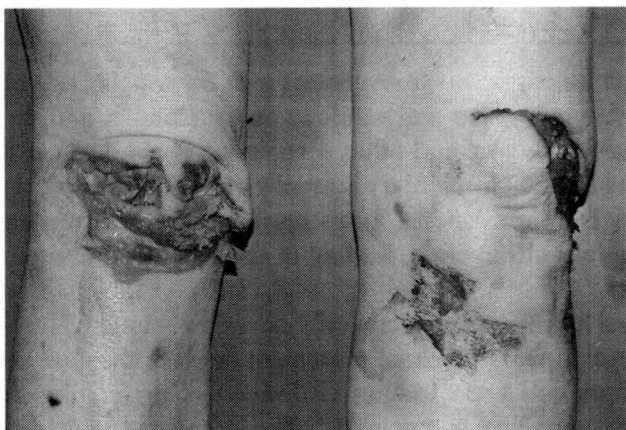

Figure 5.2 Lacerated and abraded injuries to the left and right knees from impact with the dashboard.

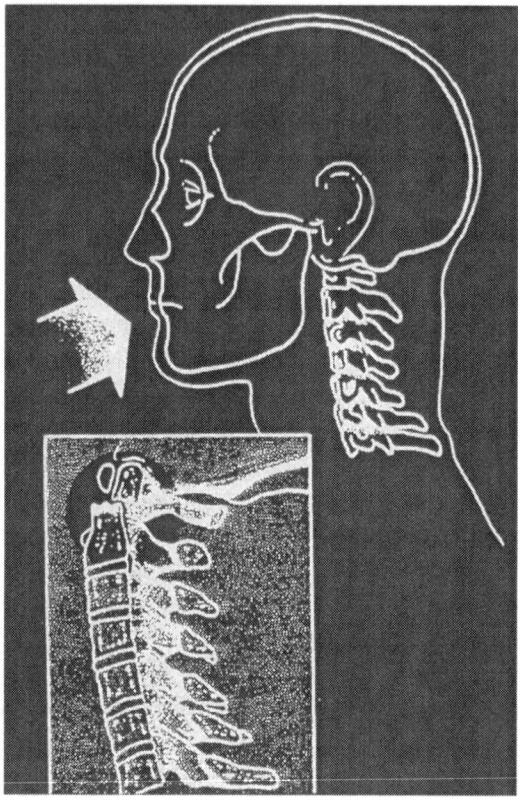

Figure 5.3 Schematic diagram of cervical spine. A common cervical spine injury is fractured odontoid process.

Head Injury

Head impact usually occurs from contact with the A-pillar, side of the vehicle roof, door frame, B-pillar and windows and surrounds, and, in the case of rollover, the vehicle roof and other occupants.[6] Rapid death at the incident scene caused by blunt head injury is usually due to diffuse axonal injury. This brain injury is from rotational forces causing differential movement within different regions of the brain, leading to damage to nerve axons and small blood vessels.

Subdural haemorrhage is classically caused by rotational forces acting on the head resulting in differential movement between the skull and relatively adherent dura, and brain leading to division of perforating small venous channels. Subdural haemorrhage is often associated with diffuse axonal injury. A subdural haemorrhage can accumulate rapidly to a volume (50 to 100 mL), resulting in compression of the underlying brain.

Traumatic subarachnoid haemorrhage over the cerebral hemispheres is caused by division of innumerable small blood vessels and, if extensive, is a marker of a significant underlying brain injury. Basal traumatic subarachnoid haemorrhage suggests rupture of the intracranial vertebral or basilar arteries or rupture of a vertebral artery within the cervical spine.

An extradural haemorrhage is classically caused by rupture of the middle meningeal artery within the squamous temporal bone. The bone shows an associated fracture in about 30% of cases. It is uncommon for an isolated extradural haemorrhage to be the sole cause of death in a motor vehicle incident. The haemorrhage has to strip the densely adherent dura from the skull and form a collection such that the underlying brain is compressed and distorted. This usually takes some hours and provides enough time for surgical evacuation of the blood clot. Extradural haemorrhage in a motor vehicle collision is usually associated with other significant forms of head injury.

A cause of death in head injury that may have subtle changes at postmortem is a tear at the pontomedullary junction in the brainstem.

Secondary Brain Injury

Secondary brain injury is common and can be as important to the survival and functional recovery of a crash victim as the primary insult. Secondary brain injury refers to brain swelling and haemorrhage that occurs as a consequence of a number of factors including, but not limited to, hypoxia, hypotension, and coagulopathy. Head injury is a recognised cause of apnea. Experimental evidence suggests the magnitude of the brain impact is directly proportional to the onset and persistence of apnea.[7]

Clinical observations have recorded an instance of life-saving artificial respiration followed by complete recovery in a motor vehicle crash victim who was observed by a medical practitioner to be apneic at the scene.[8] The absence of immediate resuscitative efforts will contribute to hypoxic secondary brain injury.

In many cases secondary injury is inevitable because of the isolated location of the motor vehicle incident.

Deceleration Injury

The uncontrolled deceleration that occurs in unrestrained vehicle occupants, primarily but not exclusive to frontal collisions, can lead to rapidly fatal deceleration injuries to the cardiovascular system. Deceleration injury is typically seen in unrestrained vehicle occupants, ejected vehicle occupants, motorcyclists, and pedestrians, but may be seen in anyone involved in collisions at speeds of greater than 60 km/hr.

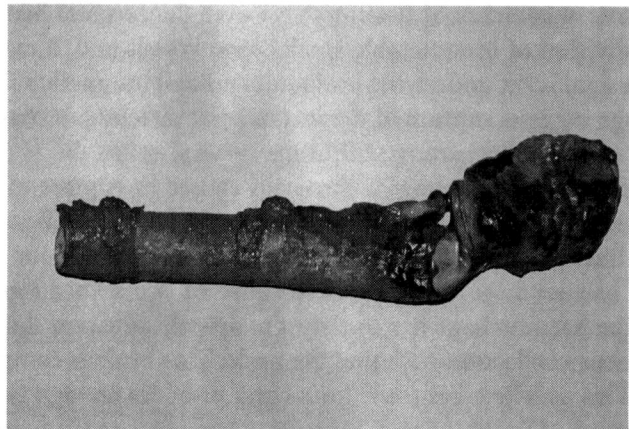

Figure 5.4   Region of traumatic rupture of the descending thoracic aorta resulting from deceleration.

The typical deceleration injury that leads to death is transection of the descending thoracic aorta (Figure 5.4). Complete rupture of the aorta results in rapid haemothorax and death in approximately 85% of cases.[9] The differential movement between the ascending aorta and arch, and the relatively fixed descending thoracic aorta, results in injuries beginning at the endothelium and extending varying degrees through the artery wall. The injury classically occurs at the level of the isthmus. An alternate explanation in the causation of the injury is a "water hammer" effect. Tears may also occur in the ascending thoracic aorta and vascular branches from the arch. Rupture of an atrial appendage is a further significant traumatic injury.

Pulmonary haemorrhage of varying severity can occur secondary to deceleration. Avulsion of major thoracic and intra-abdominal viscera including the liver, kidneys, lungs, and heart from vascular attachments are further catastrophic injuries. Tracheobronchial disruption is a further deceleration injury, which may be seen in the absence of other significant chest injuries, and may be the sole cause of death.

The introduction of crush zones to the front of cars, seat belts with energy management systems and front airbags have been designed to lengthen the duration of deceleration and subsequently reduce deceleration injury.

Restrained Occupant

The motor vehicle occupant wearing a seat belt involved in a frontal collision will also move forward following frontal impact, although obviously to a far lesser degree than unrestrained occupants. Vehicles fitted with seat belt pretensioners will have even less forward movement. Significant forces still apply to the upper cervical spine as a result of rapid movement of the victim's head. Direct blunt force is transmitted to the chest, abdomen and pelvis by the

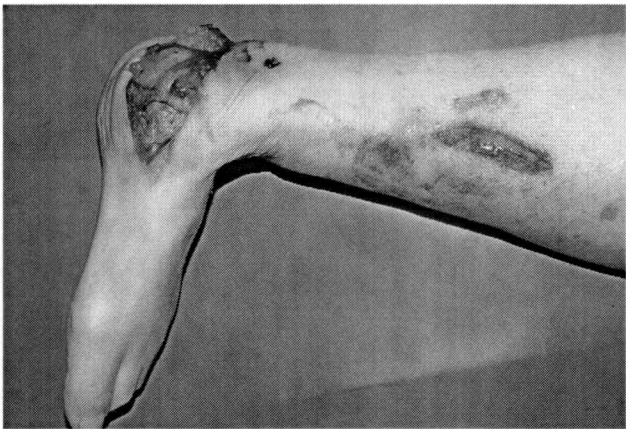

Figure 5.5 Compound fracture of the left ankle associated with floor pan intrusion in a frontal motor vehicle collision.

seatbelt. Vehicle intrusion is a further cause of blunt force injury. Direct impact between the knee and the dashboard is decreased in the restrained occupant. Floor pan intrusion is a major cause of lower limb injury (Figure 5.5).

Restrained occupants in motor vehicle collisions most commonly die as a result of head injury or deceleration injury. Other significant injuries result from the injuries described below.

Blunt Chest Trauma

Chest injury from direct blunt trauma can lead directly to death, but more commonly contributes to death in association with other injuries. Massive pulmonary contusions, ruptured pulmonary vein, ruptured heart with pericardial tamponade, and widespread rib fractures sometimes associated with lung and cardiac lacerations are injuries seen with severe chest trauma. The presence of fractures of the first and second ribs is indicative of severe blunt force to the chest, and should be a stimulus for investigation of other significant chest and abdominal injuries.

Multiple fractured ribs or fractured sternum is a significant injury in the elderly and crash victims with other major medical conditions. In these subgroups, a fractured sternum or multiple fractured ribs especially with a flail segment, there is a high morbidity and mortality rate and often a requirement for a period of ventilation in an intensive care unit with appropriate pain management. When death occurs, it is often the result of a combination of respiratory failure and bronchopneumonia.

Tension pneumothorax is a medical emergency that can lead to rapid death. Tension pneumothorax occurs when air is able to enter the potential

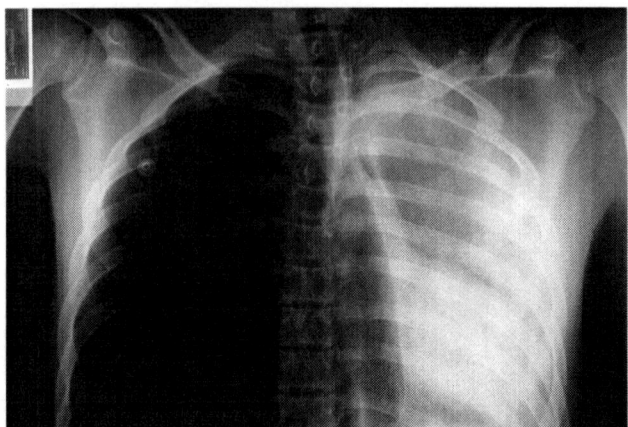

Figure 5.6 Chest radiograph showing a tension pneumothorax. Radiolucent right chest from accumulation of air within the right pleural space and showing mediastinal shift to the left side.

space between the lung and chest wall during inspiration, and is subsequently trapped during expiration. Hence the lungs and heart are increasingly compressed from the expanding volume of air, eventually leading to external compression of the heart and lungs with eventual cardiovascular collapse (Figure 5.6). The pressure can be relieved by the insertion of a cannula into the chest.

Blunt Abdominal Trauma

Blunt trauma to the abdomen can cause ruptures to abdominal viscera including the liver, spleen, bowel, and mesenteries leading to hemoperitoneum. Blunt trauma to the right side of the abdomen tends to cause liver damage, whereas trauma to the left side of the abdomen tends to cause splenic injury. Young, previously healthy trauma victims may compensate for massive abdominal injury for a significant period before the onset of cardiovascular collapse.

Abdominal trauma and haemorrhage from ruptured pelvic vessels secondary to a pelvic fracture can cause massive retroperitoneal haemorrhage. Traumatic acute pancreatitis is a relatively uncommon sequela of abdominal trauma.

Pelvic and Lower Limb Trauma

Pelvic fractures tend to occur along the direction of the application of force, though there are numerous exceptions to this general rule (Figure 5.7).

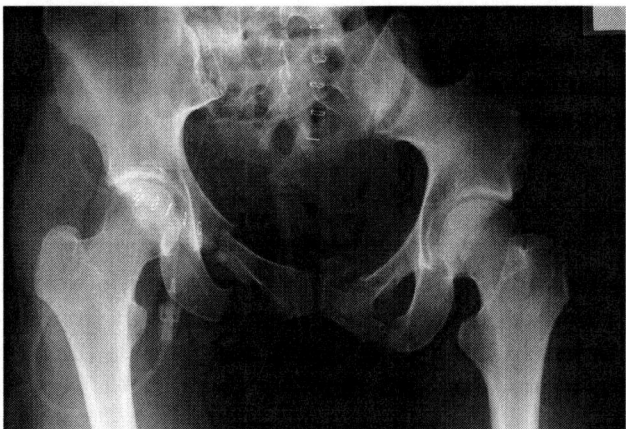

Figure 5.7 Pelvic radiograph showing fractures involving both ischiopubic rami with left sacroiliac joint dislocation.

Axial forces transmitted along the femur from a frontal impact may cause posterior dislocation of the hip joint. Posterior hip dislocation may occur from direct impact to the knee from the dashboard, though others have postulated the mechanism of injury usually results from hip flexion, adduction, and internal rotation as occurs when the driver presses hard on the brake pedal just prior to the impact.[10]

Compressive load to the femur from direct impact with the dashboard can lead to significant bending and fracture. Another common femoral fracture from direct knee impact is a longitudinal splitting fracture between the femoral condyles when the patella impacts directly with the dashboard. Forces applied to the femur from muscle contraction may contribute to femoral shaft fracture.

The tibia may undergo longitudinal compression or transverse loads from contact with the floor pan and dashboard, respectively.[11] Tibial and fibula shaft fractures occur principally from direct forces. Ankle joint and foot fractures are seen with intrusion from the floor pan, which usually causes forced dorsiflexion. A study in Germany examined fractures of the foot region of car drivers and passengers. Similar injuries were seen to both drivers and passengers with forefoot fractures most common (45%) followed by ankle (38%), mid-foot (11%), and hind-foot fractures (6%).[12] These injuries are more likely to be severe if the knee is trapped the under surface of the dashboard leading to axial loading in frontal collisions.

A later study of 480 individuals with at least moderate ankle and foot injury showed that 75% were drivers and the right ankle was most often injured, suggesting the pedals were a significant factor in the injury causation.[13] Otte and colleagues reviewed 140 cases of restrained drivers with foot and ankle injuries and found no difference in injury rate between either side.[14]

Forced inversion and eversion associated with floor pan intrusion is a prominent fracture mechanism in malleolar fractures.

Forced dorsiflexion may lead to navicular fracture and talar fracture from primary direct axial compression with floor pan intrusion.[15]

Upper Arm

Upper arm fractures in restrained front seat vehicle occupants in the absence of airbag deployment occur most commonly from direct impact and result in hand (25%), wrist (23%), and forearm (23%) injury. The elbow (9%), upper arm, and shoulder (both 10%) were injured less frequently.[16]

Airbag deployment is associated with an increased incidence of extremity injury.

Spinal Injury

Spinal injuries occur in about one third of all fatalities from road incidents. Motor vehicle collisions cause the majority (43%) of traumatic spinal cord injury in Australia.[17] Spinal cord injury is especially common in crashes in rural regions, in incidents involving four-wheel drive (4WD)/sports utility vehicles (SUV), in cases of rollover and occupant ejection.[18] The cervical spine is the most common site of spinal cord injury (61%) in occupants injured in motor vehicle incidents.[19]

Side Impact Collisions

Side impact collisions most commonly occur at road intersections. Side impact collisions caused 31% of all collisions leading to injury fatalities in the U.S. in 2002, and 36% of fatalities on Australian roads in 2003. Although these collisions often occur at lower speeds than other types of collisions, factors such as vehicle intrusion and the diminished protective effect of seat belts contribute to the relatively high rates of injury and death.[20] Older drivers have a greater risk of a side impact.[21]

The probability of injury and death varies with respect to the side and region of the vehicle that is struck, the velocity of the impacting vehicle, the mass and type of bullet and target vehicles, and the age of the target vehicle occupants.[22] The rigid body shell provides more protection from intrusion than the more yielding door structures although door reinforcement is addressing this issue.

A side impact crash results in movement of occupants toward the point of contact leading most commonly to head, neck, and thoracic injury. The target vehicle's occupants may sustain injuries from contact with their own vehicle's interior or from the impacting vehicle. The latter is a particular problem with collisions from SUV/4WD vehicles in which the bullet vehicle's bumper may override the window of the target vehicle.

Injuries in Side Impact Collisions

In side impact collisions, the vehicle occupant may sustain skin injuries from contact with shattered tempered glass. This results in typical "dicing" type punctate incised and abraded injuries (Figure 5.8).

These injuries will tend to be more prominent to the nearside occupant. A shadow effect can occur from the glass impacting another occupant or object. Direct impact with intact glass may cause lacerations or broad abrasions that may show directionality from its linear components.

Blunt force injury to the head occurs most commonly from impact with the B pillar, doors, and windows. Significant vehicle intrusion may also lead to head injury (Figure 5.9). Blunt force injury to the chest and abdomen results from impact with the door panel causing rib, lung, liver, and splenic injury.[23]

Although seat belts generally do not provide the same protection to an occupant in a side impact collision compared with a frontal collision, the use of restraints has been shown to be associated with lower rates of splenic injury in side impacts. In nearly all cases of splenic injury, the left vehicle interior is the source of injury.[24] The presence of an occupant on the near side in a side impact collision has been shown to change the injury pattern for the far side occupant, whereby injuries from contact with the opposite side interior of the vehicle are mitigated.[2]

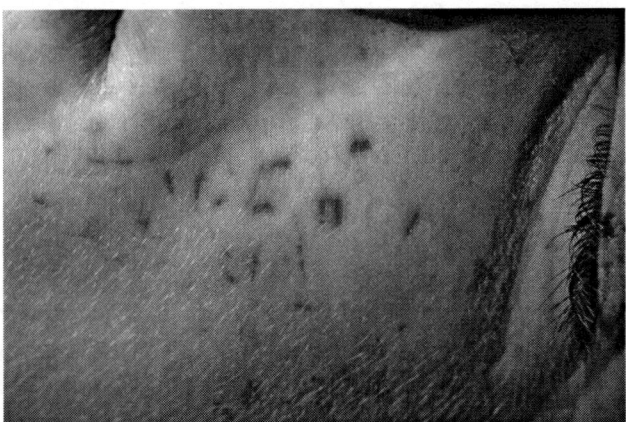

Figure 5.8 Punctate abraded injuries to the left side of the face from contact with shattered tempered glass.

Figure 5.9 Marked vehicle intrusion from side impact into pole. Injuries to the rear seat occupants may be correlated with seating position.

Side impacts causing lateral application of force may lead to transverse pelvic fractures. These fractures are seen mostly to the nearside (70.4%) occupants of the target vehicle compared with the far side (38.3%) occupants.[25] Transverse fractures of the femoral diaphysis (shaft) can occur with transverse impact from a side-on collision. Side impacts lead to an increased incidence of thigh, knee, leg, and foot/ankle injuries to the far side occupants compared with the near side occupants in a retrospective study.[25] The mechanism of injury may reflect rotation of the lower limbs toward the point of impact for far side occupant, whereas direct trauma leads to pelvic/hip injury to the near side occupants.

Children in side impact crashes suffer injuries from contact with internal cabin features and from cabin intrusion by the bullet vehicle. A combination of head, cervical spine, chest, and extremity injuries has been described.[26] The pattern of injuries to children in near side collisions is similar to the pattern observed in pediatric pedestrian incidents.[27] The injuries sustained by children who were seated near side in a side impact collision occur irrespective of the use of seat belts.

Rear Impact Collisions

Most studies have suggested that the majority of rear end collisions occur during daytime in clear weather and on straight roads. In most cases, the lead vehicle had stopped or was slowing. The vast majority of rear end collisions occurs at low speeds and is associated with minor injuries. However, collisions that occur at high speeds can lead to significant vehicle intrusion and subsequent severe

Figure 5.10 "High- speed" rear end impacts showing significant vehicle intrusion.

blunt trauma to the head, neck, and thorax (Figure 5.10). A study that corrected for exposure level showed that rear end collisions were twice as frequent in darkness when compared with daylight.[28] Approximately two thirds of rear end collisions result from inattention of the driver of the following vehicle. The contribution of environmental factors such as wet or icy roads occurs in less than 4% of cases.[28]

Passenger vehicle crashes into parked vehicles are an important subset of rear end crashes. Underlying causes include driver intoxication with alcohol and other drugs and driver inattention.[29] A particularly lethal type of rear end collision is the underrun incident in which a passenger vehicle strikes the back of a truck resulting in significant impact to the windscreen and vehicle cabin.[30] The instillation of underrun barriers to the rear of tray type trucks and trailers has decreased the severity of these crashes.

Injuries from Rear Impact

Neck injury from hyperextension in rear crashes has increased over the past two decades. Although severe trauma is uncommon in rear impacts, relatively low-speed collisions can lead to rapid neck extension especially for out of position occupants.

Recent seat design changes include high-strength designs, with "all belts to seat" configurations that have necessitated stiffer seat backs.[31] The trend toward stiffer seats has lead to increased neck displacements and may be a significant factor in the pathogenesis of flexion/extension neck injury.[32] A study by Burnett suggested that seats of mid-range seat back stiffness mini-mised neck loading and thus decreased the potential for neck injury. There is evidence to suggest that seats which yield in a rear end collision may also afford greater protection from hyperextension injury.

Rollover Collisions

A rollover event may be defined as a collision in which the vehicle rotates at least a one-quarter turn, irrespective of the resting position of the motor vehicle. The vast majority of rollover incidents occur after the motor vehicle has left the roadway.

Figures in the United States show that rollovers account for about 20% to 25% of fatal crashes. A recent report indicated that 78% of those who died in single vehicle rollover incidents were not wearing seat belts and more than half of these victims were partially or completely ejected from the vehicle.[33]

A rollover event may be the only factor in a particular motor vehicle incident or may be part of a more complex multiple incident event. In either case, rollover is associated with significant injury to the vehicle's occupants and is associated with an increased risk of occupant ejection. Injury severity and death is far more likely when a seat belt is not worn. Occasionally, some seat belt latches can disengage during a rollover and, in the absence of a prior frontal collision, additional restraint systems such as seat belt pretensioners do not function.

Rollovers are a particular issue in vehicles with a high centre of gravity such as SUV/4WD and semitrailer trucks that leave the roadway (Figure 5.11). A study on the risk of rollover in cars and light trucks after accounting for driver and environmental factors showed that some light trucks have up to twice the risk of rollover compared with cars.[34] Semitrailers with a high payload are at risk of rollover. Incidents of rollover by semitrailers are more prone to occur on roads that fall away to the shoulder, on very tight corners, and in high winds.

Figure 5.11   Truck rollover associated with sharp off-ramp from freeway.

Rollovers have been categorised into a number of subtypes, the most common of which is the tripover, which composes 57% of rollovers in passenger vehicles.[35] The next most common type of event is the fallover.

Subtypes of rollover are:

- Tipover — Occurs when the lateral movement of the vehicle is rapidly impeded (e.g., when the wheels/tires contact the curb, or gouge into soft ground)
- Fallover — Occurs when the vehicle is moving down an incline such that the vehicle's centre of gravity is beyond the outside wheels
- Flipover — Occurs when a vehicle has a rotational force imparted along its longitudinal axis; this is usually from contact with a "ramp-like" structure
- Turnover — Occurs from frictional forces from a tire on a vehicle that has rapid rotation from a sharp turn
- Postcollision — Occurs when the rollover is secondary to a motor vehicle collision
- End over end — Occurs when vehicle rotation is along its lateral axis

Injuries in Rollover Incidents

Rollover incidents lead to complicated kinematics for occupants during the vehicle's rotation. Interestingly, as the vehicle comes to rest over a longer period than in a frontal or side on collision, the vehicle occupant is somewhat protected from the effects of rapid deceleration.[36] However, because there are often multiple episodes of contact between the occupant and the vehicle's interior, blunt force injury to the head and torso is common. The frequent sources of injury include the A and B pillars, side interior and roof (Figure 5.12).

Severe injury in nonejected victims in rollover incidents have been shown to be associated with vehicle intrusion, and especially roof rail or B-pillar intrusion of greater than 30 cm.[36]

Ejection

A major risk of injury for unrestrained occupants of motor vehicles involved in a collision is ejection from the cabin.[37] It is clear that morbidity and mortality rates are markedly increased when ejection occurs. Data from the General Estimate System and the Fatality Analysis Reporting System estimated that, in 1998 in the United States, 0.8% of all motor vehicle incidents involved ejection of a vehicle occupant. Ejection was associated with 27% of all collision-related deaths and the overall fatality rate for an ejected occupant was 35%. In modern cars, it is uncommon for the door hinges to fail during

Figure 5.12 Rollover of a four-wheel drive vehicle showing roof indentation and distortion resulting in close proximity between the roof and head of the occupant.

a collision. The most common exit point from the cabin is via the side or rear window following impact damage to the tempered glass.

Injuries Associated with Seat Belts

Forensically important injuries occur from the force applied from the seat belt to the occupant.

The classical "seat belt mark" is an abrasion/intradermal bruise that extends from the region of the clavicle diagonally across the chest toward the opposite hip reflecting the path and shape of the seatbelt. A further transverse abrasion/bruised injury may be seen across the abdomen.

However, far more commonly the seatbelt/occupant interaction results in either no injury or a nonspecific bruise or abraded injury. The location and orientation of such an injury may suggest the use of a seat belt as the anterior clavicular region is not commonly injured in a motor vehicle collision. The latch mechanism overlying the lateral hip region can result in nonspecific skin injuries or rectangular, right angled, or linear abraded and bruised injuries.

Rib and sternal fractures may be caused by seat belts in a motor vehicle collision. Fractures are more likely in older females because of osteoporosis. Fractures tend to occur along the path of the seat belt, reflecting the force applied during the collision.[38] The fourth through to the ninth ribs are often fractured. A study in the 1970s showed that the ribs are fractured in an anterior location with the sixth rib the most frequently involved.[39] In surviving occupants of a motor vehicle collision, bone scintigraphy has demonstrated different patterns of rib and sternal injury to the driver and front seat passenger.[40] The imaging study showed a diagonal orientation to the rib fractures and the sternal fracture.

Incorrectly fastened and inappropriate use of seat belts is far more common in children than adults. It has been observed that in a population of children who should be restrained in a child restraint system, up to 25% were wearing seat belts that did not fit properly. Incorrectly fastened seat belts may result in submarining. Submarining refers to the situation in which the occupant is propelled underneath the seat belt during a frontal collision. Submarining commonly results when there is insufficient contact between the lap belt and the anterior lateral pelvic region. Submarining may cause significant intra-abdominal trauma including rupture of the liver, spleen and hollow viscera.[41] Wedge fractures of the lower thoracic/lumbar vertebrae (Chance fractures) occur from hyperflexion of the vertebral bodies when the occupant pivots around the lap belt. These fractures are more common in children.[42]

A clinical study evaluated the location and severity of brain injury and functional outcome with respect to seat belt use. Restrained vehicle occupants were more likely to suffer damage to the basal ganglia, corpus callosum, thalamus, and hypothalamus, whereas unrestrained vehicle occupants were more likely to sustain posterior brain lesions.[43] The use of clinical cases excludes those victims who died as a result of a head injury, and the use of seat belts probably allowed individuals to survive a severe crash that would have proved fatal in an unrestrained occupant. However, it is possible that the different anatomic locations of the head injury may reflect different mechanisms (i.e., direct blunt trauma in unrestrained individuals and flexion/hyperextension in restrained occupants).

Injuries Associated with Front Airbag Deployment

Airbag deployment is associated with a variety of injuries to victims of a motor vehicle collision. The injuries are usually minor, but may occasionally be life-threatening. Children exposed to front airbags have an increased risk of minor injuries that include facial and chest abrasions and upper extremity fractures.[44]

The types of minor injuries associated with airbag deployment are, in decreasing order of frequency, minor abrasions, bruises, lacerations, and burns. A study by Antosia and colleagues in the mid-1990s showed that the body regions most commonly injured were the face (42%), wrist (17%), forearm (16%), and chest (10%).[45] The body regions injured reflect proximity with the airbag module at the time of deployment. Abrasions, bruises, and lacerated injuries occur primarily from blunt force contact with the module cover and the airbag.

Burns have occurred from chemicals such as sodium azide or sodium hydroxide or thermal burns from hot gases liberated from vents or breaks in the airbag, though with more recent airbags these injuries are less common.[46]

Facial injuries are not unexpected in frontal crashes associated with airbag deployment because the inflated airbag is designed to extend across the face and chest. Airbags have been shown to cause eye injury including corneal abrasions, vitreous and retinal haemorrhage, chemical retinitis and traumatic cataract, retinal tears, and detachment.[47] Wearing eye glasses has been shown to present a problem in motor vehicle crashes that result in airbag deployment because the incidence of facial and eye injuries is increased in these occupants.[47]

Mouzakes and colleagues showed that the rate and severity of facial fractures decreased when drivers and passengers were protected by both seat belts and frontal airbags. A later study demonstrated that the incidence of facial fractures in motor vehicle collisions were reduced from 17% to 8% with the use of seat belts alone and reduced from 17% to 11% with the use of airbags alone. Airbags were least effective in preventing zygomaticomaxillary fractures.[48]

Airbags are associated with a reduction in hyperflexion/hyperextension injuries to the neck. The mechanism is most probably a more diffuse application of force across the head and chest, with a reduction in hyperflexion of the cervical spine. The pattern of rib fractures caused by contact from an airbag is somewhat different when compared with contact from a seatbelt in a frontal collision. Whereas rib fractures tend to follow the diagonal line of the seatbelt, the more diffuse frontal force applied to the chest by an airbag tends to cause bilateral and symmetrical lateral rib fractures.[37] The overall effect of airbag deployment in a motor vehicle collision is a reduction of fractures to the ribs, sternum, and clavicle.

Extremity injuries are increased with airbag deployment. Upper limb injuries are increased when compared with seat belts alone or when no restraining devices are used. McGovern suggested the upper limbs are not in the zone designed for protection by airbags and may be propelled around the bag, resulting in injury.[49] Front and side airbags do not protect vehicle occupants from lower extremity injuries. Burgess and colleagues showed that the use of seat belts, airbags, or combined airbag and seat belt restraints did not prevent lower extremity injuries in drivers.[50]

Fatal injury in airbag deployment occurs predominantly in children and small adults who are "out of position" because they are physically too close to the airbag at the time of deployment.[52]

Significant and lethal injuries may involve the head, neck, and chest. Head injuries reported to occur from airbag contact include intracranial haemorrhage, cerebral contusions, brainstem laceration, and transection. Ring fracture of the base of the skull and severe cervical spine injuries including atlanto-occipital dislocation have been described.[52-54] Lethal chest injury includes cardiovascular trauma with cardiac contusions, ruptured heart, valve injury, and laceration or transection of the aorta.[55-57]

Side Airbags

In side collisions, the occupant's head may impact with the B pillar, side window, and surrounds. Impact of the chest may occur with the door. Intrusion of the cabin by the bullet vehicle is a further possible source of head and chest injury. Side airbags were introduced as a specific safety system for vehicle occupants in side impact collisions to protect the head and thorax.

The introduction of side airbags may be associated with fractures to the upper limbs, especially when the hand is in situ within the hand rest of the side door. A number of cadaver, anthropomorphic, and real-world investigations have demonstrated a significant risk of entrapment injuries from the hand grip in such cases.[58] Risk of fracture increases with osteoporosis. The presence of these injuries may aid in the forensic identification of a driver in a particular incident.

Vehicle Mismatch

The probability of vehicle occupant injury is increased for the occupants of a smaller car that collides with a larger vehicle. Differences in vehicle configuration have also been shown to affect the risk of occupant injury. SUVs have a higher road clearance than average passenger cars and collisions between these vehicles leads to greater injury for the passenger car occupants even when the mass of the passenger car exceeds that of the SUV.[59,60]

Side impact from a SUV to a passenger car is particularly dangerous. Injuries to the head and upper chest are common to passenger vehicle occupants because of override of the SUV bumper above the side door reinforcement.[61] Bumper override is also a major factor in frontal collisions with passenger cars. These collisions can result in instrument panel and steering column intrusion leading to head and chest injury and a high incidence of upper extremity fractures. Bumper underride of the

SUV with the passenger vehicle can lead to marked floor pan intrusion to the passenger car, resulting in a high incidence of lower extremity fractures.

Pregnant Occupants

Motor vehicle trauma is a leading cause of hospitalisation of pregnant women in Western societies and a major cause of fetal death.[62] Motor vehicle collisions involving pregnant women have similar rates of restraint use and seat position.

Injuries sustained by pregnant women in motor vehicle incidents are similar to those in nonpregnant women. Fetal injury and death in utero can be related to direct trauma transmitted through the mother's abdomen or from an ischaemic insult if placental function is compromised from systemic maternal factors such as blood loss or accidental haemorrhage.[63]

The lap belt worn by pregnant women should be positioned beneath the abdomen and across the anterior superior iliac spines to minimise direct force to the gravid uterus. Airbag deployment has not been reported to cause fetal injury or death.

Injury Differences between Drivers and Passengers

The classical seat belt abraded/bruised injury is an important feature in differentiating between driver and passenger in serious motor vehicle collisions (Figure 5.13). The distribution of cutaneous injuries, soft-tissue bruises, and fractures sustained by a trauma victim with respect to

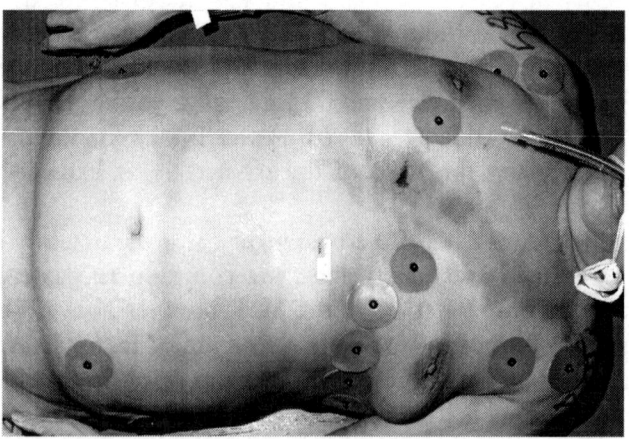

Figure 5.13 Intradermal bruise from forceful contact with seat belt.

the damage to the vehicle may allow a guarded opinion on the seating position within the vehicle. In these circumstances, all of the available information pertaining to the case should be used when offering an opinion and should include a comparison between the injuries sustained by the injured parties.

A study by Daffner and colleagues published in 1988 described the difference in the pattern of bone injuries to 250 unrestrained drivers and passengers.[64] They reported that 39 of the passengers had clavicular fractures compared with only 1 of the 250 drivers. The postulated mechanism was that the passengers raised their arms in a reflex action prior to impact. Humeral fractures were also twice as common in the passenger group.

Drivers were found to have a high incidence of hand, wrist, and elbow injuries. Of the drivers, 22 had hand fractures, 58 had wrist fractures, and 115 had fractures of the shaft of the radius or ulna.

Passengers had no hand fractures. There were 2 wrist fractures and 44 fractures of the radius or ulna. A suggested mechanism was that the driver braced his hands on the steering wheel prior to impact. The force of impact was transmitted to the hand, wrist, and forearm.

The incidence of pelvic fractures and hip dislocation were similar. Femoral fractures were less common in passengers because of a more upward component of the forward movement because of the absence of the steering wheel. Ankle and foot injuries in unrestrained drivers and passengers in high-speed collisions were generally similar to restrained vehicle occupants and were most severe when there was significant floor pan intrusion.

Injury Severity Scores

The Injury Severity Score (ISS) was created in 1974 as an indicator of anatomic injury severity based on the Abbreviated Injury Score.[65] The ISS is calculated from the most severe injury in each body region and is extensively used in hospital review committees as an objective measure in evaluating outcomes of trauma management.[66] More recently the New Injury Severity Score (NISS) has been introduced as a more accurate measure of injury severity.[67] The NISS is believed to be superior to the ISS because the calculation more accurately reflects the presence of more than one severe injury to a given body region, and the greater importance assigned to severe head and neck, chest, and abdominal injuries as opposed to extremity injury.

The Trauma and Injury Severity Score (TRISS) evaluates the severity of anatomic injury (ISS) and physiologic effect of trauma to provide a probability of survival in the trauma patient.[68,69] The documentation of injury is based on hospital investigations and autopsy reports in deceased victims of motor vehicle incidents.

Vehicle Fires

Motor vehicle fires are uncommon in gas-powered vehicles and rare in diesel vehicles. A fire requires heat, oxygen, and an ignition source. A fire may commence as a result of a fuel line fault, in which case the fire usually commences in the engine bay or as a consequence of a motor vehicle collision.

The most frequent types of collision associated with a vehicle fire are high-speed rear impact and rollover incidents. These impacts are associated with a high incidence of fuel leaks and rupture of the fuel tank.[70]

Fires are more common in older vehicles. Vehicle size is not a risk factor. Deaths from a crash with a fire may result directly from trauma or from the fire. In cases in which the fire has caused death, the victim may have been incapacitated by the collision or unable to escape because of collapse of vehicle structures or intrusion.

References

1. Smith KM, Cummings P. Passenger seating position and the risk of passenger death or injury in traffic crashes. *Accident Analysis and Prevention* 2004; 36:257–260.

2. Augenstein J, Perdeck E, Martin P, Bowen J, Stratton J, Horton T, Singer M, Digges K, Steps J. Injuries to restrained occupants in far-side crashes. 44th Annual Proceedings of the Association for the Advancement of Automotive Medicine; Chicago, Illinois, 2000.

3. King AF, King YH. Research in biomechanics of occupant protection. *The Journal of Trauma* 1995; 38:570–576.

4. Hillary FG, Schatz P, Moelter ST, Lowry JB, Ricker JH, Chute DL. Motor vehicle collision factors influence severity and type of TBI. *Brain Injury* 2002; 16:729–741.

5. Broughton J. The actual threat posed by unrestrained rear seat car passengers. *Accident Analysis and Prevention* 2004; 36:627–629.

6. Nirula R, Mok C, Kaufman R, Rivara FP, Grossman DC. Correlation of head injury to vehicle contact points using crash injury research and engineering network data. *Accident Analysis and Prevention* 2003; 35:201–210.

7. Atkinson JL, Anderson RE, Murray MJ. The early critical phase of sever head injury: importance of apnea and dysfunctional respiration. *Journal of Trauma* 1998; 45:941–945.

8. Levine JE, Becker D, Chun T. Reversal of incipient brain death from head injury apnea at the scene of accidents (letter). *New England Journal of Medicine* 179; 301:109.

9. O'Connor CE. Diagnosing traumatic rupture of the aorta in the emergency department. *Emergency Medicine Journal* 2004; 21:414–419.

10. Monma H, Sugita T. Is the mechanism of traumatic posterior dislocation of the hip a brake pedal injury rather than a dashboard injury? *Injury* 2001; 32:221–222.

11. Nyquist GW, Cheng R, El-Bohy AAR, King AI. Tibia bending: strength and response. In Backailis S, editor. *Biomechanics of Impact Injury and Injury Tolerances of the Extremities.* Warrendale, PA: SAE Publications Group, 1996.

12. Richter M, Thermann H, von Rheinbaben H, Schratt E, Otte D, Zwipp H., Tscherne H. Fractures of the foot region of car drivers and passengers. Occurrence, causes, and long term results. *Unfallchirurg* 1999; 102:429–433.

13. Morgan RM, Eppinger RH, Hennessey BC. Proceedings of the 35th Stapp Car Crash Conference. 1991. Warrendale, PA: SAE, 189-198.

14. Otte D, Rheinhaben H, Zwipp H. Biomechanics of Injuries to the Foot and Ankle Joint of Car Drivers and Improvements for an Optimal Car Floor Development, 35th Stapp Car Crash Conference, Warrendale, PA: SAE, 1992.

15. Lestina DC, Kuhlmann TP, Keats TE, Alley RM. Mechanisms of fracture in ankle and foot injuries to drivers in motor vehicle crashes. In Backailis S, editor. *Biomechanics of Impact Injury and Injury Tolerances of the Extremities.* Warrendale, PA: SAE Publications Group, 1996.

16. Richter M, Otte D, Jahanyar K, Blauth M. Upper extremity fractures in restrained front seat occupants. *The Journal of Trauma* 2000; 48:907–912.

17. O'Connor PJ. *Spinal Cord Injury.* Flinders University of South Australia, Research Centre for Injury Studies, 2000, Australian Injury Prevention Bulletin 22 Adelaide.

18. Huelke DF, Compton CP. Injury frequency and severity in rollover car crashes as related to occupant ejection, contacts and roof damage: an analysis of national crash severity study data. *Accident Analysis and Prevention* 1983; 15:395–401.

19. O'Connor PJ. Injury to the spinal cord in motor vehicle traffic crashes. *Accident Analysis and Prevention* 2002; 34:477–485.

20. Chipman ML. Side impact crashes—factors affecting incidence and severity: review of the literature. *Traffic Injury Prevention* 2004; 5:67–75.

21. Lyman S, Ferguson S, Braver ER, Williams A. Older driver involvements in police reported crashes and fatal crashes; trends and projections. *Injury Prevention* 2002; 8:116–120.

22. McLelland BA, Rizoli SB, Brenneman FD, Bouglander BR, Sharkey PW, Szalai JP. Injury pattern and severity in lateral motor vehicle collisions; a Canadian perspective. *The Journal of Trauma* 1996; 41:708–715.

23. Fildes B, Valkan P, Lane J, Lenard J. 1994. Side impact collisions in Australia. In Proceedings of the 14th International Technical Conference on the Enhanced Safety of Vehicles, Vol. 2. pp. 906–918. Washington, DC: National Highway Traffic Safety Administration.

24. Reiff DA, McGwin G Jr., Rue LW. Splenic injury in side impact motor vehicle collisions: effect of occupant restraints. *The Journal of Trauma* 2001; 51:340–345.

25. Banglmaier RF, Rouhana SW, Beillas P, Yang KH. Lower extremity injuries in lateral impact: a retrospective study. 47th Annual Proceedings of the Association for the Advancement of Automotive Medicine 2003; 425–444.

26. Orzechowski KM, Edgerton EA, Bulas DI, McLaughlin PM, Eichelberger MR. Patterns of injury to restrained children in side impact motor vehicle crashes: the side impact syndrome. *The Journal of Trauma* 2003; 54:1094–1101.

27. Howard A, Rothman L, McKeag AM, Pazmino-Canizares J, Monk B, Comeau JL, Mills D, Blazeski S, Hale I, German A. Children in side-impact motor vehicle crashes: seating positions and injury mechanisms. *The Journal of Trauma* 2004; 56:1276–1285.

28. Sullivan JM, Flannagan MJ. Risk of fatal-rear end collisions: Is there more to it than attention? Proceedings of the Second International Driving Symposium on Human Factors in Driver Assessment, Training and Vehicle Designs, July 2003, Utah, USA, pp 239–244.

29. Roberts GL, Lynn CW. *Passenger Vehicle Crashes into Stationary Large Trucks: Incidence and Possible Counter Measures.* 2003 Virginia Transportation Research Council Report No. 03-CR17.

30. Blower D. Campbell KL. *Incidence of Rear Underride in Fatal Truck Crashes 1997–1998.* NHTSA Report number HS-043 457.

31. Burnett R, Carter J, Roberts V, Myers B. The influence of seatback characteristics on cervical injury risk in severe rear impacts. *Accident Analysis and Prevention* 2004; 36:591–601.

32. Viano DC. Seat properties affecting neck responses in rear crashes: a reason why whiplash has increased. *Traffic Injury Prevention* 2003; 4:214–227.

33. NHTSA. Initiatives to Address the Mitigation of Vehicle Rollover, 2003. NHTSA, 1999. An experimental examination of selected maneuvers that may induce on-road untripped, light vehicle rollover-phase II of NHTSA 1997–1998 vehicle rollover program. DOT HS Report.

34. Farmer CM, Lund AK. Rollover risk of cars and light trucks after counting for driver and environmental factors. *Accident Analysis and Prevention* 2002; 34(2):163–173.

35. Parenteau CS, Viano DC, Shah M, Gopal M, Davies J, Nichols D, Broden J. Field relevance of a suite of rollover tests to real-world crashes and injuries. *Accident Analysis and Prevention* 2003; 35:103–110.

36. Conroy C, Hoyt DB, Eastman BA, Erwin S, Pacyna S, Holbrook TL, Vaughan T, Sise M, Kennedy F, Velky T. Rollover crashes: predicting serious injury based on occupant, vehicle, and crash characteristics. *Accident Analysis and Prevention* 2006; 38(5):835–542.

37. Gongora E, Acosta JA, Wang DS, Brandenburg K, Jablonski J, Jordan MH. Analysis of motor vehicle ejection victims admitted to a level 1 trauma centre. *The Journal of Trauma* 2001; 51:854–859.

38. Yoganandan N, Morgan RM, Eppinger RH, Pintar FA, Sances A Jr., Williams A. Mechanisms of thoracic injury in frontal impact. *Journal of Biomechanical Engineering* 1996; 118:595–597.

39. Patrick L, Andersson A. Three point harness and laboratory data comparison. 18th Stapp Car Crash Conference SAE, 1974.

40. Coel M, Sato G. Sternal fractures in motor vehicle accident victims restrained by lap-shoulder safety belts. Can bone scintigraphy distinguish passenger from driver? *Clinical Nuclear Medicine* 2000; 25:140–141.

41. Hall CEJ, Norton SA, Dixon AR. Complete small bowel transection following lap-belt injury. *Injury* 2001; 32:640–641.

42. Prince JS, LoSasso BE, Senac MO Jnr. Unusual seat-belt injuries in children. *The Journal of Trauma* 2004; 56:420–427.

43. Hillary F, Moelter ST, Schatz P, Chute DL. Seatbelts contribute to location of lesion in moderate to severe closed head trauma. *Archives of Clinical Neuropsychiatry* 2001; 16:171–181.

44. Durbin DR, Kallan M, Elliott M, Cornejo RA, Arbogast KB, Winston FK. Risk of injury to restrained children from passenger air bags. *Traffic Injury Prevention* 2003; 4:58–63.

45. Antosia RE, Partridge RA, Virk AS. Airbag safety. *Annals of Emergency Medicine* 1995; 25:794–798.

46. Suhr M, Kreusch T. Burn injuries resulting from (accidental) airbag inflation. *Journal of Cranio-Maxillofacial Surgery* 2004; 32:35–37.

47. Gault JA, Vichnin MC, Jaeger EA, Jeffers JB. Ocular Injuries associated with eye glass wear and airbag inflation. *The Journal of Trauma* 1995; 38:494–497.

48. Simoni P, Ostendorf R, Cox AJ 3rd. Effect of airbags and restraining devices on the pattern of facial fractures in motor vehicle crashes. *Archives of Facial and Plastic Surgery* 2003; 5:113–115.

49. McGovern MK, Murphy RX Jr, Okunski WJ, Wasser TE. The influence of airbags and restraining devices on extremity injuries in motor vehicle collisions. *Annals of Plastic Surgery* 2000; 34:481–485.

50. Burgess AR, Dischinger PC, O'Quinn TD, Schmidhauser CB. Lower extremity injuries in drivers of airbag-equipped automobiles: clinical and crash reconstruction correlations. *The Journal of Trauma* 1995; 38:509–516.

51. Maxeiner H, Hahn M. Airbag-induced lethal cervical trauma. *The Journal of Trauma* 1997; 42:1148–1151.

52. Bailey H, Perez N, Blank-Reid C, Kaplan LJ. Atlanto-occipital dislocation; an unusual lethal airbag injury. The *Journal of Emergency Medicine* 2000; 18:215–219.

53. Cunningham K, Brown TD, Gradwell E, Kee PA. Airbag associated fatal head injury: case report and review of the literature on airbag injuries. *Journal of Accident and Emergency Medicine* 2000; 17:139–142.

54. Gossman W, June RA, Wallace D. Fatal atlanto-occipital dislocation secondary to airbag deployment. *American Journal of Emergency Medicine* 1999; 17:741–742.

55. Sharma OP, Mousset XR. Review of tricuspid valve injury after airbag deployment: presentation of a case and discussion of mechanism of injury. *Journal of Trauma* 2000; 48:152–156.

56. Lancaster GI, De France JH, Borruso JJ. Air-bag associated rupture of the right atrium. *New England Journal of Medicine* 1993; 328:358.

57. De Guzman BJ, Morgan AS, Pharr WF. Aortic transection following air-bag deployment. *New England Journal of Medicine* 1997; 337:573–574.

58. Duma SM, Boggess BM, Crandall JR, Hurwitz SR, Seki K, Aoki T. Upper extremity interaction with a deploying side airbag; a characterisation of elbow joint loading. *Accident Analysis and Prevention* 2003; 35:417–425.

59. Broyles RW, Narine L, Clark SR, Baker DR. Factors associated with the likelihood of injury resulting from collisions between 4-wheel drive vehicles and passenger cars. *Accident Analysis and Prevention* 2003; 35:677–681.

60. Mayrose J, Jehle DVK. Vehicle weight and fatality risk for sport utility vehicle versus passenger car crashes. *The Journal of Trauma* 2002; 53:751–753.

61. Acierno S, Kaufman R, Rivara FP, Grossman DC, Mock C. Vehicle mismatch: injury patterns and severity. *Accident Analysis and Prevention* 2004; 36:761–772.

62. Weiss HB, Strotmeyer S. Characteristics of pregnant women in motor vehicle crashes. *Injury Prevention* 2002; 8:207–210.

63. Weiss H. The epidemiology of traumatic injury-related foetal mortality in Pennsylvania, 1995–1997: the role of motor vehicle crashes. *Accident Analysis and Prevention* 2001; 33:449–454.

64. Daffner RH, Deeb ZL, Lupetin AR, Rothfus WE. Patterns of high-speed impact injuries in motor vehicle occupants. *The Journal of Trauma* 1988; 28:498–501.

65. Baker SP, O'Neill B, Haddon W, Long WB. The injury severity score: a method for describing patients with multiple injuries and evaluating emergency care. *The Journal of Trauma* 1974; 14:187–196.

66. Greenspan L, McLellan BA, Greig H. Abbreviated Injury Scale and Injury Severity Score: a scoring chart. *The Journal of Trauma* 1985; 25:60–68.

67. Lavoie A, Moore L, Le Sage N, Liberman M, Sampalis JS. The New Injury Severity Score: a more accurate predictor of hospital-mortality than the Injury Severity Score. *The Journal of Trauma* 2004; 56:1312–1320.

68. Champion HR, Copes WS, Sacco WJ, Lawnick MM, Gann DS, Gennarelli T, MacKenzie E, Schwaitzberg S. The Major Trauma Outcome Study: establishing national norms for trauma care. *The Journal of Trauma* 1990; 30:1356–1365.

69. Bergeron E, Rossignol M, Osler T, Clas D and Lavoie A. Improving the TRISS methodology by reconstructing age categories and adding comorbidities. *The Journal of Trauma* 2004; 56:760–767.

70. Malliaris AC. Impact induced car fires—a comprehensive investigation. *Accident Analysis and Prevention* 1991; 23:257–273.

Additional Reading

Assal M, Huber P, Tencer AF, Rohr E, Mock, C, Kaufman R. Are drivers more likely to injure their right or left foot in a frontal car crash: a crash and biomechanical investigation. 46th Annual Proceedings Association for Advancement of Automotive Medicine 2002; 273–288.

Duma SM, Boggess BM, Crandall JR, MacMahon CB. Injury risk function for the small female wrist in axial loading. *Accident Analysis and Prevention* 2003; 35:869–875.

Farmer CM, Braver ER, Mitter EL. Two-vehicle side impact crashes: the relationship of vehicle and crash characteristics to injury severity. *Accident Analysis and Prevention* 1997; 29:399–406.

Kent RW, Crandall J, Patrie J, Ferthe J. Radiographic detection of rib fractures: a restraint based study of occupants in car crashes. *Traffic Injury Prevention* 2002; 3:49–57.

Nusholtz GS, Alem NM, Melvin JW. Impact response and injury of the pelvis. In Backailis S, editor. *Biomechanics of Impact Injury and Injury Tolerances of the Extremities.* Warrendale, PA: SAE Publications Group, 1996.

Tencer A, Kaufman R, Ryan K, Grossman DC, Henley MB, Mann F, Mock C, Rivara F, Wang S, Augenstein J, Hoyt D, Eastman B. Femur fractures in relatively low speed frontal crashes: the possible role of muscle forces. *Accident Analysis and Prevention* 2002; 34:1–11.

Traffic Safety Facts 1998. Washington DC: National Highway and Traffic Safety Administration; 1999.

Viner JG. Rollovers on side slopes and ditches. *Accident Analysis and Prevention* 1995; 27:483–491.

Wood DP, Simms CK. Car size and injury risk: a model for injury risk in frontal collisions. *Accident Analysis and Prevention* 2002; 34:93–99.

Injuries Sustained by Pedestrians

6

Introduction

Over the last decade, road fatalities have been decreasing in relative terms, whereas the number of pedestrian deaths has increased both as an absolute number and in relative terms. Collisions involving pedestrians have a high likelihood of serious morbidity and mortality. A study from South Australia, Australia, showed three distinct high-risk groups for pedestrian fatalities. The three groups identified were elderly sober pedestrians, young and middle-age intoxicated males, and male and female teenagers.[1]

An analysis of 1589 reported pedestrian crashes in Maine showed that a larger number of incidents occurred on Saturdays and more crashes were noted in the afternoon and evening.

The majority (68%) of all crashes occurred in clear conditions, with only 29% happening in inclement weather. Three-quarters of the incidents occurred on dry roads. The majority of crashes occurred on level, straight roads (71%), and most incidents were away from traffic controls or signs. Of the fatal crashes, 37% of the victims were female and 63% were male. Approximately 17% of the deceased victims and 10% of the drivers were under the influence of alcohol.[2]

A study from the United States reported that in 86% of cases the pedestrian was attempting to cross the roadway and in 60% of cases the incident occurred in a straight section of road.[3] Drivers had made no attempt to avoid the collision in 40% of the crashes. The most common avoidance manoeuver was braking. More than half of the pedestrian incidents occurred in relation to an intersection or driveway in clear weather (80%).

Pedestrian Injuries

The injuries sustained by a pedestrian in a motor vehicle collision vary considerably with respect to the age and stature of the pedestrian, the configuration of the presenting section of the motor vehicle, and the type of vehicle (e.g., passenger sedan, sport utility vehicle [SUV], flat-fronted van) and the velocity of the vehicle.

The most common cause of death in a pedestrian incident is a head or neck injury. The fatal head injury may occur from contact with the motor vehicle or from impact with the road surface although the majority of lethal head injuries occur from contact with the vehicle's windshield and surrounds. Upper cervical spine injuries are common and increase in frequency as the velocity of impact increases and if the pedestrian is thrown over the roof of the vehicle. Chest and abdominal trauma leading to rupture of vital organs and blood vessels are additional frequent injuries.

Evidence of rolling across the road may be apparent on the victim's body or clothing and associated evidence may be noted at the scene on the road surface.

Upright Pedestrians vs. Conventional Cars

This section will address the injuries sustained by an adult individual of average stature struck by a conventional passenger vehicle with a hood. Other circumstances such as pediatric victims and incidents involving vans, four-wheel drive (4WD) vehicles, and SUVs will be addressed in turn.

The most important determinant of the dynamics of a frontal impact pedestrian incident is the speed and configuration of the front of the vehicle and the centre of gravity of the pedestrian. The centre of gravity of a 70-kg adult male is just above the level of the pelvis some 1.5 m from the road surface, or about 55% of the height of the victim, approximately at the level of the umbilicus.

In a low-speed (less than 20 km/hr) incident both conventional and flat-fronted larger vehicles will tend to impart forward momentum to the pedestrian and propel them onto the road surface. In incidents involving conventional cars, the pedestrian is initially struck to the lower limbs in the vicinity of the knee joint and thigh. The pedestrian's centre of gravity is above the contact point with the vehicle, which causes the upper body to rotate toward the hood in a "scooping" action (Figure 6.1). The pelvis connects with the hood and the head may impact with the windshield and surrounds. Depending on the velocity of the vehicle, the pedestrian may continue over the roof of the vehicle or be pushed back onto the road following braking and deceleration (Figure 6.2).

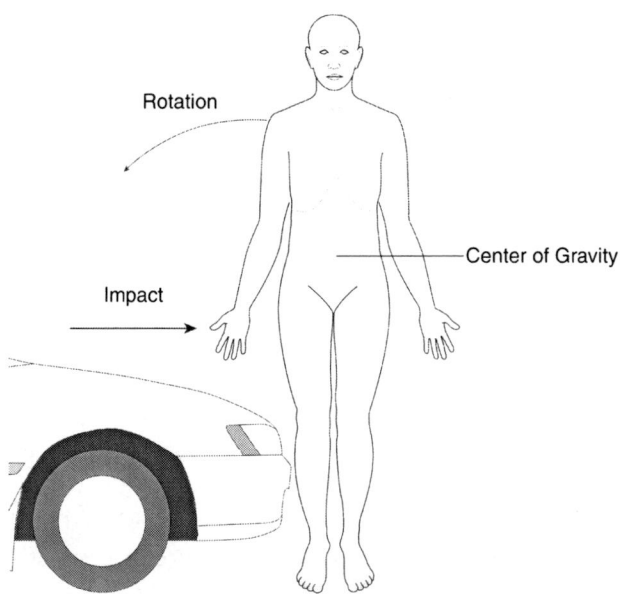

Figure 6.1 Motion of pedestrian onto conventional vehicle.

Figure 6.2 Contact damage to vehicle hood, windshield, and roof from impact with a pedestrian.

In incidents involving conventional cars at even higher speeds, the pedestrian will travel onto the hood and over the roof of the car and impact with the road behind the vehicle. This is termed a "somersault trajectory." The final resting point of the individual in such incidents tends to be some distance forward from the point of first contact, yet behind the final stopping place of the vehicle.

Bumper Injuries

Historically the injuries of particular interest to pathologists were bumper bruises, lacerations, abrasions, and associated fractures to the lower limbs (Figure 6.3). These fractures were sometimes noted to be wedge-shaped in the direction of the vehicle motion and were called Messerer fractures. The height of the injuries above the ground were believed to be a reasonable indicator as to the height of the bumper and whether the vehicle was braking at the time of the collision. The rationale was that the front of a braking vehicle would dip lower and cause injuries to a lower point on the pedestrian's leg. Differences in height between injuries to the left and right leg have been used to indicate whether a pedestrian was standing still or moving in a certain direction when struck.

Although the theories behind these assertions are sound, in practice there are considerable problems in their application.

Modern vehicles have rounded bumpers and are designed to allow considerably more deformation with subsequent restitution. Design standards have dictated that projecting features are unacceptable; therefore, it is uncommon to have a distinct patterned, abraded injury to the leg of the deceased that can be matched to a vehicle. In addition, abrasions and lacerations tend to preferentially occur over bony prominences, not necessarily indicating a distinct point of impact from the motor vehicle. Consequently, abrasions and lacerations do not lend themselves to dogmatic statements regarding height from the ground and information regarding the braking status of the vehicle.

The primary impact will cause bruises to the lower limbs. Bruising visible to the surface of the skin may be relatively minor when compared with the extent of bruising revealed by subcutaneous dissection of the deceased victim's

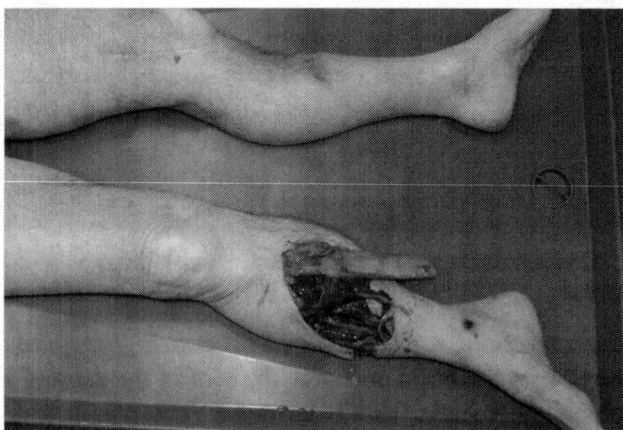

Figure 6.3 Pedestrian with compound fracture of the right lower leg with proximal tibia extending through the injury. Fractured left lower leg with marked deformity.

body or seen on magnetic resonance imaging. Further deeper dissection of skeletal muscle and demonstration of periosteal bruising can provide a more reliable guide to the region of maximum impact.

Lacerations are more common to the anterior aspect of the lower leg where the tibia is relatively exposed. Lacerations may also occur from the fractured ends of bone extending through the skin from the internal aspect of the limb. The lacerated injury produced is then clearly not necessarily an approximation of the impacting surface of the motor vehicle.

Fractures

Fractures to the shaft of the tibia are the most common fractures sustained by pedestrians. The tibial fractures result from a combination of bending from direct impact, axial loading when weight bearing, and a rotational component when the body is turning. Fracture type and location may provide information in the reconstruction of the circumstances surrounding a pedestrian death.

Experimental studies have shown that fractures of the tibia produced by direct blunt force will vary with respect to the site of the bone involved and direction of impact. A study on isolated tibia specimens confirmed the fact that fractures originate from tensile stress at the opposite site of the transverse impacting force and extend through the bone to the "region" of the applied force.[4] The study involved a localised point of application of force and yet variation in the site of fracture was demonstrable. When one considers the variation in fracture morphology that can occur to the tibia with such a localised point of applied force, it would seem reasonable to suggest that the anatomic site of the tibial fracture that results from impact with the broad surface of a car bumper in a pedestrian incident may vary considerably.

Fractures around the ankle joint are also common in pedestrian incidents. The fracture sites are highly dependent on the exact position of the foot at the moment of impact. The presence of a boot on a pedestrian can influence the location of fractures in the lower leg, with fractures more likely to be seen just above the upper margin of a boot (Figure 6.4).[5]

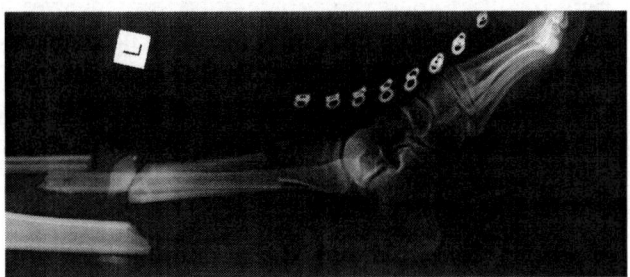

Figure 6.4 Fracture of lower leg above upper margin of the boot in a pedestrian struck by a motor vehicle.

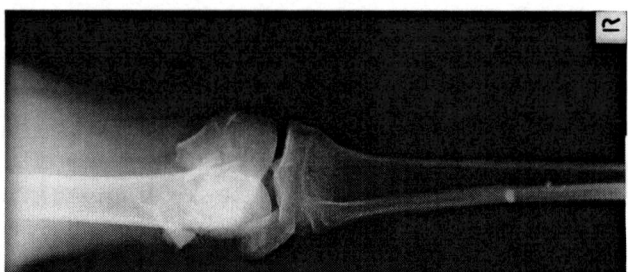

Figure 6.5 Transverse supracondylar fracture of the femur from direct impact by a motor vehicle.

The presence of femoral and pelvic injuries from primary impact is dependent on the stature of the individual and height of the presenting section of the motor vehicle. Direct trauma to the thigh may cause a transverse fracture of the femur particularly if that leg was weight bearing at the time of the impact (Figure 6.5). Impact to the lateral aspect of the hip from contact with the hood may cause the head of the femur to be driven into the acetabulum resulting in a central acetabular fracture. Although the joint can be dissected and exposed postmortem, the procedure is certainly not routine and is somewhat time-consuming. Radiographs of the joint with appropriate views can demonstrate and document the presence of fractures.

The pelvis is formed by the left and right iliac wings, ischium, and pubis, which form a ring with the sacrum. The pelvis is a very stable structure and requires significant forces to cause disruption. The Young classification of pelvic fractures incorporates the anatomic mechanism of injury and divides the fractures into lateral compression fractures, anteroposterior compression, vertical shear fractures, and combined fractures. These fractures may be associated with an acetabular fracture and may be subdivided into a number of grades.

In general, lateral compression fractures entail transverse fractures of the pubic rami with either ipsilateral or contralateral posterior injury. Increasing grade of injury is associated with ipsilateral iliac wing fracture to an open book fracture. Anteroposterior compression fractures involve diastasis or longitudinal pubic rami fractures. Increasing grade of fracture involves widening of the pubic symphysis followed by increasing sacroiliac ligament and joint disruption leading to an open book fracture. Vertical shear fractures classically result from a fall from a height and show diastasis of the pubic symphysis with vertical displacement though the sacroiliac joint, iliac wing, or sacrum.

Joint Injuries to the Lower Limb

In a series of articles, Teresinski and Madro examined various injuries to the hip, knee, and ankle joints in pedestrian deaths.[6–9] The studies described detailed dissection and examination of the joints with emphasis on the presence of injury to the joint ligaments and compression fractures to the adjacent subchondral bone. Examination of the various joint ligaments, taken in conjunction with other available information such as cutaneous and subcutaneous bruising, provides information regarding the direction of force that led to injury.

Examination of the bone immediately adjacent to ligaments can reveal bruising associated with microfractures. Tibial plateau fractures result from impact from the femur by axial loading, in adduction or abduction, and may cause fractures to the articular surface of the tibia. The presence of tibial plateau fractures suggests the lower leg was weight bearing at the time of the impact.

For example, the postmortem examination of a pedestrian may reveal a haemarthrosis of the right knee with complete or partial rupture of the posterior cruciate ligament, a complete or partial tear of the medial collateral ligament, and subchondral haemorrhage in the right lateral tibial plateau and right lateral femoral condyle. Subcutaneous dissection revealed extensive bruising to the posterior medial aspect of the right thigh. In the absence of any other significant findings, these features would be consistent with a primary impact to the posterior lateral aspect of the right thigh in an upright pedestrian with weight on the right leg.

Injuries to the Head

Head injury is common in pedestrian incidents and is a major cause of morbidity and mortality.

The head impact is most often to the windshield and surrounds. Contact with the windshield glass can cause broad abraded injuries if the glass remains intact, lacerations from blunt force, and incised injuries from broken glass. If the pedestrian's head extends through the glass, there may be severe, deep incised injuries.

Blunt force injury and rotational acceleration may result in a variety of brain injuries including contusions, intracranial haemorrhage, and diffuse axonal injury (Figure 6.6).

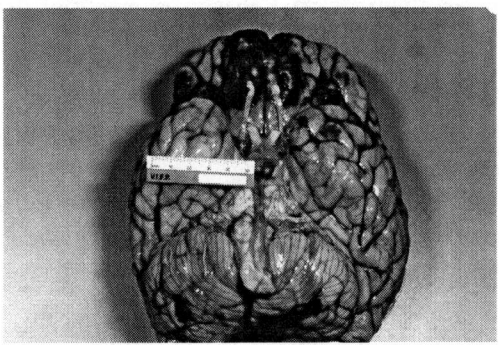

Figure 6.6 Frontal contusions to the brain after impact to the back of the head from the roadway (contrecoup contusions).

Injuries to the Neck

Injuries to the neck are common in pedestrians struck by cars. Dissection of the soft tissues and ligaments of the neck in deceased individuals can provide information regarding the direction of impact.

For example, a significant impact to the right side of an upright pedestrian will cause the head to be rapidly and forcibly turned toward the site of impact. This will tend to stretch and tear the neck muscles, including the sternomastoid and scalene muscles, on the opposite side to the impact. Similar bruises may be seen within the ligaments of the cervical spine.[10]

Bone injuries can also provide information on the forces exerted to the neck in pedestrian fatalities.

A team of radiologists in the 1980s observed that similar injuries occurred to different portions of the vertebral column depending upon the mechanism of injury. Flexion injuries led to compression and burst fractures of the vertebral bodies, radiologic "tear drop" fractures to the inferior tips of vertebral bodies, widening of the interspinous spaces, anterolisthesis, locked facets, and narrowing of intervertebral spaces at and below the level of involvement.

Injuries from hyperextension led to fractured neural arches, articular facets and pillars, widened disc spaces, and anterior ligament rupture with retrolisthesis. Shearing and rotational forces mostly occurred with flexion and led to vertebral body and pillar fractures on one side, horizontal subluxation and dislocation, and fracture transverse processes in the lumbar region. Lateral forces led to compression fractures of the articular facets and pillars in the cervical region and burst fractures of thoracic vertebral bodies. The severity of the injury was directly related to the force of the impact and position of the individual at the time of the incident.[11]

Upper cervical spine fractures and atlanto-occipital fracture/dislocation are common injuries in impacts involving the upright pedestrian and a common cause of rapid death at the scene. Karger has suggested that cervical and lumbar fractures suggest the pedestrian was in an erect posture at impact.[12]

Injuries to the Upper Limbs

Direct impact to the lateral shoulder may lead to comminuted fractures of the head of the humerus.

Most fractures of the shaft of the humerus tend to be transverse and occur mid-shaft; however, the fracture may be spiral if the arm is rotated. Direct trauma to the forearm tends to result in simple transverse fractures that may be wedge-shaped; however, identical fractures can occur with falls to the outstretched hand. In the latter case, examination of the deceased's hands may reveal broad, abraded injuries to the palm with adherent gravel.

Pedestrians vs. Larger, Flat-Fronted Vehicles (Vehicle–Pedestrian Mismatch)

Vans, 4WD vehicles, and SUVs impact with pedestrians above their centre of gravity and push the pedestrian forward at all speeds. There follows an increased risk for "runover" injuries. Children have a much lower centre of gravity compared with adults and will have dynamics identical to impact with vans, 4WD vehicles, and SUVs even when a conventional passenger car is involved.

It has been demonstrated that pedestrians who are struck by a van, 4WD vehicle, SUV, or light truck have a two to three times' greater likelihood of dying than if struck by a conventional passenger vehicle. The increase in fatality rate is related to the high propensity for significant head and chest injury.[13]

Head Injuries

The head injuries tend to be more severe in incidents involving vehicles such as 4WD vehicles compared with conventional cars.[14] The lethal head injury usually occurs from direct contact with the motor vehicle, but may result from contact with the road surface, other vehicle, or roadside object. The exact etiology of the lethal impact may be difficult or impossible in some cases. Close examination of the skin abrasions and lacerations for foreign material or a patterned quality, with correlation to the damage to the motor vehicle in question and the scene findings may indicate the precise cause of the head injury.

Abdominal Injuries

Direct impact to the abdomen often results in a surprising paucity of cutaneous injury, though bruising will be seen in subcutaneous fat and muscles. Liver and splenic ruptures are common sequelae of direct abdominal impact, especially to the right and left sides of the abdomen respectively. Organ damage can range from simple capsular tears, up to parenchymal rupture and disruption or complete vascular detachment. Ruptured stomach and small and large bowel are somewhat uncommon, though mesenteric ruptures may be more frequently seen. Kidney rupture or avulsion is seen more frequently with posterior impact.

Chest Injuries

Chest abrasions, bruises, and lacerations occur frequently with direct blunt force. Rib fractures will tend to reflect the location of the application of blunt force. Not uncommonly, direct primary impact to the chest in adult pedestrians will cause a somewhat linear arrangement of rib fractures. Significant direct blunt force may result in rupture of thoracic viscera and vasculature.

Pelvic Injury

Abrasions and bruises to the hip and pelvic region can indicate the site of primary contact between the vehicle and the pedestrian. Direct trauma to the hip can result in a variety of acetabular fractures. The acetabular fractures can be extensively comminuted and the head of the femur dislocated from the joint or into the pelvic cavity. Fractures may be seen to the trochanteric region of the femur and, in older victims of trauma, to the femoral neck.

Fractures of the pelvic ring are common. The superior and inferior pubic rami are often fractured. Multiple fractures of the pelvic rim are a common occurrence with significant blunt trauma. There is a tendency for fractures to occur in the direct of the application of force, but exceptions to this general rule abound.

Pelvic fractures are often associated with considerable haemorrhage that may extend to the retroperitoneum. Ruptures to sigmoid mesentery, ruptured bowel, and bladder, and laceration of large pelvic arteries and veins are significant visceral and vascular injuries associated with severe pelvic trauma.

Lower Limb Injuries

In the typical case of vehicle pedestrian mismatch, the knee and lower legs do not suffer the primary impact although abrasions, bruises, lacerations, and bony injury may occur from contact with the road or subsequent contact with vehicles. Fractures can result from transmitted torsion and compression forces. Knee and ankle injury, ranging from partial to complete ligament tear, to total joint disruption may also result from transmitted forces.

Upper Limbs

It is very common to see nonspecific abraded injuries to the upper limbs in pedestrian incidents. Depending on the position of the upper limb at the moment of primary impact there may be significant soft- and bony tissue injury from primary contact with the motor vehicle. Direct trauma to the shafts of long bones within the upper arm typically result in transverse fractures, although identical fractures may be seen with falls to the outstretched hand or elbow subsequent to the primary impact.

Runover Injuries

Runover incidents can cause particularly mutilating and complex injuries. The impact to a prone individual by a moving motor vehicle will lead to subsequent movement of the victim such that abrasions, bruises, and lacerations are frequently seen in multiple planes. Abrasions can result from contact with the vehicle and movement across the road surface. A patterned abrasion or intradermal bruise from contact with a tire may be evident (Figure 6.7). Deposition of grease is common to the victim's clothing, skin, and may be seen within various injuries. Contact with metallic projections of the vehicle undercarriage typically result in lacerated injuries that may have a directional quality (Figure 6.8).

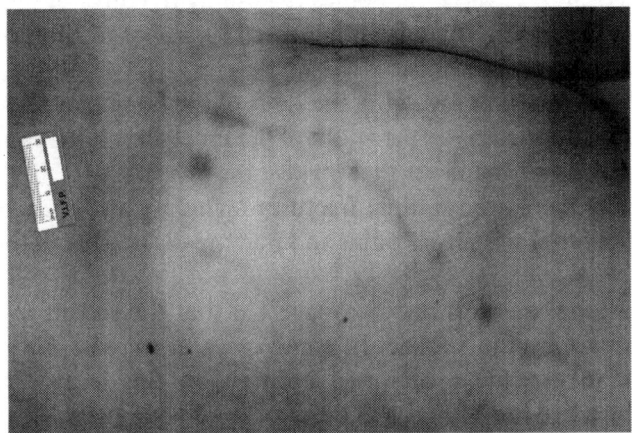

Figure 6.7 Ill-defined patterned intradermal bruise over the buttock from run over by a light truck. This injury would be associated with severe pelvic fractures with vascular and visceral injury.

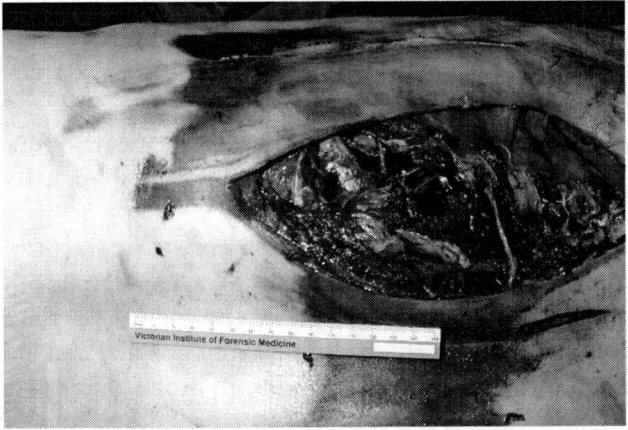

Figure 6.8 Pedestrian runover victim. Longitudinal and patterned abraded injuries with longitudinal laceration from projecting surface of vehicle undercarriage. Deposition of grease on surrounding skin.

Contact of the victim's body from a rotating tire often causes an avulsion type injury in which the skin and subcutaneous fat is torn away from an underlying tissue plane. When such contact is adjacent to a joint, there can be disarticulation and occasionally amputation of the affected limb.

Runover injuries involving the chest or abdomen typically cause severe damage to the viscera with virtual pulping of organs not uncommon. Blunt trauma from a tire running across a victim can lead to a variety of fractures. Rib fractures tend to be extensive and involve multiple fractures in anterior, lateral, and posterior locations. Blunt trauma to the spine tends to cause fracture/dislocations. Vertebral bodies may show fractures of the transverse and spinous processes. There is an increased incidence of thoracic vertebral fractures in runover incidents.

Long-bone fractures involving the shaft of the bone may show crushing in a width that approximates the width of the tire. Pelvic injuries are virtually universal in runover incidents that involve the pelvis.

Classically there are multiple fractures including an "open-book" fracture, with fractured symphysis pubis and fracture dislocation of the sacroiliac joints.

In occasional cases, it may be suggested that the victim was deceased prior to impact by the vehicle. In some cases, it may be difficult, if not impossible, to provide a reasoned opinion on this issue. The injuries sustained by a live individual will be associated with a significant amount of bruising, appropriate for the degree of force suffered by the victim. Although postmortem extravasation of blood simulating true antemortem bruising has been described, the amount of bruising seen is minor compared with the amount of trauma sustained and tends to be in loose connective tissues.[15]

Pediatric Pedestrian Injuries

Head injury is common in pediatric pedestrian incidents. Pediatric victims of head trauma have a tendency to develop cerebral edema that can be refractory to medical and surgical intervention.

Chest injury may be severe despite the absence of rib fractures. Children's ribs are extremely pliable and may not show a fracture despite other evidence of major trauma. Intrathoracic viscera can be pulped yet the ribs remain intact. Abdominal trauma can result in hepatic, splenic, and hollow viscera injury. Femoral fractures are common injuries in the older age group.

Byard examined the features of pediatric pedestrian injuries and found that severe head injury capable of causing death was present in 91.2% of cases, abdominal injury in 50%, chest injury in 47.1%, and neck injury in 38.2%.[16] The complex nature of the injuries sustained by the victims, with multiple injuries from the primary impact and various secondary injuries made understanding the sequence of traumatic events difficult to determine. The direction of primary impact could be inferred from the differential severity of the injuries in various planes or body regions.

Motor Vehicle Speed in Pedestrian Incidents

It is intuitively obvious that the greater the force of the impact to the pedestrian, the greater the degree of injury to the victim's body. The speed of the vehicle is directly related to the force of impact. A study in the U.S. examined the relationship between amputation of a limb or transection of the victim's body with the speed of the vehicle. It was found that examples of amputation or transection only occurred on highways, the inference being that such severe injury to the pedestrian's body only happens with "highway speed."[17]

A prospective study by Karger and colleagues examined injuries to pedestrian victims at postmortem with respect to impact velocity.[18] It was found that spinal fractures, ruptures of the thoracic aorta, inguinal skin ruptures from stretching, and dismemberment were associated with impact speed. The study was done on erect pedestrian victims who had been struck by a wedge- or pontoon-shaped passenger car. The authors recommended caution in the interpretation of the data but suggested: "If there was no spinal fracture, the velocity was below 70 km/hr and probably below 50 km/hr. Aortic and skin ruptures were always present if the velocity was greater than 100 km/hr but never occurred below 50–60 km/hr. Dismemberment occurred with velocities above 90 km/hr."[18]

It is important to note that the investigating police officers may be able to provide objective estimates of vehicle speed based on measurements at the scene, including the length of skidmarks and yawmarks and pedestrian "throw" distance.

References

1. Holubowycz OT. Age, sex, and blood alcohol concentration of killed and injured pedestrians. *Accident Analysis and Prevention* 1995; 27:417–422.

2. Garder PE. The impact of speed and other variables on pedestrian safety in Maine. *Accident Analysis and Prevention* 36:533–542.

3. Isenberg RA, Chidester AB, Mavros S. *Update on the Pedestrian Crash Data Study.* US Department of Transportation paper no: 98-S6-O-05.

4. Rabl W, Haid C, Krismer M. Biomechanical properties of the human tibia; fracture behaviour and morphology. *Forensic Science International* 1996; 83:39–49.

5. Eisele JW, Bonnell HJ, Reay DT. Boot top fractures in pedestrians. A forensic masquerade. *The American Journal of Forensic Medicine and Pathology* 1983; 4:181–184.

6. Teresinski G, Madro R. Ankle joint injuries as a reconstruction parameter in car-to-pedestrian accidents. *Forensic Science International* 2001; 118:65–73.

7. Teresinski G, Madro R. Pelvis and hip joint injuries as a reconstructive factor in car-to-pedestrian accidents. *Forensic Science International* 2001; 124:68–73.

8. Teresinski G, Madro R. Knee joint injuries as a reconstructive factor in car-to-pedestrian accidents. *Forensic Science International* 2001; 124:74–82.

9. Teresinski G, Madro R. Evidential value of injuries useful for reconstruction of the pedestrian-vehicle location at the moment of collision. *Forensic Science International* 2002; 128:127–135.

10. Madro R, Teresinski G. Neck injuries as a reconstructive parameter in car-to-pedestrian accidents. *Forensic Science International* 2001; 118:57–63.

11. Daffner RH, Deeb ZL, Rothfus WE. "Fingerprints" of vertebral trauma—a unifying concept based on mechanisms. *Skeletal Radiology* 1986; 15:518–525.

12. Karger B, Teige K, Fuchs M, Brinkman B. Was the pedestrian in an erect position before being run over? *Forensic Science International* 2001; 119:217–220.

13. Lefler DE, Gabler HC. The fatality and injury risk of light truck impacts with pedestrians in the United States. *Accident Analysis and Prevention* 2004; 36:295–304.

14. Tanno A, Kohno M, Ohashi N, Ono K, Aita K, Oikawa H, Oo MT, Honda K, Misawa S. Patterns and mechanisms of pedestrian injuries induced by vehicles with flat-front shape. *Legal Medicine* 2000; 2:68–74.

15. Burke MP, Olumbe A, Opeskin K. Post mortem extravasation of blood potentially simulating antemortem bruising. *The American Journal of Forensic Medicine and Pathology* 1998; 19:46–49.

16. Byard RW, Green H, James RA, Gilbert JD. Pathologic features of childhood pedestrian fatalities. *The American Journal of Forensic Medicine and Pathology* 2000; 21:101–106.

17. Zivot V, Di Maio VJ. Motor vehicle-pedestrian accidents in adults. Relationship between impact speed, injuries, and distance thrown. *The American Journal of Forensic Medicine and Pathology* 1993; 14:185–186.

18. Karger B, Teige K, Buhren W, DuChesne A. Relationship between impact velocity and injuries in fatal pedestrian-car collisions. *International Journal of Legal Medicine* 2000; 113:84–88.

Injuries Associated with Motorcycle, Bicycle, and Heavy Vehicle Incidents

7

Motorcycles

Motorcycles differ markedly from passenger motor vehicles in weight, acceleration capability, and visibility on the road, yet braking and lateral movement characteristics are not dissimilar to regular passenger vehicles. Variation in these latter parameters may be more related to a rider's ability rather than the size of the motorcycle.

Motorcyclists are 20 to 30 times more likely to be severely injured or die as a result of a crash than are motor vehicle occupants.[1] Statistics from the U.S. indicate that most motorcycle incidents tend to occur in the late afternoon and early evening and fatal crashes within the evening and early morning. Crashes and fatalities are uniform in number from Monday to Thursday, increase on Friday, and peak on Saturday then decrease slightly on Sunday.

In 2003 in Victoria, Australia, motorcycle riders and pillion passengers comprised 12% of road deaths despite the fact that motorcycles accounted for only about 3% of registered vehicles.[2] Lethal injuries usually involve severe head injury and cervical spine fracture dislocation. Nonlethal but debilitating bone, joint, and soft-tissue injuries to the lower limbs are the most common injuries sustained by motorcycle riders.

Human Factors

The Major Collision Investigation Group, a specialised team of police members who investigate serious motor vehicle incidents in Victoria, Australia, examined 47 collisions involving severe injury and fatalities to motorcycle riders. The investigations involved attendance at the scene of all fatalities and collisions causing severe injury. Of these 47 cases, 44 of the riders were male. The ages ranged from 17 to 56 years, with a mean of 32 years. There were 59.5% full licence riders, with 21.5% learner or probationary riders, and 19% unlicensed riders. The examination showed excessive speed contributed to 38% of the crashes.

Alcohol was detected in 19% of the riders, with 13% having a blood alcohol concentration of greater than 0.05 g/100 mL, the legal limit for full-licence riders in Victoria, Australia. Most of the initial collisions did not involve another vehicle and consisted principally of running off the road incidents, mainly on left-hand curves. Three quarters of the deaths and severe injuries occurred in the metropolitan region, 29% occurred on a straight section of road, and 21% were at intersections (Figure 7.1). Approximately 63% of the incidents led to impact with another vehicle, whereas 10.5% struck a fixed object such as a tree (Figure 7.2). In the study, only 4% of collisions occurred on wet roads. Overall, 75.6% of the motorcycle riders were assessed as being "at fault." The results are similar to a study on Western Australia motorcycle crash deaths, which indicated unsafe practices by motorcycle riders were implicated in 76% of at scene deaths.[3]

Possible behavioural differences between motorcyclists and a matched group of non-motorcycling car drivers were investigated in a recent study.

Figure 7.1   Collision between a motorcycle and car at an intersection with the rider coming to rest some distance from the motorcycle.

Figure 7.2 Sideswipe incident involving motorcyclist who crossed onto the wrong side of the road.

The laboratory simulator study sought to determine whether motorcyclists exhibited different behaviour while riding a motorcycle compared with a second group of motorcyclist drivers and non-motorcycling car drivers. The motorcyclists driving cars were significantly faster at detecting hazards than car drivers. Motorcyclists were found to travel at higher speeds than the matched group of car drivers, although this may have reflected the spatial and performance characteristics of motorcycles in general.[4]

Injuries to Riders in Motorcycle Incidents

In a crash of a given velocity, the motorcycle rider assumes the motorcycle's velocity and impact severity with another vehicle or fixed object. The best case scenario for a rider is a controlled "laying down" of the motorcycle with frictional forces bringing the rider to rest.

A study from Germany examined injuries of motorcycle riders presenting to the emergency room of a trauma centre during a 12-month period. It was found that 90.7% of the victims were male with an average age of 28.8 years. Helmets were worn in 98.8% cases of cases. Two patients (2.3%) died of severe head injury. The most common injuries in survivors were lower extremity injuries (46%) and, in particular, compound tibial fractures (19.7%). Fractures to the forearm involving the distal radius occurred in 18.8% of cases.[5]

Motorcycle riders who die as a consequence of a collision most commonly suffer significant head, neck, and chest injuries. Severe brain injury and fracture dislocation of the upper cervical spine commonly results in rapid death at the scene. Deceleration injury with thoracic aortic tear results in rapid exsanguination and death. Major abdominal injuries occur in up to 23% of deceased riders.

Other major injuries to motorcycle riders include pelvic fractures, often with wide separation of the symphysis pubis (open book fracture). Spinal injury occurs in just over 10% of riders injured in a collision. The thoracic spine is the region most commonly injured, with multiple spinal injuries not uncommon.[6] Spinal fractures in motorcycle riders reflect forced hyperflexion of the thoracic spine.[7] Transverse fractures of the femur and complex knee and foot injuries are common and important lower limb injuries, and fractures of the humerus, radius, and ulna are also often seen.

Rider or Pillion Passenger?

In the Yorkshire district of the U.K., approximately 4% of injured motorcycle riders were pillion passengers.[8] Occasionally, an important issue in a motorcycle fatality is to determine which of two riders was in control of the machine at the time of a collision. Similar to injuries seen in pilots of light aircraft, fractures of the hand are more common in the rider in control. Fractures and dislocations of the fingers and thumb result from contact with the handlebars and brake and clutch levers (Figure 7.3). Of course it is possible for identical injuries to occur from contact with the road and other objects.

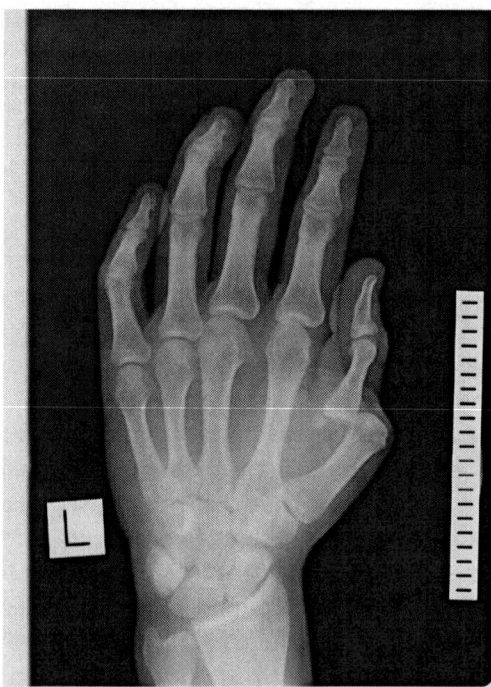

Figure 7.3 Radiograph of left hand showing dislocation of metacarpal phalangeal joint of the thumb.

Inguinal creases/abrasions or lacerations caused from impact with the fuel tank is a characteristic injury of the motorcycle driver and thus useful in differentiating between the motorcycle driver and pillion passenger.[9]

Injury Prevention through Helmet Use

The issue of helmet use by motorcycle riders ignites particularly strong opinions from lobby groups both inside and outside the motorcyclist fraternity. Issues such as decreased visual field and hearing have been raised as valid reasons not to wear helmets, although studies have shown that these factors are not significant issues. Intuitively it would appear obvious that, because head injury is a major cause of morbidity and mortality in motorcycle collisions, wearing a helmet must offer protection from head injury. The helmet provides protection from direct blunt impact to the head; however, an important issue is whether helmets provide protection from rotational brain injury.

Individuals who do not wear a helmet suffer more significant head and neck injuries, causing death and prolonged hospitalisation.[10] Several studies have examined the injury and fatality rates for motorcycle riders in relation to the introduction or abolition of mandatory helmet laws. Repeal of the mandatory helmet law was associated with an increase in the non-helmeted crash fatality rate in Arkansas and disproportionately higher hospital admission rate for non-helmeted motorcycle crash survivors.[10]

Repeal of the law applicable to helmet use in Louisiana resulted in an increased fatality rate for riders not wearing helmets. A further study using U.S. data compared states with motorcycle helmet laws and those without. The study showed that, after controlling for other significant factors in motorcycle rider deaths, fatality rates in states with mandatory helmet laws were lower on average than those without such laws.[11]

High-weight helmets (greater than 1500 g) have been associated with an increased risk of fractured base of skull.[12] Helmets have been shown to separate from the rider during crashes in 11% of cases, with 50% of these cases having the chin strap closed and 24% showing a tear or avulsion to the strap.[12] Open-face helmets have been shown to be associated with more significant head and neck injuries than full-face helmets.[13] It has also been suggested that full-face helmets may increase the risk of cervical spine fracture, although a controlled study showed this was not the case.[14]

Bicycle Incidents

The rate of bicycle incidents varies considerably depending on a particular region's use of bicycles for transportation and recreation. Belgium has a high rate of cycling with almost 10% of the population using a bicycle on a given day. Cyclists comprise 9.8% of road traffic fatalities in Belgium, whereas in the United States, the figure is 1.7%.[15] Depending on the proportion of bicycles and motor vehicles in a particular region, up to 50% of bicycle incidents requiring medical attention involve a collision with a motor vehicle.

An analysis of bicycle collisions in Great Britain showed that three-quarters of reported serious and fatal accidents occurred in 60 km/hr roads and the fatality rate of cyclists increased with increasing speed limit. Roads with a higher speed limit are associated with an increase in the incidence of rear-hit bicycle rider fatalities. More than 70% of incidents occurred at or within 20 m of a junction. The majority of injured cyclists were younger than 30 years of age and had a fatality rate of 3.4%.[16]

The most common cause of death and serious injury in cycling incidents is head injury. A study in Belgium of severely head-injured cyclists requiring neurosurgical intervention showed that skull fractures and cerebral contusions were the most common injuries encountered. More severe brain injury was associated with contact with a motor vehicle rather than a fall to the ground.[15] Fifty-seven percent of impacts were to the side of the head and 27% of impacts were to the front of the head. Examination of helmets following an incident has shown damage is most common to the front and sides of the helmet, with many cases revealing impacts to the front and side rims.[17]

A range of studies has investigated the effectiveness of bicycle helmets in head injury. Bicycle helmet design is primarily directed toward linear acceleration and relatively low-velocity impact. Most studies suggest that protection is afforded the cyclist when the principal mechanism of injury is a low-velocity fall to the ground.[18] High-speed impact with motor vehicles resulting in rotational brain injury (diffuse axonal injury) may still occur when using a helmet. Interestingly, Curnow investigated the efficacy of helmets against brain injury and concluded that the studies reported in the literature had not demonstrated definitive evidence of effectiveness.[19]

Bicycle–Pedestrian Incidents

Most accidents between bicycles and pedestrians cause relatively minor injuries and are not reported to the authorities. However serious injuries and deaths do occur.[20]

In Germany in 1997, 13 pedestrians were killed following impact from a cyclist. Invariably, the pedestrian was elderly and the cause of death was a head injury. The pedestrian's head injury is caused by a fall to the ground in the vast majority of cases.

The reconstruction of a fatal incident involving a pedestrian and cyclist may be quite difficult. Marks from the bicycle tires may be noted to the victims clothing and on the lower leg skin. Nonspecific and patterned abraded injuries to the lower legs can indicate the site of contact between the bicycle front tire and the pedestrian, and may be crucial in reconstruction. In the deceased pedestrian, subcutaneous dissection of the lower limbs may confirm the site of impact by demonstrating recent bruising.

Nonspecific abrasions and bruising may be seen to the victim's body and limbs from contact with the bicycle handlebars and the cyclist. The majority of cyclists suffer only minor soft-tissue injuries.

Heavy Vehicle Incidents

Introduction

Heavy vehicles on the road include trucks of varying size and configuration, minibuses, and large coaches. Numerically, trucks and coaches comprise a minority of vehicles on the road, but travel a disproportionately large number of kilometres per year compared with other road users. Because of their size and associated braking characteristics, trucks and coaches are significant vehicles on metropolitan and country roads, and especially so when involved in a collision. Crashes at significant speeds which involve large coaches can lead to multiple fatalities.

A large truck may be defined as a truck with a gross vehicle weight of at least 10 tons. Large trucks may be subdivided into articulated and single unit vehicles. In North America, large trucks are designated as A-, B-, and C-train vehicles. In Australia, these trucks are termed *double*.

An A indicates a single ring feeder and pin, whereas a B double has a turntable system. A C has two ring feeders and two bars. A B double has two turntable couplings and a B triple has three turntable couplings.

Overview of Truck Collisions

Most collisions with trucks occur on metropolitan roads, whereas most fatal collisions occur on country roads. Crashes involving articulated vehicles, those occurring at night and those on roads with higher speed limits tend to be more severe. Frontal collisions are associated with a high fatality rate.

Single vehicles running off the road crashes are a particular hazard for truck drivers.

In the United States, large trucks represent about 4% of all registered vehicles and 8% of total miles driven on public roads, yet are involved in 12% of all passenger vehicle occupant deaths in two vehicle collisions and 23% of passenger occupant deaths in multiple vehicle crashes.[21] Although fatal collisions have decreased per truck distance travelled over the past two decades, the reduction has been greater for truck occupants compared with passenger vehicle occupants. Clearly, the enormous difference in vehicle mass is a significant factor (Figures 7.4 and 7.5).

Figure 7.4   Collision involving a large truck and passenger vehicle.

Figure 7.5   Extensive damage to passenger vehicle following impact from a large truck.

The number of fatal collisions involving articulated and single-unit trucks in Australia has increased since 1997. During the 5-year period from 1996 to 2001, 40% of truck associated collisions involved articulated trucks and 60% involved single unit vehicles. The great majority of collisions between trucks and cars occur during daylight hours. Of these collisions, 64% of fatalities were car occupants and 20% pedestrians, motorcyclists, and cyclists.[22] In 2003 in rural Victoria, Australia, heavy vehicles were involved in 24% of fatal crashes. In more than half of the truck driver fatalities where restraint use was known, the driver was not wearing the seat belt.[2]

It is well recognised that fatigue and inattention are potential causes of motor vehicle crashes. It has been estimated that 58% of all single-vehicle truck crashes and 31% of truck driver fatalities are related to fatigue.[23] A study on trucks providing a local short-haul service that involved instrument data collection equipment showed that critical incidents on the road were identified in which the truck driver was deemed to be at fault. The study suggested fatigue was an issue prior to critical incidents. Although it was unclear why fatigue was an issue for short-haul truck drivers, it was suggested that a drivers' off-work behaviour may be a further significant issue that needs to be addressed.[24] It is in this setting that some drivers resort to the use of stimulants. The use of amphetamine and related drugs by truck drivers has been shown to be a significant problem in studies of drug use by commercial drivers.[25]

Trucks and other heavy vehicles have a higher risk for rollover incidents (Figure 7.6). Hazards on roads that increase rollover risk include ramps and inclines.

Figure 7.6 Photographs from fixed camera monitoring that recorded a truck rollover.

Vehicle Factors

Large trucks have vastly different performance characteristics compared with passenger vehicles. The marked increase in length, weight, and height leads to significant differences in acceleration, braking, turning, and stability. A questionnaire completed by truck drivers revealed that they frequently observed other road users perform unsafe driving acts in the vicinity of trucks, including changing lanes abruptly in front of a truck, following too closely and merging improperly. The other driver's actions demonstrated either a lack of knowledge or disregard to the different braking and manoeuvering ability of trucks.

Braking systems on large trucks include engine brakes and air brakes. Engine brakes work by absorbing energy on a down grade through restricting exhaust flow through the exhaust system.[26] Air brakes are the most common and important braking system in normal use and in emergency stops.

Large trucks and, especially, articulated vehicles are at increased risk of wheel lockup compared with passenger vehicles. The occurrence of lockup, especially in unfavourable road conditions, can lead to loss of control with secondary jackknife or lateral movement of the trailer. Brake failure is uncommon, but may occur with maintenance problems. A thorough mechanical examination of the brake system may be crucial in cases in which brake failure has contributed to the collision.

If the steering axle brakes lock up, the tractor trailer combination will continue forward irrespective of the wheel angle of the front wheels. If the drive wheels of the tractor lock-up the rig may jack-knife, irrespective of the steering input by the front wheels. When the rear axle wheels of the trailer lock up, directional control to the rear wheels is lost and the rig will eventually pull sideways and rotate around the tractors' driving wheels. Antilock braking systems are important in preventing lock-up situations for the steering, driving, and trailer axles.

Large trucks are associated with an increased risk of rollover and articulated trucks with jackknife incidents. Risk for jackknife increases with length of the vehicle and the risk for rollover with the height of the vehicle. A jackknife may be complicated by rollover. Rollover risk is also related to relative distribution of freight (weight), the number of trailers on an articulated vehicle, and the type of freight. Tanker trailers with partially empty tanks are at particular risk because of lateral movement of fluid during turns.[26] Rollovers can occur when outboard wheels extend onto the road shoulder and the driver attempts to steer the rig acutely back onto the paved surface. Rollover is extremely dangerous for trucks because roof crush is likely to occur.

Vehicle warning systems to alert the driver of imminent rollover are being introduced and electronic stability systems to minimise the possibility of rollover are being researched and developed.[27] Side and window airbags offer further protection to restrained drivers in the event of a partial turnover.

Large trucks have larger "blind spots" in rear view mirrors so that vehicles and other road users may not be visible when a truck driver executes a lane change or other manoeuvre. This problem can be accentuated for pedestrians when a large truck and, especially, an articulated vehicle is turning acutely. The rear wheels of the trailer track inside the primer mover/tractor. If the pedestrian is not paying attention, he or she may be struck by the rear of the vehicle and the driver may well be unaware of the incident.

Injuries in Truck Collisions

The type of injury sustained in a truck or heavy vehicle collision is somewhat dependent on the type of crash and the size of the other vehicles involved in the collision. Rollover events are a particular hazard for trucks and coaches with the potential for roof crush. Direct trauma to the head and neck leads to blunt force injury, rotational injury to the brain, and cervical spine fracture with spinal cord disruption. Rollover events with roof crush can also cause mechanical and traumatic asphyxia. Ejection from the vehicle is a particular hazard in the absence of correctly worn seat belts.

Overview of Bus Collisions

A fundamental problem in the analysis of collisions involving buses is the absence of a universal definition for coaches and buses. In general, the term *coach* is reserved for large tourist type vehicles that transport a relatively large number of passengers, often on long journeys and on rural roads. The term *bus* is usually used for vehicles that transport passengers on metropolitan roads. In a study using European data, the risk for being injured or killed when an occupant of a bus or coach was seven to nine times lower than for car occupants.[28] Bus and coach fatalities comprise about 0.5% of all road fatalities.

Not surprisingly, on city roads, crashes involving buses tend to occur at low speeds and result in relatively minor injuries. The usual disparity in vehicle size between a bus and most other road vehicles will serve to protect bus passengers; however, because many bus passengers are unrestrained and some standing at the moment of impact, this will inevitably lead to an increased risk of injury.

Many fatal incidents associated with buses are pedestrians who had alighted from the vehicle and are struck by other vehicles in the vicinity of the bus.[29] Serious incidents involving bus and coach occupants tend to occur on rural roads and involve rollover and tipover incidents.

Injuries in Bus/Coach Collisions

The most common injuries in bus and coach incidents collectively are upper and lower limb injuries (approximately 33% to 35%), and head, face, and neck injuries (38%). Lower and upper back injuries account for approximately 9% each of injuries sustained.[30] The majority of injuries are minor. Fractures are the most common serious injury.

In bus and coach incidents involving high speeds and in rollover incidents, the main risk of serious injury is ejection from the vehicle. Seat belts have been suggested as a viable means of preventing ejection in incidents involving coaches travelling at higher speeds, and the use of interior padding proposed to address injuries from passenger contact with internal surfaces in relatively slow-moving suburban buses.

References

1. McGwin G Jr, Whatley J, Metzger J, Valent F, Barbone F, Rue LW III. The effect of state motorcycle licencing laws on motorcycle drive mortality rates. *The Journal of Trauma* 2004; 56:415–419.

2. Vicroads. http://www.vicroads.vic.gov.au

3. Stella J, Cooke C, Sprivulis P. Most head injury related motorcycle crash deaths are related to poor riding practices. *Emergency Medicine* 2002; 14:58–61.

4. Horswill MS, Helman S. A behavioural comparison between motorcyclists and a matched group of non-motorcycling car drivers: factors influencing accident risk. *Accident Analysis and Prevention* 2003; 35:589–597.

5. Wick M, Muller EJ, Ekkernkamp A. The motor cyclist, easy rider or easy victim? An analysis of motor cycle accidents in Germany. *American Journal of Emergency Medicine* 1998; 16:20–323.

6. Robertson A, Giannoudis PV, Branfoot T, Barlow I, Matthews SJ, Smith RM. Spinal injuries in motor cycle crashes: patterns and outcomes. *The Journal of Trauma* 2002; 53:5–8.

7. Robertson A, Branfoot T, Barlow IF, Giannoudis PV. Spinal injury patterns resulting from car and motorcycle accidents. *Spine* 2002; 27:2825–2830.

8. Ankarath S, Giannoudis PV, Barlow I, Bellamy MC, Matthews SJ, Smith RM. Injury patterns associated with mortality following motorcycle crashes. *Injury* 2002; 33:473–477.

9. Shiono H, Akane A, Matsubara K, Tanabe K, Takahashi S. Identification of the driver in two- rider motorcycle accidents. Inguinal contusion-laceration as an indication of the driver. *The American Journal of Forensic Medicine and Pathology* 1990; 11:190–192.

10. Bledsoe GH, Schexnayder SM, Carey MJ, Dobbins WN, Gibson WD, Hindman JW, Collins T, Wallace BH, Cone JB, Ferrer TJ. The negative impact of the repeal of the Arkansas motorcycle helmet law. *The Journal of Trauma* 2002; 53:1078–1087.

11. Branas CC, Knudson MM. Helmet laws and motorcycle death rates. *Accident Analysis and Prevention* 2001; 33:641–648.

12. Richter M, Otte D, Lehmann U, Chinn B, Schuller E, Doyle D, Sturrock K, Krattek C. Head injury mechanisms in helmet-protected motorcyclists: prospective multicentre study. *The Journal of Trauma* 2001; 51:949–958.

13. Hitosugi M, Shigeta A, Takatsu A, Yokoyama T, Tokudome S. Analysis of fatal injuries to motor cyclists by helmet type. *The American Journal of Forensic Medicine and Pathology* 2004; 25:125–128.

14. O'Connor PJ, Kloeden C, McLean AJ. Do full-face helmets offer greater protection against cervical spinal cord injury than open-faced helmets? *Traffic Injury Protection* 2002; 3:247–250.

15. Depreitere B, Van Lierde C, Maene S, Plets C, Vander Sloten J, Van Audekercke R, Van Der Perre G, Goffin J. Bicycle-related head injury: a study of 86 cases. *Accident Analysis and Prevention* 2004; 36:561–567.

16. Stone M, Broughton J. Getting off your bike: cycling accidents in Great Britain in 1990–1999. *Accident Analysis and Prevention* 2003; 35:549–556.

17. Ching RP, Thompson DC, Thompson RS, Thomas DJ, Chilcott WC, Rivarra FP. Damage to bicycle helmets involved with crashes. *Accident Analysis and Prevention* 1997; 29:555–562.

18. Hansen KS, Engersater LB, Viste A. Protective effective of different types of bicycle helmets. *Traffic Injury Prevention* 2003; 4:285–290.

19. Curnow WJ. The efficacy of bicycle helmets against brain injury. *Accident Analysis and Prevention* 2003; 5:287–292.

20. Graw M, Konig HG. Fatal pedestrian-bicycle collisions. *Forensic Science International* 2002; 126:241–247.

21. Lyman S, Braver ER. Occupant deaths in large truck crashes in the United States; 25 years of experience. *Accident Analysis and Prevention* 2003; 35:731–739.

22. Haworth N, Symmons M. Review of truck safety—update of crash statistics. Report No. 205. Victoria, Australia: Monash University Accident Research Centre, 2003.

23. Schultz JD. A fatal combination. *Traffic World* 1998; 30:16.

24. Hanowski RJ, Wierwille WW, Dingus TA. An on-road study to investigate fatigue in local/short haul trucking. *Accident Analysis and Prevention* 2003; 35(2):153-160.

25. Couper FJ, Pemberton M, Jarvis A, Hughes M, Logan BK. Prevalence of drug use in commercial tractor-trailer drivers. *Journal of Forensic Sciences* 2002; 47:562–567.

26. Fricke LB. Traffic accident reconstruction. *Traffic Accident Investigation Manual*, volume 2. Evanston, IL: Northwestern University Traffic Institute; 1990.

27. Green SD. Prevent heavy truck rollover. *Traffic Safety* 2002; 2:12–13.

28. Albertsson P, Falkmer T. Is there a pattern in European bus and coach incidents? A literature analysis with special focus on injury causation and injury mechanisms. *Accident Analysis and Prevention* 2005; 37:225–233.

29. Cass DT, Ross F, Lam L. School bus related deaths and injuries in New South Wales. *Medical Journal of Australia* 1996; 165:134–137.

30. Simpson H. *National Hospital Study of Road Accident Casualties.* Crowthorne, Great Britain: TRL; 1997.

Additional Reading

Alway G, Poznanski J. Fatal and Serious Injury Motorcycle Collisions Attended by the Major Collision Investigating Group between May 2002 and April 2003.

Arboleda A, Morrow PC, Crum MR, Shelley MC II. Management practices as antecedents of safety culture within the trucking industry: similarities and differences by hierarchal level. *Journal of Safety Research* 2003; 34:189–197.

Auman KM, Kufera JA, Ballesteros MF, Smialek JE, Dischinger PC. Autopsy study of motorcyclist fatalities: the effect of the 1992 Maryland motorcycle helmet use law. *American Journal of Public Health* 2002; 92:1352–1355.

Reeder AI, Alsop JC, Langley JD, Wagenaar AC. An evaluation of the general effect of the New Zealand graduated driver licencing system on motorcycle crash hospitalisations. *Accident Analysis and Prevention* 1999; 31:651–661.

Schneider H. An analysis of motor cycle crashes 1996 to 2002. DOT S 809 576. Available online at: http://www.isds.bus.isu.edu

Postmortem Examination

8

Introduction

Under the Coroner's Act in the State of Victoria, Australia, a pathologist or medical practitioner under the supervision of a pathologist may be directed by the Coroner to perform an autopsy on the body of an individual whose remains are under the jurisdiction of the Coroner. The Coroner investigates all natural deaths in which a medical practitioner is unable to provide a death certificate, nonnatural deaths (including accident, suicide, and homicide), maternal deaths, deaths associated with an anaesthetic and deaths in custody.

The deceased's next of kin may object to full autopsy examination under Section 29 of the Coroner's Act. The objection is often related to religious or cultural beliefs. If the Coroner rejects the Section 29 application, the senior next-of-kin has the legal right to appeal to the Supreme Court of Victoria.

Furthermore, under Section 28 of the Coroner's Act, "an interested" party may request an autopsy examination following a death. Interested parties include police officers who may request an autopsy examination in cases in which criminal charges may be laid in relation to a motor vehicle incident.

Depending on the circumstances of the case, and at the discretion of the Coroner, the postmortem examination may entail a mixture of radiographic imaging, external examination and forensic photographic record, internal examination with full subcutaneous dissection, histologic, toxicologic, and microbiologic examination.

The Postmortem Examination

The routine procedures and specialized techniques used to perform a post-mortem examination will not be discussed and the reader is referred to one of a number of excellent references on the subject.[1]

Purpose of the Postmortem Examination

The purpose of the forensic autopsy, in the State of Victoria, Australia, is to discharge a legal responsibility in relation to the Coroner's Act. A primary objective of the postmortem examination is to determine the cause of death. In many deaths associated with motor vehicle incidents, this may be achieved by simply issuing the cause of death as "multiple injuries."

Individuals and groups other than the Coroner may be interested in the autopsy findings in any given case. The medical management of a victim who initially survived the motor vehicle incident, but dies some time after the attendance of ambulance personnel or in hospital, may be of interest to various parties. The autopsy examination also provides a means of audit for emergency and surgical departments where issues such as quality control can be addressed.

In the State of Victoria and funded through the Transport Accident Commission, a legislative body managing funding, research, and compensation related to motor vehicle incidents, a committee consisting of trauma surgeons, anesthetists, emergency physicians, and paramedics investigates the medical management of motor vehicle incident victims. The group determines whether the trauma victim could have survived had timely optimal care been instituted. The group reports back to the relevant government departments with recommendations for improvements in emergency and trauma management. As part of the investigation, the postmortem examinations are carefully scrutinized. It is extremely important that the autopsy report addresses all issues of interest to such groups.

The postmortem examination should seek to address all known and relevant issues pertaining to the case. Documentation of external and internal injuries and the cause of death are fundamental matters of concern during the examination. As noted previously, although the presence of natural disease is common at autopsy, it is relatively uncommon for natural disease to cause or contribute to a motor vehicle incident. The documentation of previously undiagnosed natural disease processes may also be of particular importance to the future health of the deceased's immediate family.

Ancillary Investigations

Radiographic Imaging

Preautopsy investigations may include radiographic imaging. Radiographs provide a permanent, objective record of fractures and other significant pathologic changes. In cases of pneumothorax, although special postmortem techniques may demonstrate the presence of air within the pleural space, the radiograph provides indisputable proof of the presence, size, and consequences of a pneumothorax.

The chest radiograph also provides an objective record of the position of central venous cannulae, intercostal cannulae, pacemaker wires, endotracheal tubes, and can document rib fractures. The position of the endotracheal tube may have changed from the time of death to the autopsy examination as a consequence of movement of the deceased's body at the scene, in the hospital and in the mortuary.

In some jurisdictions multislice computed tomography scanning (MSCT) and magnetic resonance imaging (MRI) are being used as an adjunct or alternative to full internal autopsy examination.[2] MSCT is particularly useful in the evaluation of bone and air (gas), whereas MRI is effective in demonstrating soft tissue (including ligamentous) injury. The cost and availability and time of MSCT and MRI examinations are currently limiting factors in their use.[3] The MSCT scan is attractive in cases where the deceased's next of kin strongly object to autopsy. The MSCT scan, in conjunction with a careful external examination of the deceased's clothing and body, can provide a significant amount of information regarding the cause of death and associated injuries.

A recent report of a fatal collision involving a cyclist struck from behind by a motor vehicle was presented by Aghayer and colleagues.[4] The soft-tissue and bony injuries sustained by the victim were evaluated using MSCT and autopsy examination and correlated to the vehicle damage. The postmortem imaging provided excellent documentation of the deceased's injuries.

Postmortem angiography can be used as an adjunct to the autopsy dissection, or as the principal investigation technique. The use of angiography is established in the investigation and documentation of vertebral artery dissection and rupture. In cases of pelvic fracture with marked pelvic and retroperitoneal haemorrhage, MSCT angiography may well record the vessel damage better than traditional dissection (Figure 8.1).

Forensic Photography

Forensic photography is an essential component of medicolegal examinations. Although the ability to derive an opinion on photographic evidence is never as absolute as personally performing the autopsy examination, one is usually able to provide a reasonable opinion using the appropriate photographs, in conjunction with the autopsy report, histologic sections, and radiographs.

A set of photographs should always include the correct identification label and include overall views to allow orientation of different injuries and other features of forensic interest. Close-up images are performed with and

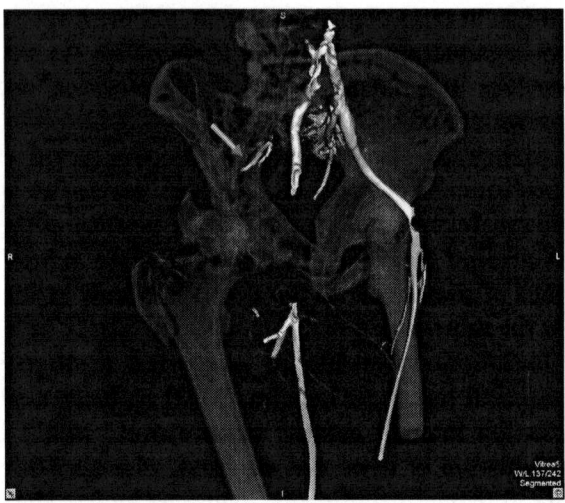

Figure 8.1   Computed tomography angiogram in pedestrian showing fractured pelvis with rupture of gluteal artery as cause of massive haemorrhage.

without the identification label to ensure that no injuries are obscured. The use of digital technology requires appropriate documentation procedures to address the issue of digital manipulation. Illustrative digital photographs and radiographs may also be sent via e-mail to relevant medical, surgical, and trauma teams for their audit and education programs.

Additional Expert Opinions

Depending on their professional experience, a pathologist may examine supplementary medical investigations such as electrocardiograms and radiographic images; however, the pathologist cannot be expected to provide expert assessment in these specialist areas. In cases in which the interpretation of medical tests may be vital to the resolution of the case, it is essential for the pathologist to have access to the appropriate medical expert.

External Examination

The external examination commences with examination of the clothing. The deceased is photographed with clothing in situ and an overall description is performed. The clothing is examined and described with resect to deposition of paint, grease, glass, dirt and vegetation.

Swabs from grease smears on skin or samples of grease stained clothing can be presented to the forensic laboratory but is of limited value. A preliminary study on the similarity of motor oils on the basis of their elemental composition showed that differences in elemental composition "do not give grounds for picking out an individual sample or a group of samples, which are fundamentally different from the rest in terms of elemental composition."[5] Defects, burns, and tears are described and photographed. Shoes from pedestrian victims may show scuff marks and the presence of "tags" of material that can suggest direction of motion at impact. In rare cases, a pedal imprint may be visible on the sole of the shoe of a driver of a motor vehicle following a collision.

The external examination section of the autopsy is objective with descriptions of the pathologic type of injury (i.e., abrasion, laceration, incised injury, or bruise). Depending on the overall circumstances of the case, each significant injury described can be photographed. The anatomic site, size, orientation, and distance from an anatomic marker, such as the heel of the foot, may be important in future legal proceedings. Injuries should be examined for the presence of foreign material. For example, an important issue in a particular case may be whether a lacerated scalp in a deceased pedestrian was from direct primary impact with a motor vehicle or from impact with the road surface. In many cases, such a determination may or may not be possible. Careful examination of the laceration may reveal loosely adherent pieces of gravel and road grime when the injury resulted from contact with the road, or less commonly flecks of paint, glass, or plastic from primary contact with a motor vehicle. The foreign material may be in the depths of the laceration and can be adherent to bone (Figure 8.2). Examination of an adjacent abrasion may also show adherent gravel or other material.

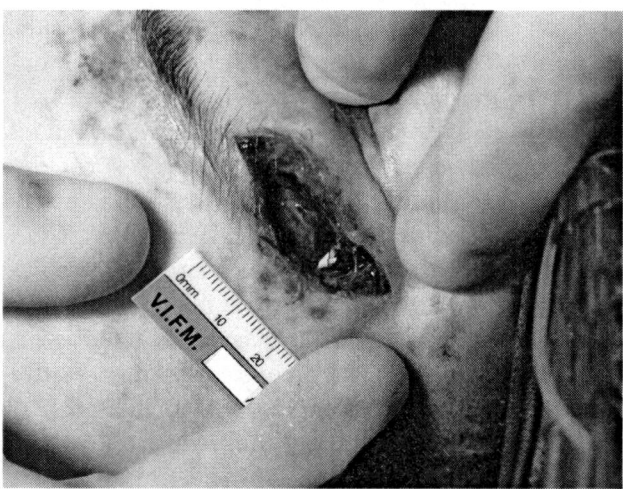

Figure 8.2 Paint flecks in depths of laceration.

Internal Examination

The abbreviated injury scale (AIS) is an anatomic scoring scale introduced in the late 1960s to categorise injury type and severity. The system has subsequently been revised and updated. In the AIS the body is divided into body regions and injuries are ranked in severity from 1 to 6. A score of 1 is of minor severity and a score of 6 is designated unsurvivable. The maximal AIS is the highest single code in the victim with multiple injuries.

The organ injury scale (OIS) is directly related to observations at autopsy. The OIS draws on the presence and severity of contusions, lacerations, and vascular injuries to various organs. The OIS can be easily derived from the autopsy report providing sufficient documentation is performed.

Cardiovascular System

The cardiovascular system includes examination of the heart and the large arteries and veins of the chest, abdomen, pelvis, neck, and cranium. In selected cases, more detailed and focused dissection of specific vessels can be performed. For example, dissection of pelvic vessels in deaths associated with fractured pelvis, and excision and decalcification of a segment of the base of the skull with the carotid siphon in suspected carotid dissection.

Natural Disease

Depending on the issues of the case in question, the heart is examined with respect to possible underlying causes of collapse, which may have lead to a motor vehicle incident, and for the presence of trauma, which may have caused or contributed to the death. The most common cause of sudden collapse and death in Western societies is coronary artery atherosclerosis.[6] However, the presence of such a common disease in the trauma victim does not, of course, mean that the disease is causal to the incident. The presence of pericardial tamponade from a ruptured acute myocardial infarct is clear evidence of natural disease causing the crash. Classic aortic dissection with pericardial tamponade or haemothorax is a further example in which natural disease is clearly connected to the incident (Figure 8.3).

The presence of coronary artery atherosclerosis is problematic. Acute coronary artery syndromes refer to atheroembolic coronary artery occlusion resulting from plaque rupture with associated thrombosis or intraplaque haemorrhage and thrombosis.[7] The presence of coronary artery thrombus occluding the vessel lumen is reported to vary from 20% to 70% of cases of sudden cardiac death.[8-10] Other authors have reported that in deaths clearly related to a sudden cardiac arrhythmia the incidence of demonstrable coronary artery thrombosis is reported to range from negligible up to 50%. Stable plaques are seen in approximately 40% of cases.[11]

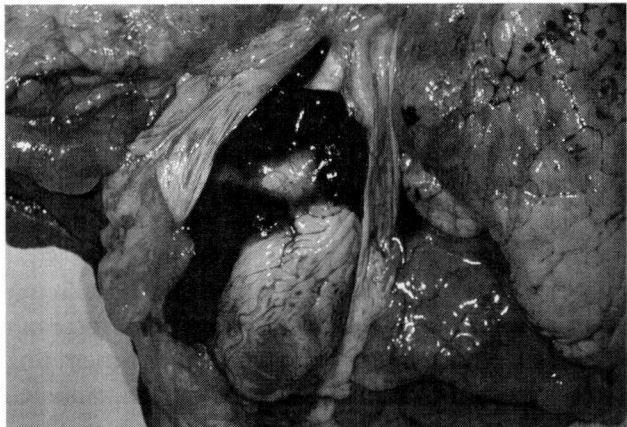

Figure 8.3 Pericardial tamponade from ruptured dissecting aortic aneurysm.

Thus in a large number of cases in which the scene findings would support a cardiac event contributing to the crash, one is unable to conclude from the autopsy findings whether the underlying heart disease was a factor. Microscopic examination of the myocardium in these cases will usually not be contributory as histologic changes take several hours to evolve. Cardiac troponin in serum is an established clinical diagnostic test for myocardial damage.[12] A preliminary study comparing antemortem and postmortem troponin levels with respect to cause of death and postmortem period showed no correlation between cardiac death and troponin level.[13] Two further studies showed elevation of postmortem serum troponin levels with morphologic evidence of myocardial damage.[14,15] The rapid nature of the death in individuals who collapse at the steering wheel implies that serum troponins would be of little value in such cases.

The macroscopic examination of the heart can reveal the presence of a cardiomyopathy, abnormal valves, high-risk coronary artery anomalies, and infiltrations such as sarcoidosis. The dissection of the heart in cases in which the cause of collapse or death is obscure should include a conduction system dissection.[16] Microscopic examination may reveal further significant pathology including the various types of myocarditis. Rarely, significant microscopic changes may be limited to the conduction system.[17]

Examination of the thoracic aorta may reveal dissection with haemothorax or pericardial tamponade. The management of a case where Marfan syndrome is suspected may include preservation of tissue for fibroblast culture and radiographs of the hand to determine metacarpal index.[18]

Trauma

Rupture of the descending thoracic aorta is a classic injury seen in cases of severe deceleration. The injury is associated with a large haemothorax that characteristically measures approximately 1000 to 1500 mL of blood. Sometimes the rupture occurs in the ascending thoracic aorta and needs to be differentiated from natural disease. The traumatic nature of the injury is supported by the presence of pericardial and cardiac injury, and adjacent bruising and fractures to the sternum and ribs.

Cardiac contusions and lacerations are usually readily seen at autopsy and can be confirmed microscopically. Pericardial tamponade is a cause of potentially treatable chest injury leading to death. Ruptures of the atrial appendages may require specific examination for their identification (Figure 8.4). Other obscure causes of pericardial tamponade include traumatic rupture of pulmonary veins through deceleration or blunt force injury.[19,20]

The OIS grade 1 cardiac injury refers to blunt or penetrating pericardial wound without cardiac involvement, herniation, or tamponade. Injuries involving myocardium but not extending to the endocardium or causing tamponade are termed grade 2 lesions. Grade 3 lesions are associated with tamponade. Injuries causing septal rupture, aortic or mitral valve incompetence, or injury to the atria or right ventricle are grade 4 injuries. Injury involving left ventricle perforation, proximal coronary artery occlusion, or less than 50% tissue loss of right ventricle or atria is a grade 5 injury. Grade 6 injuries refer to blunt avulsion of the heart.

Thoracic vascular injury is graded with respect to the vessel concerned and the magnitude of the injury. Grade 1 injuries involve a variety of arteries and veins including intercostal and mammary vessels. Trauma to major thoracic venous channels including the azygous, internal jugular, and subclavian constitute grade 2 injuries. Major arteries such as the carotid, subclavian, and innominate are damaged in grade 3 injuries. Damage to thoracic aorta, pulmonary artery, and vein and the vena cava represent grade 4 to 6 injuries. The exact classification is determined by the number and percentage circumference of the vessel injury.

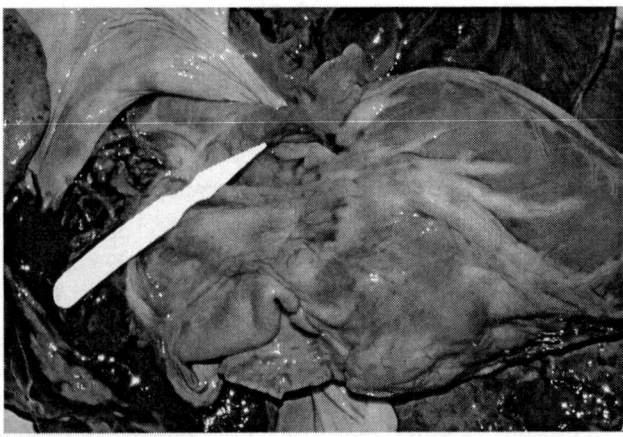

Figure 8.4   Traumatic rupture of an atrial appendage.

Trauma to the carotid and vertebral arteries leading to dissection or rupture is most probably far more common in victims of motor vehicle trauma than is recognised, documented, and reported. In crash victims who die rapidly at the scene, there are usually several other significant injuries that are consistent with causing death, and the vertebral and carotid arteries are not examined in detail. In cases of initial survival and thorough clinical examination or imaging, there may be a clinical suspicion of major vascular injury. Careful dissection or complete cervical excision followed by decalcification and transverse sections may be used to document these injuries. Radiologic imaging after cannulation and injection with contrast is technically straightforward and may be an alternative to dissection in some cases.

Arterial haemorrhage is a common cause of death in trauma victims with pelvic fracture.[21] Dissection of pelvic vessels in an area of marked haemorrhage is difficult and time-consuming. Angiography often demonstrates the damaged artery, but requires the assistance of a consultant radiologist to interpret the images.[22]

Central Nervous System

As indicated previously, the assessment of an injury commences with the external examination, with documentation of cutaneous bruises, abrasions, and lacerations indicating sites of the application of blunt force. The autopsy examination then allows for identification and measurement of subgaleal bruises and skull fractures. The course of skull fractures will tend to follow the direction of the application of blunt force.

Natural Disease

Central nervous system natural disease processes of particular interest in the investigation of a motor vehicle collision are those conditions that lead to rapid incapacitation. These include diseases such as intracranial haemorrhage and epilepsy.

Intracranial haemorrhage that causes abrupt change in conscious state results from brisk haemorrhage into the cerebral hemispheres, deep gray matter, brainstem, or subarachnoid space. Massive subarachnoid haemorrhage is usually caused by a ruptured berry aneurysm at the branching point of a major cerebral artery at the base of the brain. The aneurysm is best identified in the fresh state. Rarely, the haemorrhage may be caused by rupture of an arteriovenous malformation. Large intracerebral haemorrhages are typically associated with individuals with a history of hypertension and characteristically occur in the basal ganglia, thalamus, or pons.

Idiopathic epilepsy usually shows no abnormal underlying pathologic abnormality on examination of the brain. Hippocampal sclerosis describes neuronal loss and gliosis in the medial temporal lobe that may be seen in patients with long-term seizures.[23] Uncommonly, the postmortem examination may show an epileptiform focus such as evidence of prior brain trauma with cortical gliosis, ectopic cortical tissue, or space-occupying lesion.

The postmortem examination may also reveal nonspecific but supportive autopsy features such as bruising/laceration to the tongue, especially in the absence of facial trauma, and diffuse bilateral haemorrhages in the intercostal and abdominal musculature reflecting a generalised seizure. The evaluation of the possible involvement of epilepsy in a crash also involves the collection and assessment of the victim's clinical history of seizure frequency and severity, the type of seizure, and the usual presence of an aura.

Studies on the postmortem toxicologic analysis of anticonvulsant medications has shown varying results. Some studies suggest subtherapeutic levels of anticonvulsants are associated with sudden deaths in epilepsy, whereas others have found no association.[24] At the completion of the investigation the pathologist may or may not be able to render an opinion on the possibility/probability of a seizure contributing to the incident.

The postmortem neuropathologic examination can document the presence of significant neurologic disorders such as multiple sclerosis, prior stroke, and head injury, Parkinson's disease and various dementing disorders. The neuropathologic examination can document the pathologic extent of the disease; however, one should defer to the treating clinician for an opinion on the functional legacy of the pathology during life.

Trauma

Central nervous system trauma is the most common single cause of long-term morbidity and mortality following a motor vehicle collision. Primary brain injury causing death is most commonly from diffuse axonal injury (DAI). Traumatic subarachnoid haemorrhage and a thin film of subdural blood is commonly seen in association with DAI. Atlanto-occipital disruption is the other frequent cause of rapid death at the crash scene. Extra-axial haematomas and secondary brain injury typically contribute to death when definitive surgical management and first aid/emergency treatment are delayed.

Primary Brain Injury.   DAI is a serious consequence of blunt head trauma that results from rotational acceleration causing shear forces to axons. The severity of the injury is a spectrum ranging from clinical concussion up to persistent vegetative state and death.[25]

The pathologic findings vary with the severity of the insult. In cases of mild or moderate blunt force trauma, there may be no macroscopic features. With severe trauma macroscopic petechial haemorrhages are seen within the corpus callosum and the dorsal lateral aspect of the pons.[26] Severe DAI is associated with gliding contusions and deep gray matter haemorrhages Microscopic examination of the brain in trauma victims with DAI show petechial haemorrhages in the corpus callosum, periventricular white matter (frontal and parietal lobes), cerebellar peduncles, and dorsolateral aspect of the pons. Individuals who survive for more than a few hours after the head injury may show axonal bulbs at the terminal ends of axons. These changes are further enhanced by immunoperoxidase stains with β-amyloid precursor protein.[27] The proper interpretation of β-amyloid precursor protein stained sections of brain requires examination of a sufficient number of appropriately selected blocks.[27]

Traumatic subarachnoid haemorrhage is seen as diffuse haemorrhage beneath the arachnoid mater over the cerebral hemispheres. In the author's experience, traumatic subarachnoid haemorrhage may be the only recognisable brain injury in some crash victims who are found deceased at the scene. In most of these cases, there will be other additional evidence of severe head impact such as a hinge fracture of the base of the skull.

Atlanto-occipital fracture and dislocation are frequently seen in victims of motor vehicle collisions. Early autopsy studies suggested an incidence of approximately 5% in deceased trauma victims; however, with more recent studies the incidence of atlanto-occipital dislocation has been estimated to cause 8% to 35% of fatalities.[28] Examination of the cervical spine is best achieved by a combination of radiologic imaging and dissection (Figure 8.5). A study at the Victorian Institute of Forensic Medicine showed that plain radiographs did not demonstrate some fractures that were seen on later postmortem examination, whereas examination short of formal excision and longitudinal section also failed to demonstrate all significant injuries.[29]

The role of CT and MRI in the management of the trauma patient is evolving with the widespread availability of the technology.[30] Although plain radiographs remain the mainstay of forensic imaging in most centres, the increasing use of CT and MRI machines in the forensic setting will undoubtedly alter the practice of formal cervical spine and dissection. Recent generation CT scanners equipped with multiplanar reconstruction and three-dimensional imaging can provide extraordinary images of the cervical spine with no destruction of tissue.

Subdural haemorrhage of 50 to 100 g of blood will usually result in compression of the underlying brain with subfalcine, tentorial or tonsillar herniation, and secondary brainstem haemorrhages. The site of a subdural haemorrhage does not correlate with the site of impact. Smaller volumes of subdural blood are commonly seen in cases with other significant brain injury

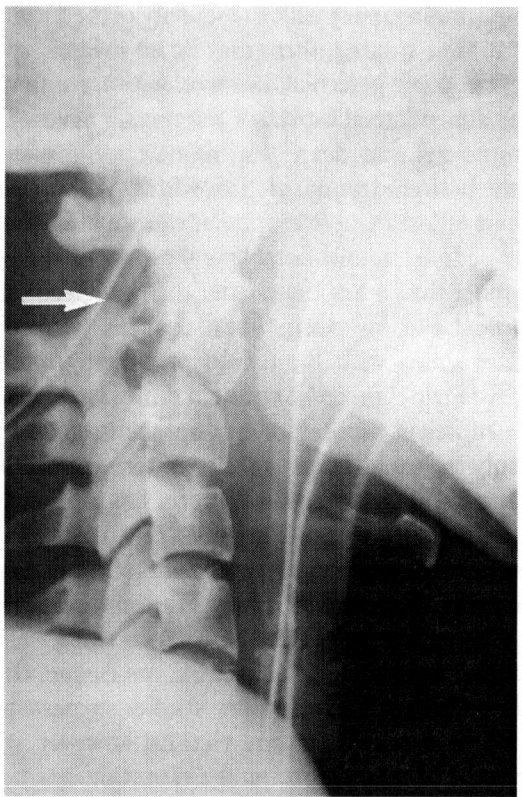

Figure 8.5   Fracture upper cervical spine (arrow) secondary to direct trauma to the chin with hyperextension of the upper neck.

(Figure 8.6). Large extradural haematomas are not frequently seen in deceased victims of motor vehicle trauma. Because the expanding haematoma has to strip the dura from the skull, the evolution of an extradural haematoma tends to be prolonged, providing sufficient time for the injured victim to be taken to hospital. Rarely posterior fossa extradural haematomas lead to more rapid death from pressure on the adjacent brainstem (Figure 8.7). These haematomas are easily overlooked if not specifically sought.

A basal subarachnoid haemorrhage may result from rupture of the basilar artery, intracranial vertebral artery, or extracranial vertebral artery. The underlying cause may be blunt force trauma to the head with rapid rotation of the head on the neck or a direct blunt force injury to the neck. There may or may not be an associated cervical fracture. Conventional postmortem angiography or CT angiography can demonstrate the region of rupture, which often occurs where the artery enters the dura. Intracranial rupture of the vertebral or basilar artery is being increasingly recognised.

Direct impact to the skull may result in contusions (bruises) to the brain. These may be associated with fractures (fracture contusions), may be directly

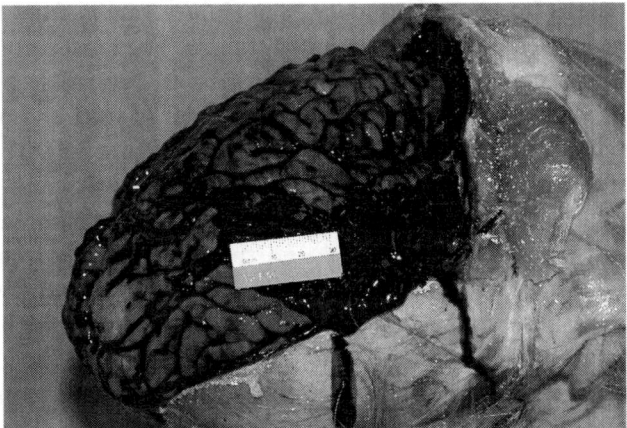

Figure 8.6 Removal of calvarium and dura to reveal underlying subdural haemorrhage.

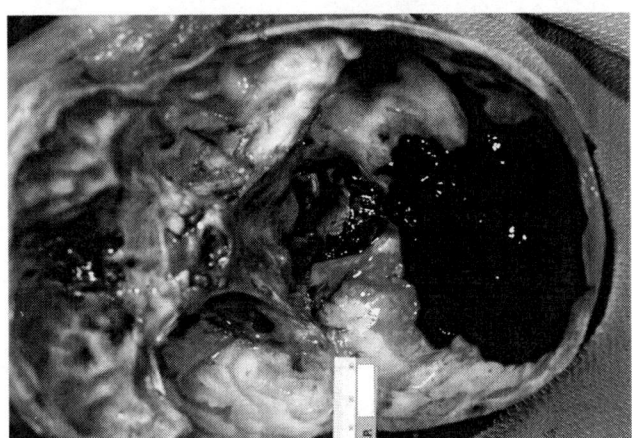

Figure 8.7 Posterior fossa extradural haemorrhage that caused compression of the brainstem.

beneath a site of impact (coup contusions), or remote from and usually opposite to a site of impact (contrecoup contusion). The classic site of a contrecoup contusion is the inferior aspect of the frontal lobes of the cerebral cortex after blunt impact to the occiput and is usually seen when the back of the head strikes a hard object such as the ground or roadway.

Hyperextension injury may cause a brainstem lesion in the absence of basal skull fracture or upper cervical spine dislocation.[31] Pontomedullary tear is a not uncommon injury in pedestrian victims of motor vehicle incidents. The injury needs to be specifically looked for, as the features may be subtle, and may require differentiation from artifact which can occur when removing the brain. Microscopic sections of the brainstem should demonstrate the presence of perivascular haemorrhages in antemortem injury.

Secondary Brain Injury. Secondary brain injury results from subsequent insults to the injured brain after the initial trauma. The most common insults are hypoxia and hypotension.[32] Cerebral edema is discernible by increased brain weight, flattening of the gyri, and effacement of sulci and parahippocampal grooving from contact with the tentorium (Figure 8.8). There may be prominence and necrosis of the cerebellar tonsils. Pediatric crash victims are especially prone to the development of cerebral edema after blunt head trauma.

Delayed traumatic intracranial haemorrhage is classically seen in trauma victims who have sustained a blunt force impact to the occiput. Typically, the patient develops haemorrhage in contre-coup contusions in the basal frontal lobes and temporal poles some 3 to 10 days after sustaining the injury.[33]

Systemic fat embolism can occur from fractures and significant soft-tissue injury and may lead to rapid clinical deterioration and death. The brain classically shows widespread petechial haemorrhages in white matter (Figure 8.9).

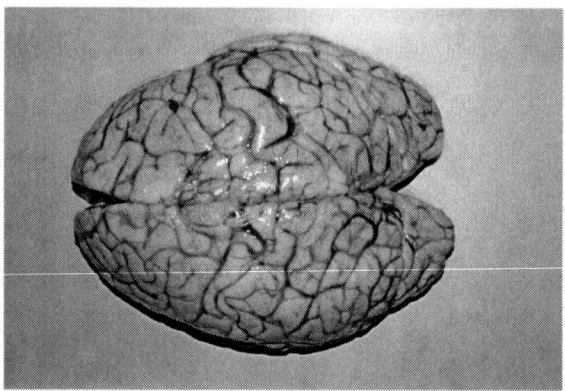

Figure 8.8 Swollen brain showing flattening of gyri.

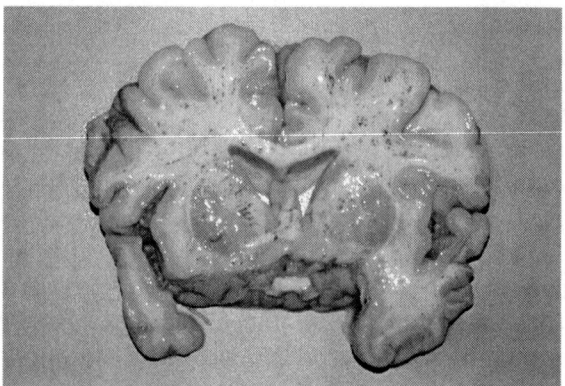

Figure 8.9 White matter petechial haemorrhages in a case of systemic fat embolism.

Musculoskeletal System

As noted previously, cutaneous abrasions, lacerations, and bruises reflect the site of the application of blunt force (Figure 8.10). The degree of bruising is determined by the magnitude of the force applied to the victim, but also their age, presence of underlying natural disease processes, and the period of survival.

Bruises within the subcutaneous fat and muscle may not be evident over the surface of the skin (Figure 8.11). Subcutaneous dissection is particularly important in showing the distribution and extent of bruises. Depending on the particular circumstances of the case in question, subcutaneous dissection

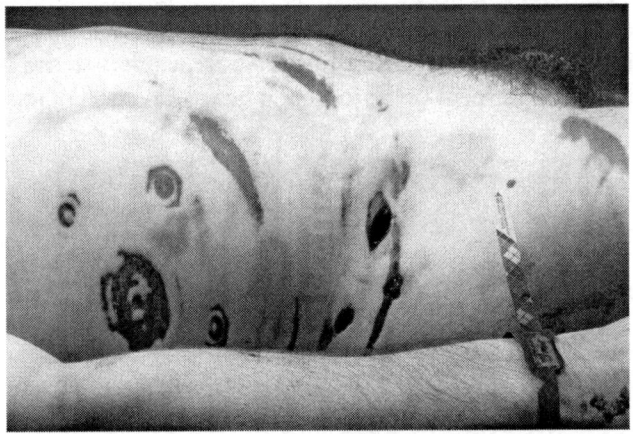

Figure 8.10 Patterned abraded injury of a wheel to the chest indicating a site of the application of blunt force.

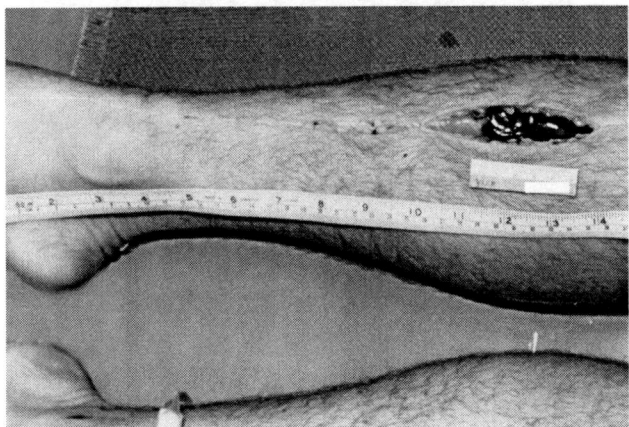

Figure 8.11 Postmortem incision into the lower leg in a region with no cutaneous injury, but showing subcutaneous bruising from blunt trauma.

may be performed over the upper and lower limbs, chest and abdomen, face, and back (Figures 8.12 and 8.13). In many cases of blunt force injury, and especially in those cases with an oblique application of force, there may be separation of the fat from the underling musculature. This can result in the formation of a cavity which can contain a large amount of blood and fluid within the traumatised tissue.

The presence of ligament injury can be demonstrated by dissection. Dissection of various joints has been described by Teresinski and Madro in a series of articles on pedestrian motor incident victims.[34–37] The demonstration of haemarthroses, avulsion and rupture of ligaments, and subchondral haemorrhage in epiphyseal bone, taken in conjunction with the other relevant case findings, can provide important information regarding the mechanism of joint injury. The tears to a joint ligament, haemorrhage or avulsion at the site of ligament insertion, and subchondral haemorrhage/crush fracture reflect abnormal forced movement of the joint and hence direction of the application

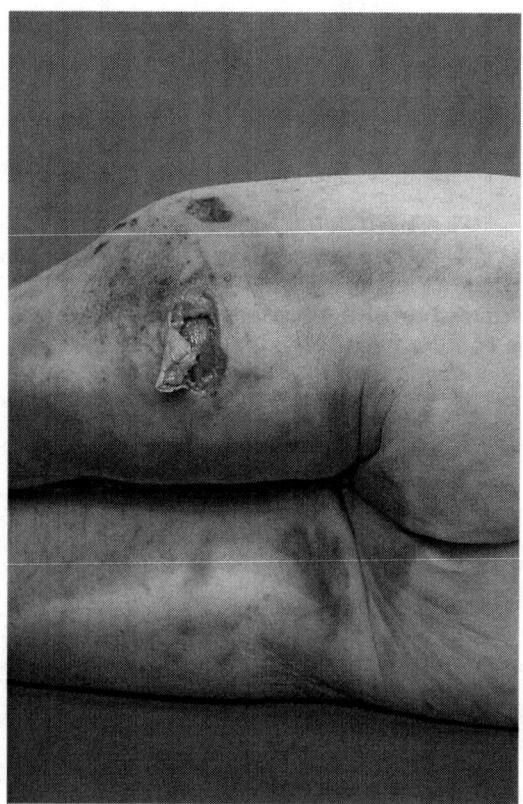

Figure 8.12 Bruising to the posterior upper thigh with a "punched out" segment of skin and subcutaneous fat from contact with a four-wheel drive motor vehicle.

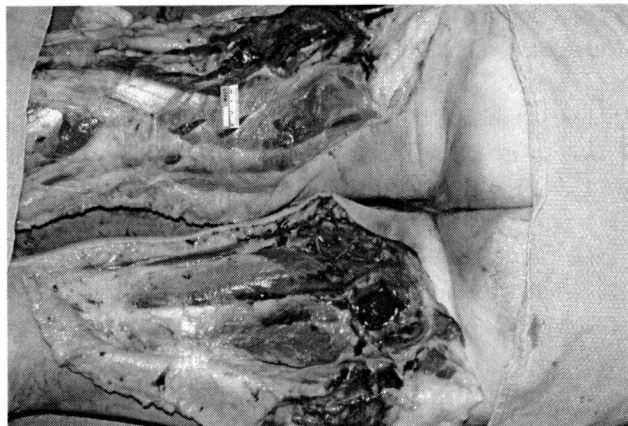

Figure 8.13 Subcutaneous dissection from Figure 8.12 demonstrating bruising within subcutaneous fat and muscle.

of force to the joint. The interpretation of these injuries cannot be done in isolation. For example, impact to the back of the lower limb in an upright pedestrian will create different stresses on the cruciate ligaments of the knee depending on whether the primary impact is above or below the knee joint.

Essentially the pathologist needs to correlate the scene/witness information, the injuries visible over the surface of the skin, and additional injuries observed on subcutaneous dissection of the body with the examination of the various joints. Furthermore, capsular tears of muscles and haemorrhages associated with muscle/tendon insertions can provide information regarding the location of impact to the body. A good example is of sternomastoid and associated anterior neck muscle haemorrhage and rupture within the muscle belly and at bony insertion sites following impact to the posterior lower limbs of the upright pedestrian. The rapid hyperextension of the head on the neck leads to soft-tissue trauma to anterior neck structures.

As noted previously, severe hyperflexion of the vertebral column leads to compression and burst fractures of the vertebral bodies, radiologic "tear drop" fractures to the inferior tips of vertebral bodies, widening of the interspinous spaces, anterolisthesis, locked facets, and narrowing of intervertebral spaces at and below the level of involvement. Severe hyperextension leads to fractured neural arches, articular facets and pillars, widened disc spaces, and anterior ligament rupture with retrolisthesis. Shearing and rotational forces mostly occur with flexion and leads to vertebral body and pillar fractures on one side, horizontal subluxation and dislocation, and fracture transverse processes in the lumbar region. Lateral forces lead to compression fractures of the articular facets and pillars in the cervical region and burst fractures of thoracic vertebral bodies.[38] Dissection or radiologic imaging can demonstrate and document these injuries.

Pelvic ring fractures may result from the application of force to the lateral, anterior, or posterior aspects of the body. Typically, the fractures correspond to lateral compression fractures or anteroposterior compression fractures. For example, side impacts in a motor vehicle collision typically lead to lateral compression fractures to the pelvic ring.[39] Motor vehicle incidents are the commonest cause of acetabular fracture. Acetabular fractures and posterior dislocation typically result from femoral shaft loading in motor vehicle incidents.[40] Lateral impact to the hip leading to severe forces to the greater trochanter of the femur can cause central acetabular fracture and dislocation.[41] Radiologic imaging provides an accurate permanent record of the injury.

The number and site of fractured ribs should be recorded. The presence of fractured first ribs is invariably a sign of significant trauma to the chest and is usually associated with important thoracic visceral injury. In elderly individuals, a fractured sternum or multiple fractured ribs and especially a flail segment can cause rapid respiratory failure and is eminently treatable.

The OIS description for a grade 1 injury is a chest wall contusion, laceration involving the subcutaneous fat, and fewer than three closed fractured ribs. Lacerations involving the full thickness of the chest to the pleura or unilateral flail segment of fewer than three ribs are termed a grade 3 injury. Grade 4 injuries relate to unilateral flail segments of more than three ribs or avulsion of chest soft tissues associated with rib fractures. A bilateral flail chest indicates a grade 5 injury.

Fractures of the skull are commonly seen in deaths from a motor vehicle incident. Fractures are usually associated with cutaneous or soft-tissue injuries to the scalp or face. Localised depressed skull fractures have been shown to result from the application of force at the site of fracture, whereas linear fractures initiate some distance from the point of impact, and extend back to the region of the impact.[42] Generally, fracture lines tend to follow the broad path of the force; however, basal skull fractures that extend across both petrous temporal bones may result from force applied to a variety of sites including the point of the chin.[43] The typical "hinge" fracture is thought to occur from the anatomical formation of the base of the skull.

Respiratory System

Intercostal cannulas should be positioned within the pleural space to drain air or blood. Incorrect placement of the tubes is not common, but may have significant consequences for the trauma victim. Cannulae may be seen within subcutaneous tissues external to the chest wall, outside the parietal pleura, within lung tissue, and in extreme circumstances may cause severe or lethal injury to major pulmonary vessels, liver, or heart.

Central venous cannulae should be identified within major central veins. Incorrect placement may result in laceration of central veins or arteries. Swan-Ganz cannulae measure pulmonary artery pressure and facilitate accurate fluid management in critically ill patients. Occasional rupture of branches of the pulmonary artery can lead to fatal haemorrhage. The rupture may be extraordinarily difficult to identify despite careful dissection. Postmortem angiography may prove successful.

A haemothorax may cause or contribute to death from blood loss and compression of chest viscera. A haemothorax can result from lacerated lung, ruptured intercostal arteries, or rupture of other thoracic vasculature. The volume of the blood should be measured. Examination of the lungs for contusions is especially important in individuals who succumb from their injuries in hospital. An estimation of the percentage of lung involved by contusion should be recorded. The integrity of the pulmonary veins should be noted in cases of haemothorax.

The integrity of the airway should be documented. Proximal tracheal injuries are usually associated with other cervical traumatic injuries, whereas distal tracheobronchial injuries are uncommon, but may be seen in isolation.[44] The trachea is usually torn in close proximity to the carina, whereas the main bronchi have been shown to tear within 2.5 cm of the carina.[45]

The OIS for lung ranges from a grade 1 injury in which unilateral contusions involve less than one lobe, to grade 2 injury in which unilateral contusions involve a single lobe, or there is lung laceration with uncomplicated pneumothorax. Grade 3 injuries refer to unilateral contusions involving more than one lobe, persistent air leak from a distal airway, or nonexpanding intraparenchymal haematoma. Injuries causing a major air leak or segmental intrapulmonary vessel disruption are designated grade 4 injuries. Grade 5 injuries occur with hilar vessel disruption and grade 6 injuries describe situations in which total hilar disruption is identified.

Diaphragmatic injury is not uncommon in blunt chest and abdominal trauma and may be overlooked at autopsy unless specifically sought. The OIS classification requires description of contusions and lacerations. The grade 1 injury refers to a contusion. Lacerations less than 2 cm are grade 2 lesions and lacerations greater than 10 cm are designated grade 3 injuries. A laceration with tissue loss greater than 25 cm^2 is a grade 5 injury (Figures 8.14 and 8.15). Bilateral injuries progress the injury severity by one.

Microscopic examination of lung tissue may show pulmonary contusions arising from blunt chest trauma. Intra-alveolar haemorrhage may also be observed when inspiratory effort is seen with blood in the trachea and bronchi. In such cases, the intra-alveolar haemorrhage appears in relation to terminal airways. Histologic examination of lung in cases of major trauma

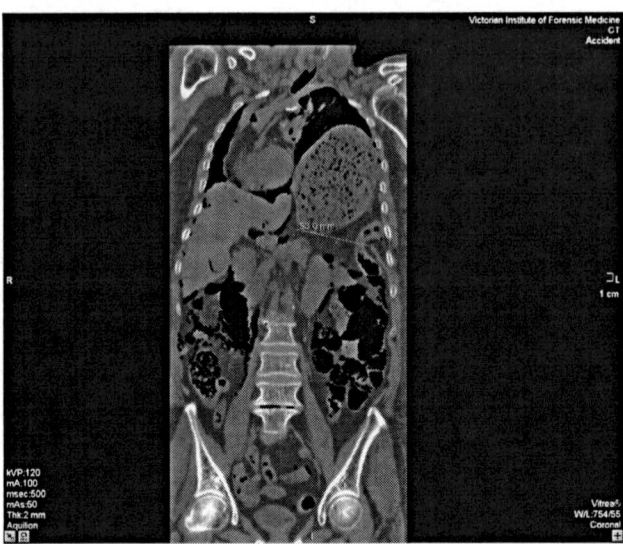

Figure 8.14 Computed tomography scan showing ruptured diaphragm with herniation of stomach into chest.

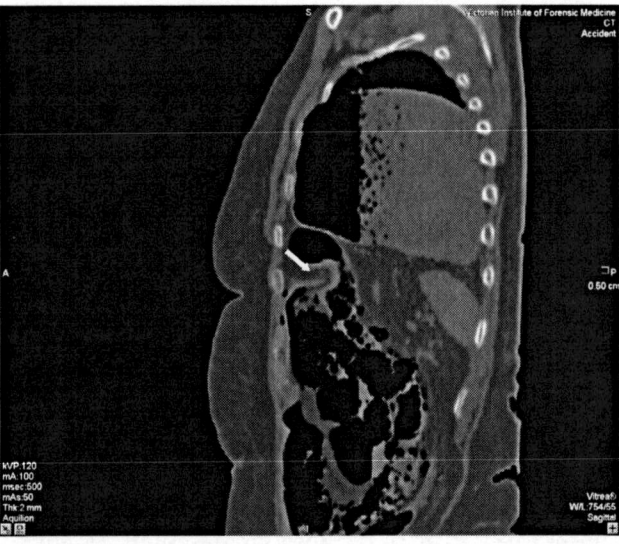

Figure 8.15 Sagittal computed tomography scan showing ruptured diaphragm.

often shows the presence of fat in pulmonary vessels. The significance of the fat requires clinicopathologic correlation with the patient's clinical observations and investigations. In patients who survive for a period of time following the incident the sections of lung often display bronchopneumonia and may show pulmonary thromboemboli.

Gastrointestinal System

The most obvious feature to document at postmortem examination of the abdominal cavity is the presence and volume of a haemoperitoneum. In the case of retroperitoneal haematoma, the volume of blood is very difficult to quantify; however, one may measure the extent of the haemorrhage, describe the limits of the haematoma from its anatomic limits, or take a photograph of the pathology.

Liver

The liver commonly shows minor capsular tears in association with other injuries to the abdomen and thoracic cavity in cases of significant blunt trauma. The description of liver injuries can include the site and percentage surface area of tears and haematomas, the depth of lacerations, the percentage degree of parenchymal disruption, and the presence of venous or arterial injury/disruption. The OIS for the liver ranges from a grade 1 injury with less than 10% subcapsular haematoma or capsular tear extending less than 1 cm into the parenchyma, to a grade 6 injury, which involves hepatic vascular avulsion.

Genitourinary System

The description of renal OIS ranges from a grade 1 injury with contusions, through to grade 5 injuries, which involve either avulsion through the hilum causing devascularisation or widespread lacerations leading to virtual disruption of the kidney. The depth and extent of lacerated injuries and the involvement of renal artery or vein are important to document. The bladder is usually injured in associated with a fractured pelvis. Lacerated injuries should be described with respect to length (less than or greater than 2 cm), position (involvement of trigone), and whether the injury is intraperitoneal.

Reticuloendothelial System

Examination of the reticuloendothelial system in cases of trauma principally involves the spleen.

The spleen is situated within the left upper abdomen below the rib cage. A number of diseases may lead to splenic enlargement, including cirrhosis of the liver with portal hypertension and infectious mononucleosis. In these cases the spleen is more exposed to traumatic injury.

Capsular rupture may be self contained. Immediate or delayed rupture of the spleen can cause catastrophic haemoperitoneum. Haematomas that occupy less than 10% of the splenic surface or lacerations causing capsular tear with less than 1cm of parenchymal involvement are termed grade 1 OIS injuries. Subcapsular haematomas involving more than 50% of surface area, lacerations extending greater than 5 cm into the splenic parenchyma, and ruptured haematomas are grade 3 lesions. Hilar lacerations that lead to more than 25% of tissue devascularisation are grade 4 lesions, whereas complete pulping of the organ or complete hilar vascular disruption is a grade 5 injury.

Death from Burns

A fire may cause rapid death from incineration, from the effects of extreme heat, lack of oxygen, carbon monoxide, and cyanide poisoning. Delayed deaths from burns usually result from sepsis or multiple organ failure.

An individual who is alive at the time of a fire and inhales smoke will have soot deposited on the airway mucosa. Toxicologic examination may reveal an elevated carbon monoxide (carboxyhaemoglobin) concentration in blood. Carbon monoxide is produced in smoldering fires when there is insufficient oxygen available for complete combustion of fuels. Hence, fires occurring in the open, and rapid fires associated with volatiles such as hydrocarbon products, may not produce appreciable amounts of carbon monoxide. In these cases, soot may also be absent from the airway mucosa.

In severe fires there can be extensive postmortem destruction of soft and bony tissues. The effect of heat to the larger flexors of the upper and lower limbs leads to postmortem flexion of the limbs.

This position is often called a "pugilistic attitude." The absence of this position may indicate some obstruction to the limbs following the incident at the time of the fire. Despite the marked destruction of the body that can occur in a severe fire, the internal organs often remain remarkably intact.

The postmortem examination may reveal injuries that would have led to immediate or rapid death from the motor vehicle collision. The demonstration of a traumatic tear of the thoracic aorta in the severely burnt remains of a crash victim would suggest that death occurred rapidly following the crash and before the onset of the fire.

Other Investigations

Various samples of body fluids and tissues may be retained for toxicologic analysis. Depending on the complexity of the case samples of organs, muscle and skin may be taken for histologic examination.

The histological sections may be reviewed by another pathologist at a later date. The microscopic sections are also invaluable in demonstrating and confirming the presence of significant occult natural disease processes.

There are limitations to the amount of information that can be gleaned from the histologic examination. For example, an individual has to survive for at least 12 hours for discernible changes of myocardial infarction to be seen on microscopic sections. Some studies have suggested that immunoperoxidase stains may allow diagnosis of myocardial infarction from 1 hour after the event. In practice, the results have not been uniformly encouraging.

Microscopic examination can document the presence of fat within pulmonary vessels, the renal glomerulus, and brain arterioles. The amount of fat deposition should be estimated and correlated with the clinical findings as fat within pulmonary vessels is a common finding in trauma.

In delayed deaths, the presence of myoglobin within renal tubules can be suggested on routine histochemical stains and confirmed using immunohistochemical stains.

Analysis of pericardial fluid for troponin and creatinine kinase has been shown to assist in the diagnosis of myocardial infarction. The presence of a myocardial contusion may result in a false-positive result.

Cause of Death

At the completion of the postmortem examination, a cause of death is issued. The cause of death may be described simply as head injury or multiple injuries. Although one may argue that the determination of the cause of death as multiple injuries provides little information, this diagnosis allows the death certificate to be issue to the deceased's family. The death certificate enables the next of kin to finalise legal and insurance matters.

The cause of death is vital for a criminal prosecution for culpable driving where it must be proven that the death was caused by trauma sustained during the collision; therefore, all other possibilities must be excluded.

Summary of Anatomic Findings

The summary of anatomic findings provides a summary in notation form highlighting the relevant injuries, significant natural disease processes, and relevant negative findings.

Comments

The comments section is the most subjective portion of the autopsy report. In the comments section, the pathologist may offer an opinion as to how the documented injuries may have occurred based on the available information. Issues raised by the treating hospital or police officers should be addressed.

The opinion can be reviewed and a supplementary report released if further important information becomes available after the original report had been finalised.

References

1. Ludwig J. *Handbook of Autopsy Practice*. 3rd edition. Ottowa, NJ: Humana Press; 2002.

2. Thali MJ, Yen K, Schweitzer W, Vock P, Boesch C, Ozdoba C et al. Virtopsy, a new imaging horizon in forensic pathology: virtual autopsy by post mortem multislice computed tomography (MSCT) and magnetic resonance imaging (MRI)—a feasibility study. *Journal of Forensic Sciences* 2003; 48:386–403.

3. Yen K, Vock P, Tiefenthaler B, Ranner G, Scheurer E, Thali MJ, Zwygart K, Sonnerschein M, Wiltgen M, Dirnhofer R. Virtopsy: forensic traumatology of the subcutaneous fatty tissue; multislice computed tomography (MSCT) and magnetic resonance imaging (MRI) as diagnostic tools. *Journal of Forensic Sciences* 2004; 49:799–806.

4. Aghayer E, Thali M, Jackowski C, Sonnenschein M, Yen K, Vock P, Dirnhofer R. Virtopsy—fatal motor vehicle accident with head injury. *Journal of Forensic Sciences* 2004; 49:809–813.

5. Zieba-Palus J, Koscielniak P. An analysis of the similarity of motor oils on the basis of their elemental composition. *Forensic Science International* 2000; 112:81–90.

6. McGwin G Jr., Sims RV, Pulley L, Roseman JM. Relations among chronic medical conditions, medications, and automobile crashes in the elderly: a population-based case-control study. *American Journal of Epidemiology* 2000; 152:424–431.

7. Gotlieb AI. Atherosclerosis and acute coronary syndromes. *Cardiovascular Pathology* 2005; 14:181–184.

8. Farb A, Tang AL, Burke AP, Sessums L, Liang Y, Virmani R. Sudden coronary death. Frequency of active coronary lesions, inactive coronary lesions, and myocardial infarction. *Circulation* 1995; 92:1701–1709.

9. Scott RF, Briggs TS. Pathologic findings in pre-hospital deaths due to coronary atherosclerosis. *American Journal of Cardiology* 1971; 29:782–787.

10. Davies MJ, Thomas A. Thrombosis and acute coronary artery lesions in sudden cardiac ischemic death. *New England Journal of Medicine* 1984; 310:1137–1140.

11. Virmani R, Burke AP, Farb A. Coronary heart disease and its syndroms, in *Cardiovascular Pathology* 2nd ed., Virmani R, Sounders P, Eds. 2001; 10:211–218.

12. Malasky BR, Alpert JS. Diagnosis of myocardial injury by biochemical markers: problems and promises. *Cardiology Reviews* 2002; 10:306–317.

13. Davies SJ, Gaze DC, Collinson PO. Investigation of cardiac troponins in post mortem subjects: comparing antemortem and post mortem levels. *American Journal of Forensic Medicine and Pathology* 2005; 26:213–215.

14. Zhu BL, Ishikawa T, Michiue T, Li DR, Zhao D, Oritani S, Kamikodai Y, Tsuda K, Okazaki S, Maeda H. Post mortem cardiac troponin T levels in the blood and pericardial fluid. Part 1. Analysis with special regard to traumatic causes of death. *Legal Medicine* (Tokyo) 2006; 8(2):86–93.

15. Ellingsen CL, Hetland O. Serum concentrations of cardiac troponin T in sudden death. *American Journal of Forensic Medicine and Pathology* 2004; 25:213–215.

16. Song Y, Zhu J, Laaksonen H, Saukko P. A modified method for examining the cardiac conduction system. *Forensic Science International* 1997; 86:135–138.

17. Song Y, Laaksonen H, Saukko P, Toivonen S, Zhu J. Histopathological findings of cardiac conduction system of 150 Finns. *Forensic Science International* 2001; 119:310–317.

18. Thomas SM, Younger KA, Child A, Wilson AG. Is the metacarpal index useful in the diagnosis of Marfan syndrome? *Clinical Radiology* 1996; 51:570–574.

19. Le Guyader A, Bertin F, Laskar M, Cornu E. Blunt chest trauma: a right pulmonary vein rupture. *European Journal of Cardio-thoracic Surgery* 2001; 20:1054–1056.

20. Varghese D, Patel H, Cameron EW, Robson M. *Annals of Thoracic Surgery* 2000; 70:656–658.

21. Hagiwara A, Minakawa K, Fukushima H, Murata A, Masudo H, Shimazaki S. Predictors of death in patients with life-threatening pelvic hemorrhage after successful transcatheter arterial embolization. *Journal of Trauma* 2003; 55:696–703.

22. Yoon W, Kim JK, Jeong YY, Jeong JS, Park JG, Kang HK. Pelvic arterial hemorrhage in patients with pelvic fractures: detection with contrast-enhanced CT. *Radiographics* 2004; 24:1591–1606.

23. Thom M, Zhou J, Martinian L, Sisodiya S. Quantitative post-mortem study of the hippocampus in chronic epilepsy: seizures do not inevitably cause neuronal loss. *Brain* 2005; 128:1344–1357.

24. Opeskin K, Burke MP, Cordner SM, Berkovic SF. *Epilepsia* 1999; 40:1795–1798.

25. Smith DH, Meaney DF, Shull WH. Diffuse axonal injury in head trauma. *Journal of Head Trauma and Rehabilitation* 2003; 18:307–316.

26. Adams JH, Doyle D, Ford I, Gennarelli TA, Graham DI, McLellan DR. Diffuse axonal injury in head injury: definition, diagnosis and grading. *Histopathology* 1989; 15:49–59.

27. Graham DI, Smith C, Reichard R, Leclercq PD, Gentleman SM. Trials and tribulations of using -amyloid precursor protein immunohistochemistry to evaluate traumatic brain injury in adults. *Forensic Science International* 2004; 146:89–96.

28. Fisher CG, Sun JCL, Dvorak M. Recognition and management of atlanto-occipital dislocation: improving survival from an often fatal condition. *Canadian Journal of Surgery* 2001; 44:412–420.

29. Leditschke J. *The Cervical Spine Injuries in Fatal Road Traffic Accident. A Pathological and Radiological Study.* PhD Thesis. Monash University Department of Forensic Medicine, Victoria, Australia; 1995.

30. Tins BJ, Cassar-Pullicino VN. Imaging of acute cervical spine injuries: review and outlook. *Clinical Radiology* 2004; 59:865–880.

31. Ohshima T, Kondo T. Forensic pathological observations on fatal injuries to the brainstem and/or upper cervical spinal cord in traffic accidents. *Journal of Clinical Forensic Medicine* 1998; 5:129–134.

32. Marshall LF. Head injury: recent past, present, and future. *Neurosurgery* 2000; 47:546–561.

33. Kaplan M, Ozveren MF, Topsakal C, Erol FS, Akdemir I. Asymptomatic interval in delayed traumatic intracerebral hemorrhage: report of two cases. *Clinical Neurology and Neurosurgery* 2003; 105:153–155.

34. Teresinski G, Madro R. Ankle joint injuries as a reconstruction parameter in car-to-pedestrian accidents. *Forensic Science International* 2001; 118:65–73.

35. Teresinski G, Madro R. Pelvis and hip joint injuries as a reconstructive factor in car-to-pedestrian accidents. *Forensic Science International* 2001; 124:68–73.

36. Teresinski G, Madro R. Knee joint injuries as a reconstructive factor in car-to-pedestrian accidents. *Forensic Science International* 2001; 124:74–82.

37. Teresinski G, Madro R. Evidential value of injuries useful for reconstruction of the pedestrian-vehicle location at the moment of collision. *Forensic Science International* 2002; 128:127–135.

38. Daffner RH, Deeb ZL, Rothfus WE. "Fingerprints" of vertebral trauma—a unifying concept based on mechanisms. *Skeletal Radiology* 1986; 15:518–525.

39. Gokcen EC, Burgess AR, Siegel JH, Mason-Gonzales S, Dischinger PC, Ho SM. Pelvic fracture mechanism of injury in vehicular trauma patients. *Journal of Trauma* 1994; 36:789–796.

40. Grattan E, Hobbs JA. Injuries to hip joint in car occupants. *British Medical Journal* 1969; 1:71–73

41. Dakin GJ, Eberhardt AW, Alonso JE, Stannard JP, Mann KA. Acetabular fracture patterns: associations with motor vehicle crash information. *Journal of Trauma* 1999; 47:1063–1079.

42. Shapiro HA. Adult skull fracture: magnitude of forces and mechanism involved. *Legal Medicine Annual* 1974; 33–44.

43. Harvey FH, Jones AM. "Typical" basal skull fracture of both petrous bones: an unreliable indicator of head impact site. *Journal of Forensic Science* 1980; 25:280–286.

44. Bertelsen S, Howitz P. Injuries of the trachea and bronchi. Thorax 1972; 27:188–194.

45. Rossbach MM, Johnson SB, Gomez MA. Management of major tracheobronchial injuries: a 28-year experience. *Annals of Thoracic Surgery* 1998; 65:186.

Toxicology 9

Introduction

It has been recognised for some time that the presence of alcohol within the blood of a driver is associated with an increased risk of motor vehicle collisions, injuries, and fatalities.

The issue of alcohol-associated motor vehicle collisions is a worldwide problem; however, recent evidence suggests that the prevalence of drunk driving is decreasing in many Western societies. It is in this setting that an increasing interest in the contribution of illicit and therapeutic drugs to motor vehicle collisions has evolved. The varying proportion of both illicit and therapeutic medications within the blood of drivers will vary in different localities depending on many factors, including the inherent drug culture and drug availability, availability of over-the-counter medications, and prescribing habits of the medical profession.

It is clear from epidemiologic and laboratory driving skill performance studies that the concentration of alcohol within a driver's blood is directly proportional to the risk of collision and death. The contribution of the effects of illicit and therapeutic drugs to road collisions and deaths is a more vexing question. Because the central nervous system effects of both stimulants and depressants carry a theoretical risk for significant cognitive effects, and some drugs have been demonstrated to impair simulated driving performance in laboratory studies, there is conflicting evidence as to which of these drugs is associated with an increased risk of motor vehicle collisions.

Numerous studies investigating the problem of drug related motor vehicle incidents have analysed the raw data relating to road deaths and the presence of illicit and therapeutic drugs within blood and urine.

By simply comparing injury and fatality rates with drug use, the possible contributing effects—such as culpability of other road users and environmental and vehicle factors—are not addressed. More recent studies using culpability analysis have investigated the risk from both illicit and therapeutic drugs to vehicle collisions.

The use of urine as a biologic medium for drug analysis has introduced problems in determining the contribution of a particular drug to road collisions. The concentration of a drug in urine is influenced by many factors, including the time the bladder was last emptied, the volume of fluid ingested, and the active secretion of different drugs by the renal tubules in different individuals. Furthermore, the concentration of drugs within blood in different studies may reflect differences in analytic methods, anatomic site of the sample in deceased individuals, and the time the sample was obtained with respect to the time of drug administration.

Ethanol (Alcohol)

Introduction

Ethanol (ethyl alcohol) is a simple molecule with a hydrocarbon chain and a hydroxyl (OH) group. Ethanol is a volatile liquid and is highly water soluble.

Pharmacokinetics

Ethanol is rapidly absorbed from the stomach and the small intestine. The peak blood alcohol concentration (BAC) after a standard alcoholic drink is reached about 30 minutes after ingestion. A very rough guide for the BAC in the 30 minutes after a single standard drink is 0.01% (0.01 g/100 mL); however, the BAC of a given individual after the consumption of alcoholic beverages is highly variable because of a number of factors. The rate of absorption of ethanol is decreased when gastric emptying is delayed. Consumption of food and the ingestion of high concentrations of alcohol significantly delays gastric emptying.[1] Also, when alcohol is diluted within a large volume of other liquid, the absorption is decreased.

Metabolism of ethanol occurs principally within the liver. The hepatic enzyme alcohol dehydrogenase converts ethanol to acetaldehyde, which in turn is metabolised to acetate. The metabolism of ethanol is proportional to the serum concentration up to concentrations of approximately 1.5 mmol/L (i.e., first-order kinetics). The metabolism is very nearly zero-order for concentrations greater than 3 mmol/L.[2] The elimination of alcohol roughly occurs at a rate of 0.01% per hour, although there is considerable individual variation.[3]

Actions of Ethanol

Ethanol is a central nervous system depressant. Because of its high water solubility, alcohol is quickly distributed throughout the water component of body fluids and tissues and is able to rapidly cross the blood-brain barrier resulting in the classic signs of intoxication.

Individuals with a history of chronic excessive alcohol intake may appear relatively sober to the lay observer, even with significant concentrations of alcohol within their blood; however, formal tests will always reveal a reduction in motor and cognitive ability.

Social Factors

In the State of Victoria, Australia, a coordinated education program and law enforcement campaign changed community attitudes concerning the social acceptance of drinking and driving. The advertising campaign involved television commercials, newspaper and magazine advertisements, and billboards within the metropolitan zone and along major highways. The high-profile commercials showed graphic, realistic recreations of motor vehicle collisions and displayed the human consequences of such behaviour. In a relatively short period, it became generally socially unacceptable to drink and drive. A subgroup of individuals continue to drink and drive with significantly elevated BAC, and evidence suggests that binge drinking and driving is a major problem with teenage drivers.

It has been suggested that breath testing campaigns and fear-based advertising have a saturation limit and the effect on the community may wane over time, whereas others believe a permanent change in community social norms can occur.[4] A review article on the effectiveness of sobriety checkpoints indicated that the deterrence value of random breath-testing checkpoints are effective in decreasing alcohol related crashes, injuries, and deaths.[5] A study on a sustained compulsory breath testing and media campaign in New Zealand showed a combination of compulsory breath testing, zero alcohol tolerance, media blitzes, and booze buses halved late-night serious and fatal injury crashes.[6]

Legislation

In the State of Victoria, Australia, the legal limit for alcohol in the blood of an adult nonprobationary driver is 0.05 mg/100 mL (0.05%). The legal limit for a probationary driver is zero alcohol concentration. The probationary period is 3 years from acquiring a driver's licence.

Commercial truck drivers, bus drivers, and taxi drivers are prohibited to have alcohol in their blood. Some Scandinavian countries have imposed a zero BAC for all drivers. From a road safety perspective, it is clear that a zero

BAC for all drivers is a common sense goal, which would undoubtedly lead to a reduction in motor vehicle collisions, injuries and deaths.

In Victoria police officers have the legal right to enforce random preliminary breath testing for alcohol (PBT) and, if the individual is over the legal limit, to perform an evidentiary breath test or blood test. Drivers who present to hospital following a motor vehicle collision must provide a blood sample for alcohol analysis.

Individuals who have been convicted of a drink driving offense in Victoria, Australia may incur penalties including loss of licence for significant periods in addition to monetary penalties and at times imprisonment. However, research has shown that the majority of offenders proven to have driven under the influence of alcohol and had their licences revoked will continue to drive unlicenced, and are at risk of driving whilst intoxicated.[7]

Recent legislation has led to the installation of breath immobiliser locks in recurrent offenders and in individuals with a markedly high blood alcohol concentration resulting in conviction at court.

Methods of Analysis

Individuals who die as a result of a motor vehicle incident come under the authority of the State Coroner of Victoria and the body is transported and admitted to the Victorian Institute of Forensic Medicine for coronal autopsy. Pedestrians and drivers killed in motor vehicle incidents have a full toxicological examination including head space gas chromatography and liquid chromatography with positive results after screening confirmed by gas chromatography with mass spectrometry. All results are quantified within 95% confidence using two independent modalities.

Blood from post mortem examinations should be drawn from the femoral vein within the groin. In some individuals who have died from massive blood loss, it may be extremely difficult to obtain a reasonable sample of femoral vein blood at the post mortem examination. In these circumstances some centres use blood from the chest cavity. The BAC measured on chest cavity blood may be artifactually raised because of the close proximity of the stomach and its contents, and the liver.

The Alcohol Breath Test

In the State of Victoria if a motorist is stopped by police and asked to undergo a breath test he or she must comply. Failure to do so may result in charges being laid, a fine and disqualification from driving for at least two years. Drivers with severe respiratory disability may have difficulty in providing an adequate sample for the breath test.[8] In these cases blood must be drawn for toxicological analysis.

The preliminary breath test (PBT) is used as a screening test to detect drivers with an elevated blood alcohol concentration. The Victorian Police Force uses the SD 400 PA Lion Alcolmeter machine. The concentration of alcohol in the breath sample is determined by absorption of infrared radiation at wave lengths of 348, 339, and 386 nM. After a PBT that shows a result above the prescribed limit, an evidential breath test is performed using the Drager Alcotest 7110 machine. A driver may request a blood test to confirm the breath test. Immediate loss of licence is applied to full-licenced drivers with an alcohol level of >0.15 g/100 mL or when the evidential breath test above the prescribed limit is the driver's second offence. There is a correlation between breath and blood alcohol concentrations and when there is a discrepancy between the PBT and the BAC, the PBT tends to provide a lower concentration for a given blood alcohol concentration.[9]

Physiologic studies have allowed better understanding of the alcohol exchange process within the pulmonary system. It was previously believed that the alcohol content of the exhaled breath was derived from alveolar diffusion. Studies have shown that alcohol exchange occurs within the proximal conducting airways via diffusion from the bronchial arteries of the systemic circulation.[10] The physiologic mechanism of alcohol exchange explains some factors that may cause variation in PBT from changes in breathing before and during an alcohol breath test. Hyperventilation for 20 seconds before providing the breath sample has been shown to decrease the breath alcohol concentration by 11% and holding one's breath for 30 seconds before exhaling may increase the measured alcohol concentration result by up to 16%.[11] These effects can be explained by the changes in ventilation over the airway mucosa causing local alterations in mucosal alcohol concentration with time. In practice, these effects are negated by routine instructions from police officers to drivers to obtain a uniform sample.

Alcohol Interlock Devices

An interlock device is a breath testing device that is connected to the vehicle's ignition system. If the device detects alcohol in the breath of an individual beyond the specified parameters, the vehicle will not start.

A study in recidivism rates of drivers who had their driver's licence revoked because of alcohol-impaired driving demonstrated an 80% reduction in arrests for "driving while under the influence" offences during the 12-month study period when an interlock device was fitted to their vehicle. However, repeat offenders, including those in the study group, rapidly returned to driving when intoxicated after the devices were removed.[12] In some cases, the driver may recruit another individual to breathe into the device so the vehicle will start. System improvements in interlock devices to address such issues include temperature and pressure sensors, repeat tests while driving, and data recorders.[13]

The National Highway Traffic Safety Administration (NHTSA) reported that about 10 to 20% of all drunk drivers in fatal crashes were repeat drunk-driving offenders. The approach to the problem of drunk driving requires a sustained multifactorial response including education, treatment of those with alcohol-dependence issues, concerted law enforcement, and appropriate management in the courts, with mandatory alcohol interlock devices for recurrent offenders and those with very high BAC when apprehended.

Interpretation of Toxicology Results

The physiologic effects of alcohol are generally predictable and described in many texts of forensic medicine, internal medicine, and toxicology. Low BAC levels are classically associated with mild euphoria and disinhibition, moderate levels with varying degrees of incoordination, ataxia and slurring of the speech, and high levels with marked incoordination, and eventually a reduction in conscious state. Extremely high levels can result in death secondary to respiratory depression. Because of the tolerance that develops with habitual exposure to many drugs including alcohol, an alcoholic with a high BAC may appear outwardly sober, whereas a novice drinker may show significant features of intoxication. It is extremely difficult to assess the degree of intoxication from ethanol by clinical means.[14]

It is difficult to attribute definite physiologic effects to an individual from a measured toxicologic result. It would appear prudent to make general comments relating to the effects of alcohol and provide general statements such as "the measured BAC is 0.10 g/100 mL, twice the legal limit in this jurisdiction and would be expected to cause significant impairment in one's ability to safely control a motor vehicle."

Some drivers who have been involved in a serious motor vehicle incident, and especially after a hit-and-run collision, may claim that they consumed an alcoholic beverage after the incident. A group in Germany has addressed this issue using the identification of congeners, small molecules that provide the taste and smell to the alcoholic drink, to investigate the validity of the claim. The forensic toxicology analysis uses a quantitative and qualitative study of ethanol, methanol, n-propanol, and isomers of butanol in the blood and urine from the driver, with a comparison to the putative postcollision drink.[15] Although the interpretation requires detailed knowledge of the absorption, metabolism, and elimination of these molecules, the group asserts that the examination can resolve this particular issue.

In the postmortem situation, the effects of decomposition can occur relatively quickly if a deceased individual was in a warm environment for some time before extrication from the motor vehicle. Decomposition may result in production or destruction of alcohol by the metabolic activities of bacteria and yeasts. This is especially likely to occur in obese individuals who, even after refrigeration, may maintain a relatively normal core temperature for a considerable period after death, which will tend to increase the decomposition process.

The analysis of vitreous humour is important in such circumstances as the vitreous is less likely to be affected by decomposition because of its protected position. Vitreous humour may have a lag phase with respect to blood concentration of alcohol and other drugs. It may take some time for equilibrium to occur between the blood and vitreous humour.

Forensic Calculations

A calculation that is useful as a guide to the amount of alcohol consumed by an individual is the Widmark formula.[16] This equation provides an estimation of blood alcohol levels from the consumption of an amount of alcohol.

Back calculations of the amount of alcohol consumed with respect to a given BAC and duration of time is expressed by the formula:

$$a = r \times p \times (Ct + (\beta \times t))$$

where a = amount of alcohol in grams, r = constant analogous to the volume of distribution, p = body weight in kilograms, Ct = blood alcohol concentration, and β = ethanol elimination constant.[17]

Individual variation is seen in the constant r between men and women. The constant for men is 0.68 and for women is 0.55. One reported study investigating the amount of alcohol consumed using an analysis of a single blood alcohol concentration using Widmark's equation showed an error rate of ±20%.[18]

The breath alcohol concentration can be substituted for the blood alcohol concentration in the formula. This substitution will inevitably lead to error, because the breath and blood alcohol concentrations are closely related but not identical. A study using 115 subjects, which analysed the reliability of the Widmark equation, demonstrated that using the formula underestimated the actual ethanol dose when breath alcohol concentrations were used.[17]

An equation to approximate the BAC at a particular time (T_0) by extrapolation from a measured BAC (T_1) is given by the equation:

$$BAC (T_0) = BAC (T_1) + K (T_1 - T_0).$$

where K = elimination constant.

Laboratory studies have shown that back extrapolation error increases with length of the extrapolation period and the K constant, which may vary significantly in different individuals.

Back estimations are more precise when the driver is in the postabsorptive phase. A laboratory study by Stowell indicated that back estimations of BAC could seldom be performed with great accuracy.[19] However, the authors stated that back estimates were unlikely to be subject to gross errors if the individual in question was in a normal social drinking situation. The following equation applied:

$$BAC = (D/TBW) \times Blw \times 100 - \beta \times t$$

where BAC = blood alcohol concentration, D = dose of alcohol, TBW = total body water volume, Blw = the fraction of water in the blood (v/v), β = blood alcohol clearance rate, and t = the time (hours) between the start of drinking and the event in question

The authors state that "the results given by the formula must be interpreted according to the circumstances surrounding the drinking situation."[19] The Widmark equation assumes a linear constant elimination rate after peak alcohol absorption of approximately 0.01% to 0.02% every hour. Although this is a reasonable estimate, there may be variation in a particular case. Furthermore, absorption rates of alcohol will vary depending on the presence of food in the stomach, the volume of liquid ingested, effects of injury in the trauma victim, and other factors. Hence the estimates of alcohol concentration provided by equations such as the Widmark formula are best given as a range of possible values.

Non- Alcohol Drugs and Driving

Introduction

Epidemiologic, laboratory, and experimental studies have examined the contribution of the use of various drugs while driving to the incidence of motor vehicle collisions, injuries and fatalities. Epidemiologic studies provide information on the incidence and prevalence of the particular drug in relation to motor vehicle collisions. Case-controlled epidemiologic studies and culpability analyses give information concerning the extent of the drug-driving problem. Experimental studies using a battery of performance tests, simulated driving tests, and "on-road" driving tests assess the drug's effects on the process of driving a motor vehicle.

Although some broad general observations and conclusions may be drawn from the literature, one should consider the practical limitations of a proportion of the work. Even with case-controlled studies and culpability analysis, one may be observing the association of a particular drug with motor vehicle collisions and not a direct causative link. The association may reflect the underlying psychologic and social reasons as to why the individual was taking the particular drug or drugs, rather than a purely pharmacologic cause for the deterioration in performance.

Furthermore, many studies analysed urine for the presence of drugs. The presence of a drug within urine cannot be used as a definite measure of impairment. A classic example would be the use of urine to detect cannabinoids in a driver's system, where a positive result indicates exposure to the drug within weeks before the sample was taken. The concentration of the drug in blood provides far more accurate information, but even in this situation data such as the dose of the particular drug, the time of dose, and duration of therapy are important for reliable interpretation.

Most experimental driving tests are performed on healthy volunteers. The long-term effects of drug use, the issue of drug withdrawal, and the effects of multiple drugs are usually not addressed.

Cannabis

Pharmacokinetics

Tetrahydrocannabinol (THC) is the principal active component of cannabis. The drug can be ingested orally, but is most commonly smoked. Smoking provides the greatest bioavailability and rapidity of action. An average inhaled dose will generally lead to clinical effects within 15 to 20 minutes and last for a couple of hours. The measured peak THC concentration declines considerably sooner than the clinical effects. Laboratory studies have revealed a strong association of a THC level >2 ng/mL and the use of cannabis within a couple of hours.

The metabolism of THC results in compounds with THC-like activity in addition to inactive metabolites. THC has a high affinity for fatty tissues, which results in the elimination of THC from blood. Carboxytetrahydrocannabinol is a major metabolite and is an inactive compound that may be detected within urine for weeks after exposure to a dose of cannabis.

Effects of THC

The acute effects of THC include relaxation, mild euphoria, a desire for social interaction, and increased appetite. There is demonstrable short-term impairment of memory and motor coordination, increased reaction time, altered perception, and impaired judgement.

Examination of the literature reveals conflicting views as to the effects of THC on driving and subsequent motor vehicle incidents.[20–23] In a review of driver simulator performance studies, Smiley showed that alcohol intoxication led to increased speeds and overtaking maneuvers, whereas THC was associated with reduction in speed and a decrease in overtaking maneuvers.[24] Simulated real-world tests showed increased reaction times, including those relating to emergency situations. It has been shown that THC has a negative effect on the standard deviation of lateral position, an operative function of driving not under voluntary control.

Driver culpability studies with respect to intoxication with THC alone have shown a slight percentage increase in driver injury, although no statistically significant difference was noted in two recent studies. The apparent paradox of decrease in driving skill yet no statistically proven increase in the rate of collisions leading to injury has been explained by the behavioural affects of THC, in which the affected driver may compensate for the impairment of driving skill with decreased aggression and risk-taking behaviour.[21,25] Other studies have suggested that the use of THC alone does not increase the risk of culpability for significant injury or death, but there may be an increased incidence of motor vehicle collisions leading to less severe injuries and property damage.

In a thorough literature review, Morland indicated that "based on present knowledge, it can be stated that the use of cannabis constitutes a risk to traffic safety at least for the first few hours after cannabis intake" and "the prevalence of cannabis among the general driving population, drivers suspected of impaired driving, and drivers involved in non-fatal and fatal accidents, indicates a substantial quantitative safety traffic problem."[22]

Central Nervous Stimulants

Illicit central nervous system stimulants include amphetamine and its derivatives and cocaine.

Amphetamine derivatives include methamphetamine, methylenedioxyamphetamine (Ecstasy) and 3,4-methylenedioxyamphetamine.

A study in Washington examined the prevalence of drug use in commercial tractor-trailer drivers using analysis of urine specimens and showed 9.5% of cases were positive for stimulants (methamphetamine, amphetamine, phentermine, ephedrine, and cocaine). Interestingly, the second most frequently encountered drug class was cannabinoids, with 4.3% of drivers testing positive for marijuana metabolites. Only 1.3% of drivers were positive for alcohol.[26] Crash culpability studies have shown a higher percentage in illicit central nervous system stimulant–positive drivers compared with non–drug-affected drivers; however, the increase was not statistically significant.

Actions of Central Nervous System Stimulants

The central nervous system stimulants cause a number of physiologic responses, including increased awareness, increased heart rate and blood pressure, and increased vigilance, but may also cause increased risk-taking behaviour and can be associated with withdrawal-related fatigue.[27]

Laboratory studies on the use of stimulants have been inconclusive. Some performance tasks have shown improvement with stimulant use, whereas others have suggested the perception of enhanced alertness by stimulant users is largely incorrect; in fact, no real improvement in performance can be demonstrated.[28] A review of methamphetamine and driving impairment in the mid-1990s showed that drivers using methamphetamine demonstrated a variety of aberrant driving behaviour, including weaving, erratic driving, speeding, and drifting off the road.[26] Chipman found that cocaine use was associated with "at-fault" collisions.[28]

A further study showed that the use of central nervous system stimulants resulted in a twofold increase in the risk for motor vehicle accidents, though this was not statistically significant.[30] Drummer demonstrated that central nervous stimulants had a strong association with culpability.[23] The odds for a driver using stimulants being culpable for a motor vehicle incident were 2.3 times those of a drug and alcohol free driver and was marginally statistically significant.

The available evidence would suggest that the overall crash risk for drivers affected by central nervous system stimulants would appear to be increased compared with other road users.

Opiates

The most common opiate abused as an illicit drug in most communities is heroin. Heroin is an acetylated morphine derivative with rapid onset that may be injected, inhaled, and snorted. Heroin is rapidly metabolised to morphine through the metabolite 6-monoacetyl morphine. 6-monoacetyl morphine is present in urine and can be analysed in most toxicologic laboratories. The presence of 6-monoacetyl morphine indicates the recent use of heroin.

Morphine is used extensively in medical practice and palliative care in the treatment of cancer. Synthetic opiates include dextroproxyphene and methadone, a long-acting narcotic used in drug treatment programs and in palliative care. Patients may require large doses of morphine to control pain as tolerance to the effects of opiates develops over time. Although opiates have significant targeted central nervous system effects, low to moderate doses have not been shown to cause a significant detriment in performance, although initiation of therapy can result in cognitive impairment.[31]

A case-controlled laboratory study on the effects of methadone use on psychophysical performance tests showed poor performance in the methadone group.[32] However, Chesser and colleagues did not demonstrate any performance deficit.[33] A case-controlled study that examined morphine and codeine in the blood of injured drivers admitted to the emergency room of a major hospital showed a twofold increase in risk of injury in the drug-using drivers.[30] A culpability analysis study did not demonstrate a strong positive association with opiates; however, the study was influenced by the fact that 65% of opiate positive drivers in the study were using other drugs.[23]

The available evidence would suggest that the overall crash risk for drivers using opiates is higher than other road users. The risk is probably greater for those commencing a significant dose of an opiate and includes those abusing opiates.

Benzodiazepines

The benzodiazepines are a group of central nervous system depressant drugs used in the treatment of anxiety and associated disorders and in the management of alcohol and other drug withdrawal programs. Benzodiazepines may be abused by individuals with substance abuse problems when their drug of choice is not readily available. The benzodiazepine class of drugs is also commonly abused in those with behavioural issues.

Simulated driving studies have shown impairment associated with the use of benzodiazepines.[34] Effects on driving have been demonstrated in the morning after the use of benzodiazepines at night. The degree of impairment has been compared with a BAC of up to 0.05 to 0.10 g/100 mL. Furthermore, deficits in standard deviation of lateral position is adversely affected by members of the benzodiazepine group.[35]

Epidemiologic studies have shown an increased risk of motor vehicle collision in those receiving prescriptions for benzodiazepines and especially during the first week of therapy. In general, epidemiologic studies have shown a five to sixfold increase in risk of motor vehicle collisions in those using benzodiazepines.[23]

The effect of benzodiazepines is related to the particular drug and the duration of therapy. The risk is especially significant in those commencing therapy and with the illicit use of the drug.

Summary

The evidence for impaired driving performance and increased risk of motor vehicle collision has been clearly demonstrated for the benzodiazepine group of drugs. Driving within a few hours after the use of cannabis poses a risk to road users. The use of central nervous system stimulants in significant doses may well constitute a risk. Drivers who are inexperienced with opiate drugs are a risk on the road.

Individuals who use comparatively large doses of any of the groups of drugs and those who use multiple "illicit" drugs clearly pose a risk on the road.

References

1. Wilkinson PK, Sedman AJ, Sakmar E, Kay DR, Wagner JG. Pharmacokinetics of ethanol after oral administration in the fasting state. *Journal of Pharmacokinetics and Biopharmacokinetics* 1997; 5:207–214.

2. Levitt MD, Levitt DG. Appropriate use and misuse of blood concentration measurements to quantitate first-pass metabolism. *Journal of Laboratory and Clinical Medicine* 2000; 136:275–280.

3. Holfort NHG. Clinical pharmacokinetics of ethanol. *Clinical Pharmacokinetics* 1987; 13:273–292.

4. Ross HL. The deterrent capability of sobriety checkpoints: summary of the American literature. NHTSA Report DOT HS 807–862.

5. Elder RW, Shults RA, Sleet DA, Nichols JL, Zaza S, Thompson RS. Effectiveness of sobriety checkpoints for reducing alcohol-involved crashes. *Traffic Injury Prevention* 2002; 3:266–274.

6. Miller T, Blewden M, Zhang J-F. Cost savings from a sustained compulsory breath testing and media campaign in New Zealand. *Accident Analysis and Prevention* 2004; 36:783–794.

7. Tashima HN, Helander CJ. *1999 annual report of the California DUI management information system.* Report No. CAL-DMV-RSS-1999-179 Research and Development Section, California Department of Motor Vehicles, Sacramento.

8. Odell MS, McDonald CF, Farrar J, Natsis JS, Pretto JF. Breath testing in patients with respiratory disability. *Journal of Clinical Forensic Medicine* 1998; 5:45–48.

9. Jones AW, Andersson L. Comparison of ethanol concentrations in venous blood and end-expired breath during a controlled drinking study. *Forensic Science International* 2003; 132:18–25.

10. Hlastala MP. The alcohol breath test-a review. *Journal of Applied Physiology* 1998; 84:401–408.

11. Jones AW. Role of re-breathing in determination of the blood-breath ratio of expired ethanol. *Journal of Applied Physiology* 1983; 55:1237–1241.

12. Raub RA, Lucke RE, Wark RI. Breath alcohol ignition interlock devices: controlling the recidivist. *Traffic Injury Prevention* 2003; 4:199–205.

13. Beirness DJ, Simpson HM, Robertson RD. International Symposium on Enhancing the Effectiveness of Alcohol Ignition Interlock Programs. *Traffic Injury Prevention* 2003; 4:179–182.

14. McKnight AJ, Langton EA, Marque PR, Tippetts AJ. Estimating blood alcohol level from observable signs. *Accident Analysis and Prevention* 1997; 29:247–255.

15. Iffland R, Jones AW. Evaluating alleged drinking after driving - the hip flask defence. Part 2. Congener analysis. *Medicine, Science and the Law* 203: 43(1):39-68.

16. Widmark EMP. Principals and applications of medico-legal alcohol determination. Davis, CA: Biochemical Publications; 1981.

17. Friel PN, Logan BK, Baer J. An evaluation of the reliability of the Widmark calculations based on breath alcohol measurements. *Journal of the Forensic Sciences* 1995; 40:91–94.

18. Gullberg RG, Jones AW. Guidelines for estimating the amount of alcohol consumed from a single measurement of blood alcohol concentration: re-evaluation of Widmark's equation. *Forensic Science International* 1994; 69:119–130.

19. Stowell AR, Stowell LI. Estimation of blood alcohol concentrations after social drinking. *Journal of Forensic Sciences* 1998; 43:14–21.

20. Fergusson DM, Horwood LJ. Cannabis use and traffic accidents in a birth cohort of young adults. *Accident Analysis and Prevention* 2001; 33:703–711.

21. Bates, MN, Blakely TA. Role of cannabis in motor vehicle crashes. *Epidemiology Reviews* 1999; 21:222–232.

22. Morland J. Driving under the influence of non-alcohol drugs. *Forensic Science Review* 2000; 12:80–105.

23. Drummer OF, Gerostamoulos J, Batzris H, Chu M, Caplehorn J, Robertson MD, Swann P. The involvement of drugs in drivers of motor vehicles killed in Australia in road traffic crashes. *Accident Analysis and Prevention* 2004; 36:239–248.

24. Smiley A. Marijuana; on-road and driving-simulator studies. In Kalant H, Corrigall W, Hore R. eds. *The health effects of cannabis.* Toronto, Ontario, Canada; Addiction Research Foundation; 1999, pp. 173–191.

25. Smiley A. Marijuana on road and simulator studies. *Alcohol Drugs Driving* 1986; 2:121–134.

26. Couper FJ, Pemberton M, Jarvis A, Hughes M, Logan BK. Prevalence of drug use in commercial tractor-trailer drivers. *Journal of Forensic Sciences* 2002; 47:562–567.

27. Logan BK, Schwilke EW. Drug and alcohol drug in fatally injured drivers in Washington State. *Journal of Forensic Sciences* 1996; 41:505–510.

28. Fischman MW. Cocaine and the amphetamines, in Meltzer HY, ed. *Psychopharmacology: a third generation of progress.* New York: Raven Press; 1987.

29. Chipman ML, MacDonald S, Mann RE. Being "at fault" in traffic crashes: does alcohol, cannabis, cocaine, or polydrug abuse make a difference? *Injury Prevention* 2003; 9:343–348.

30. Movig KLL., Mathijssen MPM, Nagel PHA, Van Egmond T, De Gier JJ, Leufkens HGM, Egberts ACG. Psychoactive substance use and the risk of motor vehicle accidents. *Accident Analysis and Prevention* 2004; 36:631–636.

31. McKim, W. *Drugs and Behaviour.* Englewood Cliffs, NJ: Prentice-Hall; 1986.

32. Berghaus G, Staak M, Glazinski R, Hower K, Joo S, Friedel B. Complementary empirical study on the driver fitness of Methadone substitution patients. In

Utzelmann H-D, Berghaus G, Krog, editors. *Alcohol, Drugs and Traffic Safety.* T92, Tüv Rheinland GmbH Köhn, pp. 120–132.

33. Chesser GB, Lemon J, Gomel M, Murphy G. Are the driving related skills of clients in a methadone maintenance program affected by methadone? *Alcohol, Drugs and Traffic Safety,* Kloden CN, McClean AJ, eds. Adelaide Australia Technical Report No. 3.

34. Willumeit HP, Ott H, Neubert W. Simulated car driving as a useful technique for the determination of residual effects and alcohol interaction after short- and long-acting benzodiazepines. *Psychopharmacology Supplement* 1984; 1:182.

35. O'Hanlon JF, Brookhuis KA, Louwerens JW, Volkerts ER. Performance testing as part of drug registration, In O'Hanlon JF, deGrier JJ, eds. *Drugs and driving.* London, UK: Taylor and Francis; 1986. p. 311.

Additional Reading

Al-Lanquawi Y, Moreland TA, McEwen J, Halliday F, Durnin CJ, Stevenson IH. Ethanol kinetics: extent of error in back extrapolation procedures. *British Journal of Clinical Pharmacology* 1992; 34:316–321.

Darke S, Kelly E, Ross J. Drug driving among injecting drug users in Sydney, Australia; prevalence, risk factors and risk perceptions. *Addiction* 2004; 99:175–185.

Jones AW, Andersson L. Variation of the blood/breath alcohol ratio in drinking drivers. *Journal of Forensic Sciences* 1996; 41:916–9121.

Longo MC , Hunter CE, Lokan RJ, White JM, White MA. Prevalence of alcohol, cannabinoids, benzodiazepines and stimulants amongst injured drivers and their role in driver culpability. Part II: the relationship between drug prevalence and drug concentration, and driver culpability. *Accident Analysis and Prevention* 2000; 32:623–632.

Lowenstein SR, Koziol-Mclian J. Drugs and traffic crash responsibility: a study of injured motorists in Colorado. *The Journal of Trauma* 2001; 50:313–320.

Mason M, Dubowski K. Breath-alcohol analysis; uses, methods and some forensic problems—review and opinion. *Journal of Forensic Sciences* 1976; 21:9–41.

Retchin SR, Cox J, Fox M, Irwin L. Performance based measurements among elderly drivers and non-drivers. *Journal of the American Geriatrics Society* 1988; 36:813–819.

Tehrune KW, Ippolito CA, Hendricks DL, Michalovic JG, Bogema SC, Santinga P, et al. *The incidence and role of drugs in fatally injured drivers.* Washington, DC: US Department of Transportation, National Highway Traffic Safety Administration; 2003.

Vingilis E, MacDonald S. Review: drugs and traffic collisions. *Traffic Injury Prevention* 2002; 3:1–11.

Wilkinson PK. Pharmacokinetics of ethanol; a review. *Clinical and Experimental Research* 1980; 4:6–20.

Cause of Death 10

Introduction

A death resulting from a motor vehicle incident may be rapid or delayed. The most common traumatic insults leading to rapid death at the scene include severe head injury with diffuse axonal injury, fracture dislocation of the upper cervical spine, and transection of the thoracic aorta. Victims of trauma who survive the initial collision and subsequently die before active treatment by medical and paramedical personnel can be instituted usually succumb to blood loss. Delayed deaths in hospital result from various combinations of irreversible brain injury, organ failure, and sepsis.

Older victims of trauma who have coexisting chronic medical conditions are at greater risk of death from relatively mild trauma compared with those with no underlying medical problems.[1] The individual victim's diminished physiologic reserve is the underlying factor for the increased risk.

Deaths at the Collision Scene

Immediate death is a consequence of major disruption of the body following crashes at high speed and in some pedestrian and motorcycle incidents. As noted previously, severe blunt trauma/rapid deceleration can cause swift death from head injury with diffuse axonal injury, fracture/dislocation of the atlanto-occipital joint/upper cervical spine, and complete rupture of the thoracic aorta.

Experimental evidence in laboratory animals has shown that blunt head trauma may cause disturbed respiratory function and apnea. Separate groups of anesthetized but spontaneously breathing rats were subjected to increasing severity of blunt force trauma to the brain. It was shown that lesser degrees of blunt force injury were associated with disturbance of respiration, which spontaneously resolved. However, greater degrees of blunt force trauma led to serious respiratory dysfunction and apnea, which was proportional to the magnitude of the head injury. At the severe end of the injury spectrum, there was prolonged apnea leading to profound hypoxia.[2] Furthermore, a clinical report of medical practitioners at the scene of a motor vehicle incident described apneic patients who responded to artificial ventilation with subsequent full recovery. The doctors stated that the patients would have died if immediate artificial respiration was not performed.[3]

Other motor vehicle crash victims may be noted to be conscious and responding to bystanders and paramedical personnel or with a decreased conscious state but clearly breathing, moving, or actively bleeding, prior to obvious clinical deterioration and death. Injuries that lead to death in these circumstances include a complication of an unstable upper cervical fracture and catastrophic blood loss. Blood loss may be external or internal. The likelihood of survival of a victim of motor vehicle trauma with haemorrhagic shock is dependent on many factors, including their age, general medical state, the presence of other injuries, and the timeliness of resuscitation and appropriate injury management. Typical causes of haemorrhagic shock include intrathoracic haemorrhage, haemoperitoneum, and retroperitoneal haematoma. Rapid blood loss can also arise from a large number of less severe injuries involving multiple systems.

Asphyxial processes may result in death at the scene. Traumatic and mechanical asphyxia are pathologic processes that require accurate scene information and thorough autopsy examination for a correct diagnosis to be made. Asphyxia in the broadest sense refers to a lack of oxygen within the blood. Mechanical asphyxia occurs in any situation in which the chest is unable to expand because of a constricting object. Asphyxia may also occur from a situation that leads to forced irreversible flexion of the neck or pressure to the neck leading to upper airway obstruction.[4] In other occasions, a motor vehicle may come to rest over the body of an ejected vehicle occupant. The postmortem examination will usually, but not always, show some objective evidence of injury to the chest or neck.

A pneumothorax is not uncommon in trauma victims with chest injuries. Most healthy individuals will tolerate an uncomplicated pneumothorax; however, the presence of other significant injuries or underlying natural disease processes may lead to a pneumothorax contributing to death at the scene of the collision. A tension pneumothorax is a medical emergency that requires rapid decompression otherwise death will rapidly ensue. Recent reports suggest needle decompression is not always reliable and that tube thoracostomy is preferred.[5]

Early Deaths from Motor Vehicle Incidents

Early deaths after injury sustained in motor vehicle incident are usually a consequence of primary head injury or catastrophic blood loss. Severe diffuse axonal injury (grade 3) with brainstem involvement is associated with immediate loss of consciousness in adults.[6] Extra-axial collections can reach a crucial volume leading to midline shift, caudal herniation with subsequent brainstem dysfunction. In the great majority of these cases, there is associated traumatic subarachnoid haemorrhage and axonal injury. Rupture of a vertebral artery secondary to direct neck blunt trauma, or more commonly from extension and rotation of the head on the neck may also lead to early death.

Haemorrhagic shock may cause death of the patient despite the best efforts of paramedical and medical personnel. The bleeding may be ongoing from the moment of the crash, may arise from a limited number or numerous vessels, or result from delayed rupture of an aortic tear. About 15% of traumatic aortic tears are self-contained, allowing the victim to get to hospital alive prior to rupture. It has been estimated that 15% of patients die within the first hour and 30% of these initial survivors will die within 6 hours.[7]

Tension pneumothorax, traumatic pericardial tamponade, myocardial contusion, and tracheobronchial disruption may be seen as the principal injury leading to early death in a crash victim, but more commonly are associated with a number of other significant injuries.[8]

Delayed Deaths from Motor Vehicle Incidents

Introduction

Delayed mortality after a motor vehicle incident occurs primarily from secondary brain injury or multiple organ failure. A substantial research effort has examined the stimulation and effects of various cytokines and chemokines that lead to systemic inflammation in addition to parallel anti-inflammatory mediators. The imbalance of these mediators is believed to be the basis for secondary brain injury, other organ dysfunction, and death in victims who later succumb to the effects of multiple trauma.

Trauma Pathophysiology

Trauma causes soft-tissue and organ injury, fractures, hypoxia, and blood loss and induces both local and systemic inflammatory responses. These processes are intended to activate host immune mechanisms and stimulate the repair process and involve the local and systemic release of inflammatory cytokines and chemokines, stimulation and activation of leukocytes, activation of the complement cascade, the kallikrein-kinin system, and the coagulation cascade.[9,10] If the trauma is severe enough, the patient may develop excess inflammation with clinical features of the systemic inflammatory response syndrome. The clinical diagnosis of systemic inflammatory response syndrome, as defined by the American College of Chest Physicians/Society of Critical Care Medicine, requires the presence of at least two of four clinical parameters: tachycardia greater than 90/min, tachypnea greater than 20/minute, temperature greater than 38°C or less than 36°C, and number of leukocytes greater than 12,000 mm^3 or less than 4,000 mm^3.

In the two-hit hypothesis of subsequent organ dysfunction, the primary impact represents the "first hit," with local tissue trauma and activation of inflammation, and the "second hit" is represented by succeeding insults including hypoxia, metabolic acidosis, ischaemia and reperfusion, and sepsis.[9] In concert with the proinflammatory processes, anti-inflammatory mediators are stimulated in a negative feedback response. The balance between these functions is vital to the patient's recovery.

An imbalance of the two systems leading to a proinflammatory state with necrosis of parenchymal cells may lead to the multiple organ dysfunction syndrome (MODS). Multiple organ dysfunction syndrome can resolve or progress to multiple organ failure (MOF).[11] Conversely, if the anti-inflammatory state is excessive the patient may develop a relative immunosuppressed state termed the compensatory anti-inflammatory response syndrome (CARS).

Historically, the central nervous system was believed to be in an immunologically privileged position because of the blood-brain barrier. Recent research has shown that neurons, astrocytes, and microglia are able to produce an array of inflammatory mediators similar to those in the peripheral circulation.[12] Brain edema secondary to diffuse mechanical brain injury is believed to result primarily from cytotoxic injury, with astrocytic and neuronal swelling derived from increased membrane permeability to sodium and potassium, failure of the active ion pump, and sustained uptake of osmotically active solutes.[13]

The goal of trauma care is to as rapidly as possible facilitate an environment in which normal body system homeostasis can be obtained. To this end, the trauma victim must be promptly transported to a trauma care centre where appropriate resuscitation, examination, investigation, and surgical management can commence. Surgical intervention at the scene is limited to fundamental principals of resuscitation (i.e., airway, breathing, and circulation). Lifesaving procedures such as intercostal cannula insertion for suspected tension pneumothorax and endotracheal intubation to maintain adequate ventilation are obviously essential in the appropriate clinical circumstances. It is, however, extremely important that the patient is conveyed without delay to hospital to control blood loss and minimise secondary brain injury.

Damage Control Surgery

Victims of motor vehicle trauma who are transported to a major trauma centre are managed with respect to the principles of damage control surgery. First described in the early 1990s by Rotondo and Schwab in the management of penetrating abdominal trauma, damage control surgery has evolved into principles for immediate care in patients who require emergency neurosurgery, abdominal and thoracic surgery, and orthopaedic surgery.[14–18]

In essence, the aim of damage control surgery is to control haemorrhage and minimize the potential for further metabolic insults to the trauma victim from metabolic acidosis, coagulopathy, and hypothermia. In damage control laparotomy, the surgeon endeavours to control haemorrhage with rapid packing of the abdomen, followed by definitive haemorrhage control by an appropriate rapid surgical technique, which may include splenectomy, nephrectomy, clamping of major blood vessels, and packing of the liver. Depending on the particular clinical situation, the surgeon may employ control of fecal contamination with a diversion procedure followed by temporary closure of the abdomen.[18] The abdomen may be closed around sterile drapes or prosthetic materials.

The patient is resuscitated in the operating room and intensive care unit where further restoration of normal temperature, maintenance of proper ventilation and blood pressure, and correction of coagulopathy is performed. The patient is then returned to the operating room for removal of packs, a definitive surgical procedure, and formal abdominal closure in a much safer physiologic state.

The optimal management of the trauma patient is best served by the expertise of a team of surgeons and medical intensivists trained in trauma care. As noted previously, the priority of initial surgery is to control bleeding with emergency laparotomy/thoracotomy. Damage control surgery for abdominal injuries may use temporary expedient surgical management, whereas damage control thoracotomy usually requires initial definitive surgical repair.[19] The technique of choice is still the easiest and fastest available in the particular circumstances. In the emergency department, the primary goals of emergency thoracotomy are to evacuate a pericardial tamponade, cross-clamp the descending thoracic aorta, control intrathoracic haemorrhage, and address massive air embolism.[20]

If the neurosurgeon believes that an emergency craniotomy is needed to evacuate an extra-axial haematoma, this can be performed in concert with other procedures. Damage control orthopaedics aims for early stabilisation of fractures, which serves to decrease tissue damage and blood loss. Definitive orthopaedic management is timed to follow physiologic recovery.[21] The choice of intramedullary fixation or temporary external fixation depends on all of the patient's clinical features.[22]

Clinical studies have provided valuable information regarding the effects of serious metabolic disturbance on the prognosis of the patient undergoing damage control surgery. It has been shown that the inability to correct pH above 7.21 and the presence of marked coagulopathy (activated partial thromboplastin time (APTT) greater than 78 seconds) at the completion of damage control laparotomy, was predictive of 100% mortality.[23]

Organ Failure

Adult Respiratory Distress Syndrome (ARDS) is a relatively common complication of chest and multiple trauma and may be seen as an isolated clinical problem. Adult Respiratory Distress Syndrome is characterised clinically by progressive and profound hypoxia despite artificial ventilation. Ventilator-associated pneumonia is a particularly important cause of mortality and morbidity in patients in the intensive care environment.[24]

A head injury can be associated with myocardial dysfunction (stunned myocardium). This potentially reversible condition causes a reduction in cardiac function and is believed to result from autonomic nervous system stimulation.[25] In rare cases, head injury can be associated with symptomatic metabolic disturbance including hypomagnesaemia, hypocalcaemia, and hypophosphataemia which may manifest as ventricular arrhythmias.[26]

The effects of trauma on the kidneys will vary depending on the magnitude of the insult and the presence of natural renal disease. Factors that may precipitate renal dysfunction in the trauma victim include myoglobinuria from significant crush injury to skeletal muscle, hypovolaemia with poor renal perfusion, and the effects of intravenous contrast in various imaging modalities. In some cases, renal insufficiency occurs as a consequence of liver dysfunction (hepatorenal syndrome).

Acute adrenal dysfunction may contribute to normovolaemic shock in victims of trauma. Postmortem examination has shown infarction of pituitary or adrenal tissue, and clinical studies have suggested some benefit from corticosteroid therapy in some victims of trauma.

Sepsis

Sepsis is a common problem in patients who suffer severe injury and require prolonged hospitalisation, often with the requirement for intravenous and intra-arterial cannulae and urinary and chest catheters.

Despite aseptic techniques to minimise colonisation of bacteria to indwelling cannulae and catheters, such foreign bodies pose a particular risk to patients as they provide a focus for nosocomial infection.[27] As noted previously, there are complex pro- and anti-inflammatory responses in the trauma victim and dysregulation causing a decrease in host immunity may render the patient susceptible to sepsis.[28]

Fat Embolism

Fat embolism is an uncommon but well recognised cause of death from trauma. Fat embolism is characterised by the presence of fat within the circulation and is usually, but not exclusively, associated with fractures, typically of long bones. Fat embolism is believed to result from, in varying degrees, mechanically derived fat from fractures and soft-tissue trauma and enzyme-originated circulating free fatty acids.[29] In acute cases, macroscopic fat may be seen in the pulmonary circulation on transoesophageal echocardiography and on macroscopic examination of the pulmonary arteries at autopsy.

Typical clinical findings in acute cases are the rapid development of hypoxia and haemodynamic dysfunction. In the more usual case of fat embolism syndrome, the onset of clinical deterioration is delayed 12 to 24 hours after injury. The patient classically presents with progressive respiratory failure, change in mental state, and often a petechial rash over the chest. Postmortem examination shows petechial haemorrhages within the white matter of the brain and microscopic fat globules within small blood vessels.

Pulmonary Thromboembolism

Delayed death from pulmonary thromboembolism is well recognised in victims of trauma. Risk factors for peripheral venous thrombosis include bed rest, smoking, endothelial damage, a hypercoagulable state, and inherited coagulopathies. Trauma is recognised as a cause of a hypercoagulable state.[30] Acute pulmonary thromboembolism has been described to occur approximately 2 hours following the occurrence of a leg injury in a young male in a motor vehicle collision.[31]

The clinical effects of thromboembolism vary depending upon the size of the thrombus and the underlying health of the affected individual. Large thrombi that acutely occlude the left and right pulmonary arteries or main pulmonary trunk are associated with sudden cardiovascular collapse and rapid demise.

Iatrogenic injury

A patient's medical therapy may contribute to his or her death. The most common examples include patients on anticoagulation therapy who suffer increased bleeding from blunt and sharp force trauma. A case of delayed onset subarachnoid haemorrhage arising from a cerebral contusion was seen in a middle-age trauma victim. The subarachnoid haemorrhage was associated with anticoagulation therapy for a prosthetic heart valve.[32]

Various therapeutic medications have recognised dose-related and idiosyncratic adverse effects on many different organs. The author has examined a case of propofol infusion syndrome in a young man who suffered a mild head injury and seizures following a single vehicle motor vehicle incident. Prolonged propofol infusion at high doses has been associated with bizarre electrocardiograph changes, metabolic acidosis, and refractory heart failure.[33]

Occasional victims of motor vehicle trauma may suffer an iatrogenic injury that contributes to or leads directly to death. Such iatrogenic injuries include malplacement of central venous cannulae leading to vascular injury or pneumothorax. In a moribund patient who is clearly dying from injuries sustained in the collision, an iatrogenic injury may be coincidental to the death. The decision as to whether an iatrogenic injury either contributes to or is directly related to the death relies on careful analysis of the medical records in conjunction with the autopsy findings. In some cases, the medical and surgical issues may be complex and beyond the area of expertise of the pathologist. In such cases it would be prudent to seek an independent expert opinion from the appropriate college.

Summary

The medical investigation of every individual who dies in relation to a motor vehicle collision is an individual case with its own set of variables. The age of the victim, the presence of significant underlying natural disease processes, and the rapidity with which resuscitative measures and definitive treatments are instituted may be as important as the constellation of injuries for a particular case. Multiple fractured ribs should not normally be life-threatening in a fit young male driver, yet the same injuries are life-threatening for an elderly frail man with underlying emphysema.

The pathologist cannot be expected to have expert knowledge in all areas of medicine and surgery. The correct documentation of the deceased's injuries will facilitate an expert opinion from an appropriate expert in cases in which the issues in question are beyond the expertise of the pathologist.

References

1. McGwin G Jr., MacLennan PA, Fife JB, Davis GG, Rue LW III. Pre-existing conditions and mortality in older trauma patients. *The Journal of Trauma* 2004; 56:1291–296.

2. Atkinson JL, Anderson RE, Murray MJ. The early critical phase of sever head injury: importance of apnea and dysfunctional respiration. *Journal of Trauma* 1998; 45:941–945.

3. Levine JE, Becker D, Chun T. Reversal of incipient brain death from head-injury apnea at the scene of accidents (letter). *New England Journal of Medicine* 1979; 301:109.

4. Vega RS, Adams VI. Suffocation in motor vehicle crashes. *The American Journal of Forensic Medicine and Pathology* 2004; 45:101–107.

5. Leigh-Smith S, Harris T. Tension pneumothorax-time for a re-think? *Emergency Medicine Journal* 2005; 22:8–16.

6. Gennarelli TA, Thibault LE, Adams JH, Graham DI, Thompson CJ, Marcinin RP. Diffuse axonal injury and traumatic coma in the primate. *Annals of Neurology* 1982; 12:564–574.

7. Beel T, Harwood AL. Traumatic rupture of the thoracic aorta. *Annals of Emergency Medicine* 1980; 9:483–486.

8. Swan KG Jr, Swan BC, Swan KG. Decelerational thoracic injury. *The Journal of Trauma* 2001; 51:970–974.

9. Keel M, Trentz O. Pathophysiology of polytrauma. *Injury* 2005; 36:691–709.

10. DeLong WG, Born CT. Cytokines in patients with polytrauma. *Clinical Orthopaedics* 2004; 422:57–65.

11. Rensing H, Bauer M. Multiple organ failure. Mechanisms, clinical manifestation and therapeutic strategies. *Anaesthetist* 2001; 50:819–841.

12. Schmidt OI, Heyde CE, Ertel W, Stahel PF. Closed head injury—an inflammatory disease? *Brain Research Reviews* 2005; 48:388–399.

13. Unterberg AW, Stover J, Kress B, Kiening KL. Edema and brain trauma. *Neuroscience* 2004; 129:1021–1029.

14. Rotondo M, Schwab CW, McGonigal M, et al. "Damage control." An approach for improved survival in exsanguinating penetrating abdominal injury. *Journal of Trauma* 1993; 35:375–382.

15. Bose D, Tejwani NC. Evolving trends in the care of polytrauma patients. *Injury* 2006; 37:20–28.

16. Rosenfeld JV. Damage control neurosurgery. *Injury* 2004; 35:655–660.

17. Tzovaras G, Hatzitheofilou C. New trends in the management of colonic trauma. *Injury* 2005; 36:1011–1015.

18. Sugrue M, D'Amours SK, Joshipura M. Damage control surgery and the abdomen. *Injury* 2004; 35:642–648.

19. Rotondo MF, Bard MR. Damage control surgery for thoracic injuries. *Injury* 2004; 35:649–654.

20. Biffl WL, Moore EE, Harken AH. Emergency department thoracotomy. In Mattox KL, Feliciano DV, Moore EE, Editors. *Trauma*. New York: McGraw-Hill; 2000. pp. 245–259.

21. Hildebrand F, Giannoudis P, Krettek C, Pape H-C. Damage control: extremities. *Injury* 35:678–689.

22. Giannoudis PV, Smith RM, Bellamy MC, Morrison JF, Dickson RA, Guillou PJ. Stimulation of the inflammatory system by reamed and unreamed nailing of femoral fractures. An analysis of the second hit. *Journal of Bone and Joint Surgery, British Volume* 1999; 81:356–361.

23. Aoki N, Wall M, Demsar J. Predictive model for survival at the conclusion of a damage control laparotomy. *American Journal of Surgery* 2001; 180:540–545.

24. Miller PR, Johnson JC 3rd, Karchmer T, Hoth JJ, Meredith JW, Chang MC. National nosocomial infection surveillance system: from benchmark to bedside in trauma patients. *Journal of Trauma* 2006; 60:98–103.

25. Ohtsuka T, Hamada M, Kodama K, Sasaki O, Suzuki M, Hara Y, Shigematsu Y, Hiwada K. Images in Cardiovascular Medicine. Neurogenic stunned myocardium. *Circulation* 2000; 101:2122–2124.

26. Khogali SS, Townsend JN, Marshal H. Ventricular tachycardia following head injury. *Heart* 2003; 89:829.

27. Verdier R, Parer S, Jean-Pierre H, Dujols P, Picot MC. Impact of an infection control program in an intensive care unit in France. *Infection Control and Epidemiology* 2006; 27:60–66.

28. Ni Choileain N, Redmond HP. The immunological consequences of injury. *Surgeon* 2006; 4:23–31.

29. Huber-Lang M, Brinkmann A, Straeter J, Beck A, Gauss A, Gebhard F. Case report. An unusual case of early fulminant post-traumatic fat embolism syndrome. *Anaesthesia* 2005; 60:1141–1143.

30. Schmidt U, Enderson BL, Chen JP, Muall KI. D-dimer levels correlate with pathologic thrombosis in trauma patients. *Journal of Trauma* 1992; 33:312–320.

31. Rogers FB, Turner OM, Shackford SR. Immediate pulmonary embolism after trauma: case report. *The Journal of Trauma* 2000; 48:146–147.

32. Lopez AE, Barnard JJ, White CL III, Oeberst JL, Prahlow JA. Motor-vehicle collision-related death due to delayed-onset subarachnoid haemorrhage associated with anticoagulant therapy. *Journal of Forensic Sciences* 2004; 49:807–808.

33. Vasile B, Rasulo F, Candiani A, Latronico N. The pathophysiology of propofol infusion syndrome: a simple name for a complex syndrome. *Intensive Care Medicine* 2003; 29:1417–1428.

Appendix 1

Scene Examination

Overview

The purpose of the scene investigation is to identify and document the relevant features of the incident scene. This entails an analysis of environmental factors and physical evidence from the roadway and identification and documentation of external and interior damage to motor vehicles involved in the incident. Physical evidence includes identification and measurement of collision debris and tire marks, the position of rest of vehicles, ejected occupants, and pedestrians. The initial collision point (point of first contact) is determined and recorded.

At the earliest practical time, the scene must be secured. It is assumed that most scenes are contaminated by the time the investigation unit arrives on site because vehicles in the vicinity of the incident have often driven through the scene within moments of the collision. Members of the public and emergency personnel have usually attended victims of the incident.

Environmental Factors

It is important to document basic environmental factors such as:

- Weather conditions
- Road signage
- Road factors

Weather Conditions

Adverse weather conditions increase the risk of being involved in a motor vehicle collision. Adverse weather conditions include rain, sleet and hail, fog, high winds, and sun glare.

A comparison of studies in the literature on motor vehicle collisions and adverse weather conditions is complicated by variations in methodologies, and problems in defining and measuring such basic issues as the amount of rainfall in a specified period. However, a number of generalizations can be made with respect to the effects of rain and snowfall.

1. Collision risk increases with rainfall and the risk increases with the intensity of rain. On average, the risk of a traffic collision increases by 75% during rain compared to normal driving conditions.[1] The risk of injury during rainy weather is increased by 45%.
2. A study from Israel confirmed a widely held impression that the risk of collision in rain is increased after a prolonged period of dry weather.[2] This may be due to the accumulation of road grime. Furthermore, oil deposited by vehicles is spread by rain and that appears as a rainbow effect on top of the residual water.
3. Collisions in rain tend to be rear end collisions, tend to occur on curved roads and at signalized intersections, at night, and involve multiple vehicles.
4. Collision risk increases with snowfall and with intensity of snowfall, though injury severity tends to decrease, presumably because of the lower speeds involved.
5. Collisions in snow involve a higher proportion of run off the road incidents.[1]

High winds have been shown to contribute to motor vehicle crashes and are a particular hazard for trucks, buses, and vans. High winds typically cause overturning, sideswipe incidents, and spins.[3] Fog and sun glare can both cause a significant reduction in visibility. In foggy conditions, the driver can slow down, although this can lead to subsequent rear end collisions.

Statistics suggest that collision risk is increased at both dawn and dusk. Although a number of factors contribute to the increased risk, problems with sun glare and visibility are potential factors. The problem of visibility is of particular concern in motorcycle/bicycle incidents and pedestrian fatalities. A study using the time changes that occur in daylight savings has shown that motor vehicle incidents increase with decreasing ambient light, and a rapid reduction in collision rate occurs with the introduction of daylight savings time.

A laboratory simulation study showed that glare caused from the lights of oncoming cars caused a significant reduction in a driver's ability to detect pedestrians by the roadside.[4] The scene examination, incorporating the point of first contact and preceding roadway and considering the degree of glare associated with an oncoming vehicle may be crucial in a particular case.

Road Factors

The presence of significant irregularities and abnormalities to the road surface can contribute to the motor vehicle incident. This is more likely to be relevant when high speeds are involved.

Black ice can be a particularly dangerous problem on freeways, highways, and country roads. Black ice is a thin layer of clear ice on the road surface that is not readily apparent to the driver. The presence of black ice can lead to extremely slippery conditions with loss of steering and braking control. Areas prone to black ice are often known to local residents who in turn can provide valuable information to investigators. Factors that are conducive to the formation of black ice include near freezing conditions, fog, and sections of road in deep cuttings.[5]

Potholes are caused by defects in the road surface that increase in size and depth from wear by traffic flow. When a driving wheel enters a large pothole, such that the driving edge of the wheel completely leaves the normal road surface, the subsequent jolt through the front end suspension will tend to make the motor vehicle move in the direction of the affected wheel. In general, road irregularities and potholes do not cause loss of vehicle control for most drivers. In cases in which it is suggested an issue with the road surface contributed to the collision, close examination of the road for tire marks may provide important corroborative information.

A number of other significant road surface issues may affect a vehicle's handling characteristics:

1. White painted lines, arrows, and other road markings can cause a loss of friction and may be significant issue, especially for motorcycles. The degree of slip is magnified in wet conditions.
2. Rutting of the road surface through traffic use can cause vehicles to travel along a regular driving line. Rutting also holds water, which can raise further problems in rainy conditions.
3. Rippling of the road surface from heat, and vehicles slowing rapidly over time, causes vehicles to travel over the top of the ripples, and often leads to loss of friction and can cause wheels to slip. Rippling occurs on bitumen and unmade roads.
4. Bitumen bleed refers to liquid bitumen rising to the top of the paved surface, which manifests as a smooth black surface. The surface can become extremely slippery when wet and often causes tires to lose grip very quickly.

Surface Water

The presence of water across a roadway will affect a motor vehicle differently depending on the depth of the water and speed of the motor vehicle when the water is encountered.

The term *hydroplaning* refers to loss of contact between the tire contact patch and the road surface by a wedge of water that cannot escape from beneath the tire as it rotates. Hydroplaning is uncommon, but is prone to occur when there is little or no tread on the tire to deflect the water away from the road surface, and in vehicles travelling at high speed (>100 km/hr). There is usually a history of recent heavy rain and possibly problems with the design or function of the drainage from a section of roadway.[6] Because the tire rubber is no longer in contact with the road surface, the lack of friction will result in complete loss of steering and braking capabilities.

A deep layer of water over a road can impart significant drag on a motor vehicle. This can result in marked changes in the handling of the vehicle and can lead to loss of control, especially with inexperienced drivers. The vehicle may pull sharply to one side and lead to overcorrection error, causing side-swipe collisions and run off the road incidents.

Evidence from the Roadway

Assessment of the roadway leading up to the incident, at the incident point, and distal to the incident will provide the investigator with information regarding the causation and in the reconstruction of a particular collision. Essential observations include:

- Tire marks
- Collision debris
- Gouge and scrape marks
- Fluid run off
- Place(s) of rest

Tire Marks

Tire marks are commonly associated with motor vehicle incidents. Important tipes of tire marks include skidmarks, yawmarks, collision marks, acceleration marks, flat tire marks, and rolling prints.

Skidmark

A skidmark is a tire mark that occurs when a tire, instead of rotating, slides over the road surface. Thus skidmarks commonly occur when a driver applies the brakes firmly and abruptly causing a wheel to "lock up." The characteristic features of the skidmark are that the mark gradually increases in intensity with distance, is usually in a straight line, and usually terminates abruptly at the point of collision. Groove marks from the tread pattern run parallel to the edges of the skid mark (Figure A1.1).

In modern passenger motor vehicles, the braking distribution is about 60% to the front wheels and about 40% to the back wheels. In the case of a "lock up," there is a tendency for the front wheels to skid, although this is not always the case. Whether a skidmark occurs depends on many factors, including the maintenance history of the motor vehicle, the type and condition of the tires, and the condition of the road surface. There is a tendency for the locked rear wheels to rotate around the vehicle's longitudinal axis so that rear skidmarks tend to be curved.

Antilock braking systems are a system of optimal braking efficiency. When the driver applies the brake abruptly and severely, the system applies the brakes to the point of "lock up" and then releases the brake to allow the wheel to rotate, which optimises the braking ability of the motor vehicle. Because the wheel is allowed to rotate, skidmarks will not be present, instead a series of off-and-on deceleration scuff marks may be present on the road surface. This may have the appearance of a regular pattern on the road surface.

Skidmarks from a motorcycle differ from a passenger vehicle in a number of ways. The motorcycle tire mark is usually a single skidmark derived from the rear tire. A locked front wheel can leave a skidmark; when this occurs, it is often more prominent because of forward pitching of the machine. However,

Figure A1.1 Typical skidmark demonstrating increase in intensity of tire mark with distance.

Figure A1.2   Typical single skid mark from a motorcycle.

a locked front wheel results in an unstable machine hence these skidmarks tend to be short.

The motorcycle skidmark is thinner than a passenger vehicle skidmark and may have a weaving quality (Figure A1.2). At the point of first contact, there may be a collision tire mark and, analogous to motor vehicle collisions, examination of the motorcycle tire may show a corresponding flat spot from skidding and tire damage secondary to direct impact.

Yawmark

A yawmark is a tire mark that results from a tire rotating and sliding at the same time. The sliding occurs at an angle to the vehicle's direction of motion. A yawmark occurs when a driver is attempting to turn the motor vehicle, hence yawmarks are curved (Figure A1.3). Generally the yawmarks arise from the outboard tires. Close inspection of the yawmark will reveal parallel striations at an angle different to the direction of travel (Figure A1.4). A yawmark tends to be thinner at the beginning and increase in width as loss of control worsens. The striations may become transverse if loss of control reaches such a point that the vehicle rotates into a "spin."

Figure A1.3 Yawmark from vehicle commencing in gravel (position of police officer). Two skidmarks from skid test to determine road surface friction.

Figure A1.4 Close-up of parallel striations in a yawmark.

Figure A1.5   Collision tire mark showing rapid alteration in direction of skidmark.

Collision Mark

A collision mark is a tire mark that occurs during the motor vehicle collision. The sudden application of significant force to the motor vehicle is transmitted through the tires, resulting in the abrupt appearance or alteration in the direction of tire marks. The collision mark is important as it may indicate the site of first contact, which is a significant factor in collision reconstruction analysis (Figure A1.5).

Acceleration Mark

An acceleration mark is a tire mark that occurs from a tire spinning on its axis. The acceleration mark is usually in a straight line. The characteristic

Figure A1.6   Acceleration mark showing characteristic abrupt, dark origin.

features of an acceleration mark are that it is dark at the beginning and becomes lighter as the mark continues (Figure A1.6). This is the opposite to what one sees with skidmarks. Acceleration marks are reasonably common on some roads and it is important not to confuse remote acceleration marks with skidmarks from the collision.

Flat Tire Mark

A flat tire mark is a tire mark that occurs from rapid deflation of a tire on the revolving wheel rim.

The revolving deflated tire results in the production of heat, which is most prominent over the wheel rims. The mark produced will therefore tend to be faint at the beginning and become stronger with distance travelled and will be pronounced at both parallel longitudinal edges of the tire. It can have the appearance of a series of scallops on the road (Figure A1.7).

Figure A1.7   Scalloped appearance of revolving deflated tire.

Rolling Print

Rolling prints are tire marks that are left by a tire rolling in a normal manner. The marks are usually visible through soft surfaces such as grass, sand, and dirt, but can be visible as a tire pattern through oil, water, or other fluid on the road surface.

Collision Debris

The distribution of collision debris is an important marker for the point of first contact in the incident.

The debris is produced at the time of the collision and hence the material will generally maintain its direction of motion. A somewhat "cone-shaped" region of debris will tend to point back a variable distance to the point of first contact. This distance depends on the characteristics of the collision including the speed of the vehicles involved. Small pieces of debris tend to move further than large pieces, although the actual distance travelled also depends on the nature and shape of the object (Figure A1.8).

Often the underbody dirt from a motor vehicle involved in a collision is immediately deposited at impact and can be seen on the road surface. The position and nature of the material (e.g., headlight or taillight glass) or underbody dirt may be of great importance in the analysis of a complex incident involving multiple vehicles and multiple impacts.

Figure A1.8   Collision debris some considerable distance from the vehicle in a "high-speed" collision with a pole.

Trace Evidence

Trace evidence is particularly important in hit run matters. The evidence gathered at the scene may often be the only indicator to successfully identify the vehicle involved. Trace evidence can include paint, plastic, glass, and other vehicle components, pieces of clothing, jewelry, and other material from victims related to the incident (Figure A1.9).

An important feature of interest at the scene is the colour of vehicle paint. A paint specimen can be analysed by the forensic science laboratory to determine class characteristics (i.e., characteristics that are common to a group of

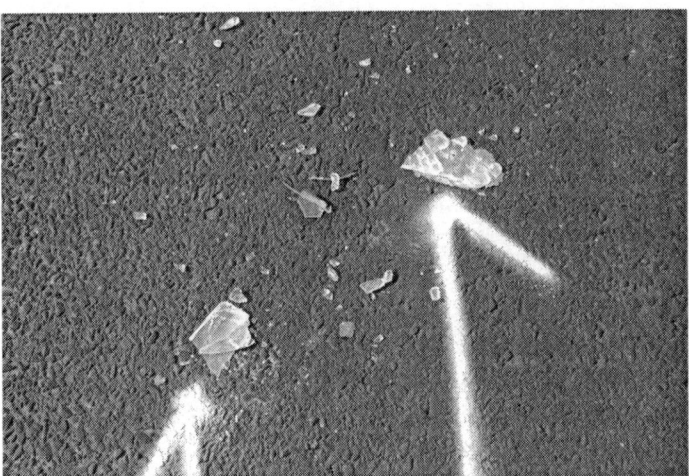

Figure A1.9   Pieces of glass at the scene of a hit-and-run pedestrian incident.

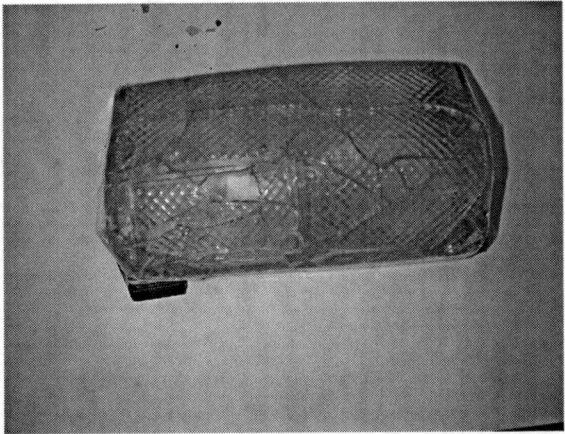

Figure A1.10   Reconstruction of indicator assembly from evidence recovered at the scene of a hit-and-run pedestrian death.

motor vehicles). Occasionally, individual characteristics may be identified by the forensic laboratory to allow positive identification to a particular vehicle in question.

Headlight and indicator glass can give class and sometimes individual characteristics, provided enough material is available for examination. Small fragments of headlight glass may suggest or identify the manufacturer of the vehicle concerned. Depending on the fragments of indicator material recovered, one may deduce the location of damage to the vehicle (Figure A1.10). If sufficient material is recovered such that reconstruction of the damaged item is possible, toolmark analysis of the exhibits may permit a definitive match to a suspect vehicle.

Gouge and Scrape Marks

Gouge and scrape marks refer to deep and superficial damage to the roadway from contact to the vehicle's undercarriage and other vehicle components. A broad surface of metal such as a panel tends to cause a shallow scuff mark, whereas deeper grooves are caused by projections such as bolts.

- Curved grooves suggest rotation by the vehicle (Figure A1.11).
- A variety of changes may be seen to the road surface from contact with parts of a motorcycle.
- Deep gouges occur from contact with hard metallic portions of the machine such as the foot stand.
- Rounded metallic guards and fiberglass may result in finer scratches to the road surface.

Figure A1.11   Point of first contact in a motor vehicle incident with tire marks and roadway scrapes.

Fluid Runoff

Deposits of oil, hydraulic fluid, and petrol tend to pool at the point of rest. The most common type of fluid run off is radiator fluid. The fluid flows to the lowest point and can fill gouge marks and obscure tire marks.

Point of Rest

The term *point of rest* refers to the final resting point of the motor vehicles involved in the incident, in addition to the bodies of pedestrians and occupants ejected from motor vehicles. Accurate documentation of the resting points of motor vehicles and pedestrians is important for accident reconstruction and estimation of speed.

Pedestrian Incidents — Evidence from the Roadway

The scene examination of a pedestrian incident needs to address a number of issues including, the point of impact, regions of the motor vehicle that came into contact with the pedestrian, speed of the vehicle, and any other factors that may have contributed to the incident.

Determination of the point of first contact may be difficult. This is primarily because of the massive difference between the mass of a motor vehicle and a human body, so the velocity of the motor vehicle will not be significantly altered as a consequence of impact. Scuff marks from the victim's shoes may be seen on the road surface. These marks can rapidly disappear in rainy weather. Skid marks produced during braking will tend to pass the point of first contact. In such instances, a slight increase in width of the skidmark may occur as a result of over deflection of the tire from the weight of the pedestrian on the vehicle.

The point of first contact may also be evaluated from the spread of headlight/indicator glass, flecks of paint, and plastic materials, although small pieces of material such as flecks of paint can be found a considerable distance from the point of first contact. The deposition of human tissue and blood on the roadway may also extend back toward the point of first contact.

References

1. Andrey J, Mills B, Leahy M, Suggett J. Weather as a chronic hazard for road transportation in Canadian cities. *Natural Hazards* 2003; 28:319–343.
2. Brodsky H, Hakkert AS. Risk of a road accident in rainy weather. *Accident Analysis and Prevention* 1988; 20:161–176.

3. Baker CJ, Reynolds S. Wind-induced accidents of road vehicles. *Accident Analysis and Prevention* 1992; 24:559–575.

4. Theeuwes J, Alferdinck J, Perel M. Relation between glare and driving performance. *Human Factors* 2002; 44:95–108.

5. White A, Warrick R, Baldock J. Treatment of black ice on a major freeway. Proceedings of the 21st ARRB and 11th REAAA Conference. Transport, Our Highway to a Sustainable Future, Cairns, Australia, May 2003.

6. Huebner RS, Anderson DA, Warner JC. Proposed design guidelines for reducing hydroplaning on new and rehabilitated pavements. *NCHRP Research Results Digest* 1999; 243.

Appendix 2

Motor Vehicle Examination

Exterior

The features of interest in the external examination of the motor vehicle include:

- Contact damage
- Induced damage
- Windshield damage
- Tire damage
- Headlight and tail light damage

Contact Damage

Contact damage to a motor vehicle refers to a change to the surface of the vehicle from direct contact/impact with an object in an incident. The object involved is usually another motor vehicle or a pedestrian, but may also be a street pole or tree. The spectrum of damage seen to the motor vehicle can range from minor paint transfer to various degrees of indentation and intrusion up to "separation" of the car.

Paint Transfer

Paint transfer can occur with various types of collisions ranging from minor sideswipes to severe head-on collisions. In minor tangential contact between

Figure A2.1 Transfer of paint from vehicle to vehicle.

motor vehicles, smears of paint may be deposited from one vehicle to another (Figure A2.1). Paint smears have directionality. The smear tends to be light and thin at the point of contact and become heavier along the direction of contact because of the production of heat and friction. Transfer may also occur from, and onto, the rubber of a tire and the clothing of a pedestrian. Less commonly, the pattern weave of a pedestrian's clothing may be imprinted to the paint surface or tire of a vehicle.[1,2]

The presence of recent paint transfer to a motor vehicle which is not explained by the involvement of the other known vehicles in the collision may suggest the involvement of another vehicle that left the scene.

Indentation

Indentation of the exterior surface of the motor vehicle is the most visually apparent manifestation of a collision. The position, nature, and degree of indentation can provide valuable information to the reconstruction of the incident and, after detailed measurements of the indentation, can also provide information regarding the speed of the vehicles at the time of the collision through accident reconstruction.

Impacts with light and electricity poles typically cause "rounded" indentations with a diameter approximating that of the causative object (Figure A2.2). Frontal contact with a pedestrian will result in a smaller frontal indentation and, depending on the speed of the vehicle, with adjacent deformation of the bonnet and damage to the windscreen and surrounds.

Rollover results in various degrees of vehicle body indentation and roof crush, paint loss and scrapes, transfer of road grime, gravel or grass, dirt, and other vegetation to the vehicle. There may be buckling of the A, B, and C pillars from impact to the roof and induced damage to other body panels.

Figure A2.2 Marked cabin intrusion with a side impact into a power pole.

Induced Damage

Induced damage refers to changes to the motor vehicle that occur as a consequence of direct damage at another location on the motor vehicle (Figure A2.3). For example, a high-speed impact to the right front corner panel of a motor vehicle will result in contact damage to this region of the vehicle, but

Figure A2.3 Induced damage to the right front panel associated with a left offset frontal impact.

may also cause folds in the sheet metal and body at another remote part of the vehicle through transmitted forces.

Windshield Damage

The front windshield is composed of laminated glass. Laminated glass consists of two layers of annealed glass on each side of a middle layer of thin plastic. The plastic material is a polyvinyl butyral polymer. Laminated glass may also be manufactured by pouring resin between two sheets of glass. Annealed glass refers to glass that has undergone a controlled cooling process during manufacture.[3] The glass fragments produced after impact have razor-sharp edges that can result in severe and potentially fatal incised and stab injuries to vehicle occupants after a collision.

The presence of the polyvinyl butyral polymer layer maintains the integrity of the glass preventing the formation of independent mobile shards of glass and contributes to occupant safety by providing additional protection from ejection from the vehicle.

Direct impact to laminated glass is easily recognizable. Blunt impact to laminated glass results in a "star pattern." Such damage to the glass windshield is most commonly seen with head impact from a pedestrian, but may also occur from contact with other objects such as a pedestrian's shoulders and hips (Figure A2.4).

Most vehicle side and rear windows are made from tempered glass. Tempered glass is heat-strengthened glass that is two to four times as strong as annealed glass.[3] The production of tempered glass causes significant internal stress to the glass. Blunt impact to tempered glass results in the glass shat-

Figure A2.4 Typical windshield damage from impact from the head of a pedestrian.

tering into innumerable small pieces. Tempered glass may shatter with minimal force if it has been previously damaged. Disintegration of the glass may then allow ejection of an unrestrained vehicle occupant. It has been demonstrated that the use of laminated glass in side windows results in less occupant ejection after impact to side windows.

Tire Damage

Inspection of a vehicle's tires after a collision may provide information with respect to the cause and dynamics of the collision. Rapid deflation of a tire and "blow out" are relatively uncommon but potentially significant factors in the causation of an incident. A blow out is classically caused by sudden failure in a tire that had been previously damaged or was showing significant wear (Figure A2.5). A blow out will leave typical tire marks on the road surface. These consist of a scalloping effect as the wheel rotates and causes the sidewalls to impact the road surface as the tire moves on the rim.

A tire that "blows out" from underinflation usually ruptures in the tire wall. If underinflation has been a longstanding problem, there may be associated discoloration to the tire wall at the point of maximum bending. Material fatigue may be evident from uneven dishevelled cord fibers at the damaged area of the tire.

Factors of interest in the examination of tires of a vehicle involved in a collision include the degree of inflation of the tire and the wear and integrity of the tread pattern. Information relevant to the dynamics of the incident include "flat spots," contact damage, and transfer of material onto the tire rubber. A skidmark left on the roadway during a motor vehicle incident by a particular vehicle may also result in an associated mark on the tires involved.

Figure A2.5   Partial tread separation due to excessive speed on a "retread" tire.

Figure A2.6 An extreme example of a flat spot on a tire from a high-speed skid test conducted in excess of 100 km/hr.

This will manifest as a "flat spot," a region of rubber loss with possible striation in the longitudinal axis of the tire (Figure A2.6). A yawmark left on the roadway will cause oblique to transverse striations to the tires involved.

Direct impact to a tire in an incident will produce marks to the tire surface often with associated damage to the wheel rim. Direct impact tends to result in radial damage to the periphery of the rim, which extends toward the axle. Because the inflated tire can absorb a significant amount of energy from a direct impact, the presence of adjacent tire and rim damage indicates the application of a large amount of force to the wheel. Damage to wheel rims may also be caused by sliding on the paved surface leading to scratching around the circumference of the outer edge of the rim, particularly if the wheel was rotating. Impact with a gutter leaves a tell-tale sign of concrete dust visible on the rim or tire.

Headlights and Tail Lights

Examination of headlights and tail lights may provide important information on the collision and the subsequent reconstruction. The examination may determine whether a vehicle's lights were functioning at the time of the incident, whether the high or low beam was operating, and, in some cases, whether the brakes were employed.

Halogen lamps are composed of a tightly coiled, arched, or straight tungsten filament or filaments bonded between two steel wire supports. Individual lamps may incorporate more than one function. Headlights may have high and low beam functions, whereas tail lights may include rearlight

Figure A2.7   Lamp showing discolored glass and deformed filament.

and brake functions. The filament assembly is encased within a quartz or heat-resistant glass bulb that contains a halogenated gas. Operation of the lamp results in the filament heating to a temperature of about 1500°F, which causes the filament to glow.

The damage caused to a lamp during a collision is highly dependent on a number of factors, including whether the lamp was operating at or just before the collision, whether the glass bulb was broken during the crash, the characteristics of the collision, and preimpact condition of the lamp. If the lamp was operating around the time of the crash, the filament would be extremely hot and tend to bend in the direction of the impact. The degree of deformation is related to the heat and change in velocity during the collision.

If the operating filament is broken during the crash, the fractured ends of the filament will tend to have a rounded or blunted appearance. When the bulb is broken while operating, the tungsten filament will rapidly oxidize, leading to the deposition of colored tungsten oxides on the inner aspect of the bulb and immediately adjacent regions of the vehicle (Figure A2.7).[4] It is important to note that similar oxidation will occur if a lamp with a broken bulb is turned on. Because of the very high temperatures involved in the operation of lamps, when the bulb is broken during operation microscopic and macroscopic droplets of glass may be deposited on the filament.

Pedestrian Incidents—Evidence from the Motor Vehicle

The damage sustained to a motor vehicle in a pedestrian incident varies with respect to the speed involved in the incident, the type of vehicle involved, and the position on the vehicle where the pedestrian was struck. The evidence from the motor vehicle may be scanty, consisting of paint transfer, retained fibers of clothing or the deposition of blood or human tissue.

Contact damage will be seen where the motor vehicle impacts the upright pedestrian (Figure A2.8). Examination of the motor vehicle may reveal broken headlights/indicator lights, fascia, and grill components. Indentation may be evident when the passenger has been scooped upward onto the hood. In the

Figure A2.8   Blood and tissue from pedestrian victim to bumper and light assembly of motor vehicle.

absence of indentation, one may see longitudinal scratches from contact with clothing or deposition of clothing pigment. One may also observe imprints and transfer of clothing and dye to the vehicle bumper, hood, or roof.

The windshield may show typical stellate fractures from contact with the pedestrian's head, shoulders, or other body part. There may be deposition of hair, blood, and tissue on the glass surface and within glass fractures. A further common site or deposition of human tissue and clothing is the window frame. In high-speed incidents, damage to the vehicle, transfer of paint, and deposit of human tissue may be seen over the roof and trunk of the motor vehicle. In runover incidents, tissue may be recovered from the vehicle undercarriage, often on projections such as bolts, and within wheel wells (Figure A2.9).

Figure A2.9   Human tissue in wheel well in a runover incident.

Interior

Interior vehicle damage can often be associated with the distribution of driver and passenger injuries. The laminated glass of the windshield can show damage from contact by an occupant or from material within the cabin. Contact from an occupant may result in deposit of blood, hair, or other body tissue.

Damage to the dashboard and fascia, sides of doors, steering wheel, floor pan, and pedals may be seen.

Detection of a suspect's DNA within the cabin of a motor vehicle in which the suspect denies any previous contact is of obvious interest to the investigators and courts in a criminal or civil case. Experiments have shown that the DNA from the individual who last handled an object will tend to preferentially deposit over those who previously handled the object.[5] Thus the last person to drive a motor vehicle will tend to preferentially deposit their DNA on the vehicle's steering wheel.

Contact with interior structures some distance from the occupant's seat may raise the possibility that the seat belt was not worn, although studies with anthropomorphic dummies have shown significant movement of vehicle occupants still occurs during collisions even when seat belts are worn.

Restraint System Examination

The seat belt is composed of a woven nylon or polyester fabric webbing finished with selvages. The webbing extends through an oval guide called a D-ring, which is usually attached to the B pillar, although some seat belts are incorporated into the seat. Some D-rings are made of plastic, whereas others have a plastic coating. The belt locks into a retractor of which there are a number of different types. The emergency locking retractor relies on an inertial sensor to lock the retractor and prevent the belt spooling out when sudden deceleration is detected. These are most effective in collisions in the longitudinal plane; however, spool out has been noted to occur in rollover incidents.[6] The vehicle sensitive retractor detects deceleration in all directions and is not subject to spool out during a rollover.

Pretensioner devices take up excess webbing as may occur when an individual is out of normal position at the time of the collision or when wearing bulky clothing. A sensor detects the change in velocity immediately after the collision and fires an explosive charge that takes up the slack in the seat belt so that the individual is held firmly in the seat.

The general examination of the seat belt in an older vehicle may show wearing consistent with a history of compliance with seat belt use. It is very uncommon for the seat belt to fail during the collision; most seat belt defects occur from paramedics cutting the belt to attend the victim. In these cases, the clean straight edge to the damaged region is characteristic. Occasionally, a belt will fail and show frayed, feathery edges. In difficult cases, microscopic or electron microscopic examination at the forensic laboratory is usually conclusive.

The presence of blood or other human tissue over the length of the belt suggests it was extended and in place during the incident. Examination of the belt webbing may reveal abraded or melted material from contact with the D-ring from the forces applied to the belt in a severe collision.[7]

The lap belt webbing may show deposition of seat material from contact with the edge of the seat. Further signs of belt loading may be seen from interaction of the webbing with the occupant's chest and shoulder, and the metallic tongue section of the shoulder belt. Loading from the chest may cause transfer of skin or clothing fabric. The position of these load marks may also provide information on the performance of the retractor system. Examination of attachment points of the belt to the motor vehicle may show bending and buckling.

Detailed examination of the retractor systems requires removal of the devices and expert laboratory examination. In a severe impact, the retracting mechanism often locks and it is easy to determine whether a restraint had been worn, even after it has been cut for rescue.

Airbag Examination

The various airbags within the motor vehicle should be examined to verify deployment and correlated with the principal direction of force applied to the vehicle. It should be noted that current frontal airbags have two possible deployment events, so that airbags may deploy during the first, less serious collision in a multiple incident crash, before the most severe part of the collision.

Swabs can be taken from the surface of a deployed airbag to provide objective evidence regarding the seating positions of the occupants in a motor vehicle collision.[5] Recent studies have demonstrated recovery of DNA from the surface of airbags that deployed after a collision. The recovery of DNA was demonstrated from driver and passenger airbags from recognizable human stains and from random swabs. However, contamination of unrelated DNA was also demonstrated in a number of cases. This was believed to have arisen from ambulance or police personnel or even during the manufacturing process.[8]

Mechanical Issues

A qualified mechanic may be required to examine the various motor vehicles with respect to appropriate maintenance, suspected defects and defective repairs (e.g., substandard welds). The most common issues of vehicle maintenance that can contribute to a crash are inadequate tire tread depth, under-inflated tires, worn brake pads, and insufficient vehicle fluids. The mechanic can offer an opinion as to the cause of component failure (e.g., a consequence of the impact, fatigue, or faulty production or maintenance).

References

1. Drummond FC, Pizzola PA. An unusual case involving the individualisation of a clothing impression on a motor vehicle. *Journal of Forensic Sciences* 1990; 35:746–752.

2. Kuppuswamy R, Ponnuswamy PK. Note on fabric marks in motor vehicle collisions. *Science and Justice* 2000; 40:45–47.

3. Sances A Jr, Carlin FH, Kumaresan S, Enz B. Biomedical engineering analysis of glass impact injuries. *Critical Reviews in Biomedical Engineering* 2002; 30:345–377.

4. Baker JS, Lindquist TL. Lamp examination for on off in traffic accidents. Evanston, IL: Traffic Institute, Northwestern University, 1972.

5. Lowe A, Murray C, Whitaker J, Tully G, Gill P. The propensity of individuals to deposit DNA and secondary transfer of low level DNA from individuals to inert surfaces. *Forensic Science International* 2002; 129:25–34.

6. Meyer SE, Hock D, Forrest S, Herbst B, Sances A Jr, Kumaresan S. Motor vehicle seatbelt restraint system analysis during rollover. *Biomechanical Sciences Instrumentation* 2003; 437:229–240.

7. Gorski ZM, German A, Nowak ES. Examination and analysis of seat belt loading marks. *Journal of Forensic Sciences* 1990; 35:69–79.

8. Grubwieser P, Pavlic M, Gunther M, Rabl W. Airbag contact in traffic accidents: DNA detection to determine the driver identity. *International Journal of Legal Medicine* 2004; 118:9–13.

Appendix 3

Collision Reconstruction

Overview

The collision reconstructionist is an expert police investigator or engineer trained in the interpretation of a motor vehicle incident scene and provides an independent, objective analysis of the sequence of events that culminated in the collision and its aftermath. The reconstructionist evaluates the scene evidence leading up to the collision, the position, type and degree of damage to the vehicles, and postcollision movements of vehicles, pedestrians, and other victims.

At the completion of the examination, the collision reconstruction expert can provide scientific evidence that can corroborate or refute the testimonies of witnesses to the incident.

Precollision Evaluation

The precollision analysis includes assessment of a number of different factors including vehicle positions, preimpact velocities, human factors, and road and weather conditions.

Skidmarks indicate the position and direction of a vehicle and can also provide information on the vehicle's velocity. Simple equations can estimate minimum velocity from the length of skidmarks. The calculated velocity is a minimum velocity and less than true velocity, as time elapses and velocity decreases from the time the driver releases the throttle and engages the brake, and the significant braking that occurs up to the point of wheel lock up.

The presence of yawmarks indicates a situation in which a vehicle's tires are slipping and rotating and point to the driver having lost control and is moving sideways with respect to the desired direction of travel. The accurate measurement of yawmark length and radius can yield information on vehicle velocity. The radius can be derived from a calculation after chord and middle ordinate measurements of the yawmark are taken at the scene or with the assistance of computer drafting software.

Roadway geometry issues may include horizontal and vertical curvature, the designated speed limit for the prevailing conditions, intersection and lane merge designs, traffic signals and signs, debris or water on the road, and other road hazards. Because the incident may have commenced some distance proximal to the actual collision point, it is important to assess an adequate length of roadway. A particularly deep step between the bitumen surface and the gravel shoulder of the roadway could have caused a driver to lose control of the motor vehicle some considerable distance from the actual collision point before the production of yawmarks and skidmarks.

In motorcycle incidents, the determination of preimpact velocity is difficult. The slide distance of the motorcycle, or resting point of the riders, can be used in a variety of calculations. Slide distance of a motorcycle after an incident is associated with a number of variables, including episodes of vaults and spins with variation in secondary contact points with the road surface. Estimation of speed from resting points of the riders has been performed using assumed trajectories, although such assumptions may not be valid. In some cases frontal impact of the front wheel of the motorcycle can cause a vault action from the rear of the machine. Damage analysis of the motorcycle has been attempted, but the marked variation in contact between the machine and other vehicles seriously question its accuracy.

If witness statements suggest tire failure as a cause or contributing factor to the collision, the investigator can correlate the presence or absence of typical tire marks with the damage to the vehicle's tires and rims. The investigator can liaise with mechanics to address the issue of brake, steering, suspension, or other vehicle component failure.

Collision Evaluation

The analysis of the collision environment and vehicle damage includes the point of first contact in the incident, the principal direction of the force of impact, and the consequences of collision to vehicles, occupants, and pedestrians. Examination of the roadway for collision tire marks, scrapes and gouges, scuff marks, and collision debris is important to determine the first contact point.

The position of the point of first contact can serve as an indicator as to which vehicle was at fault in a crash. When the point of contact is on one side of the road in a two-car, head-on collision, it may suggest one of the vehicles crossed onto the wrong side of the road before impact. The absence of skidmarks from the target vehicle may indicate that the bullet vehicle crossed quickly into the wrong lane. Frontal impact to the target vehicle may suggest the driver had no time to attempt any evasive action, whereas an oblique offset frontal impact to the target vehicle may indicate attempted evasive action. The direction of the impact forces and position of the collision site must be correlated with all of the available scene information.

The principal direction of force causing contact damage to a motor vehicle is correlated with the contact damage to other vehicles involved in the collision. The principal direction of force should be readily explicable when related to the precollision directions and post-impact trajectories. Because most motor vehicle collisions do not pass through each vehicle's center of mass, the vehicles will be subject to varying degrees of rotation around their center of mass. The change in velocity and rotation will depend on the initial velocity and mass of the respective vehicles.

The amount of damage to a vehicle is also dependant on the region that is impacted and the stiffness of the vehicle. The same impact velocity to the front of a vehicle will cause considerably less damage than an identical impact to the side or rear of the vehicle. Furthermore some vehicles such as sports utility vehicles are inherently stiffer than others.

Postcollision Evaluation

The postcollision examination includes the documentation and analysis of postcollision trajectories, distance traveled after impact, and the resting positions of vehicles and incident victims. The rest positions should be consistent with the postcollision trajectories, the damage patterns to the vehicles, and preimpact velocities.

The examination of the scene and vehicles may reveal direct damage to a vehicle's wheels, which may be free-turning or remain locked from the impact damage. Damaged and locked wheels increase frictional forces between the tire and the road and have consequences in the determination of preimpact velocity.

Collision Reconstruction

Several computer software programs are available to investigators to assist in a reconstruction of the collision. The programs can simulate single and multiple vehicle collisions with various types of vehicles (e.g., passenger car, sport utility vehicles, heavy trucks) and fixed objects. They provide an estimate of delta V based on vehicle damage and scene measurements. Most systems use conservation of linear momentum, damage analysis and established crush stiffness coefficients, and conservation of energy methods. The programs can allow trajectory simulations and different environmental and vehicle conditions.

Some software programs provide time versus distance estimates for pedestrians or vehicles and can provide information regarding visibility between different objects with respect to time and distance. Other products furnish information on vehicle occupant or pedestrian kinematics during a collision.

The principal concepts in relation to the physics of motor vehicle collisions are the following.

Damage Analysis

The analysis of damage to a vehicle can be used to estimate impact velocity (delta V). The linear relationship between residual vehicle crush and delta V in wide contact collisions was originally detailed in a number of articles from the late 1960s. The inception of these programs was as a research tool in the evaluation, testing, and implementation of safety systems. Later reviews suggested confidence limits in estimated delta V ranged from 9 to 25%. The accuracy of the these computer programs were directly related to the crush stiffness coefficients employed.[1] More extensive crash test results are now available on a larger range of vehicles for frontal, offset frontal, and side impact collisions, including side impact pole tests.

Government and industry sources provide information on stiffness coefficients of different motor vehicles. Cars have different degrees of stiffness at different points. For example, a side-impact collision may involve the door, or the side of a wheel which has a significantly increased stiffness profile.

The damage analysis is performed by measuring the amount of contact damage to a vehicle. The indentation is measured from the normal preimpact position of the deformed metal, usually at up to six equal points across the area of damage. The measurements may be done manually or with electronic measuring equipment. Vehicles which have considerable longitudinal bowing distortion have an additional bowing constant applied to the measurements. This constant is derived from the normal preimpact position of the sheet metal of the vehicle, compared to the distorted or bowed shape. The bowing constant serves to allow for the energy expended in deforming the metal, which is separate from the area of intrusion.

Conservation of Momentum

The Law of Conservation of Momentum states that the total momentum of a system before a collision is equal to the total momentum after the collision. Momentum is a vector with a direction and a magnitude.

Momentum (p) = velocity (m/s) × mass (kg)

The law can be expressed as a simple equation for a two-vehicle colinear collision:

$$M1V1 + M2V2 = M1V1' + M2V2'$$

where M1 = mass of first vehicle, V1 = velocity of first vehicle, M2 = mass of second vehicle, V2 = velocity of second vehicle, and V1' = postimpact velocity of first vehicle, and V2' = postimpact velocity of second vehicle.

Any loss of momentum by one vehicle in a collision is gained by the other vehicle. Because the masses of the vehicles are constant, there are corresponding changes in velocity. Conservation of linear momentum is used to determine the impact velocity of motor vehicles in a collision, and hence the severity of the collision. As noted previously, momentum is a vector and the preimpact and postimpact directions must be solved in the analysis.

Conservation of Energy Analysis

The first law of thermodynamics states that energy must be conserved in a system. Before a motor vehicle collision, two moving vehicles will possess kinetic energy. The kinetic energy (KE) is directly related to the vehicle's mass (m) and the square of the velocity (v) by the equation:

$$KE = \frac{1}{2} mv^2.$$

Kinetic energy is converted into work during a collision with residual crush damage to the vehicles (plastic deformation), skidding, and braking. A relatively small amount of energy is converted into the work of vibration, heat, and restitution (elastic deformation). If the crush damage of the vehicles is calculated, and the postimpact trajectories, deceleration, and positions of rest are known, then the preimpact velocities can be determined.

Pedestrian Collisions

Pedestrian incidents that result in serious injury or death are challenging cases. When skidmarks are present, an estimation of the preimpact velocity may be performed. A very rough guide to vehicle speed is indicated by the position of impact to the vehicle's hood or windshield by the victim's head or shoulder. An estimation of vehicle speed can be achieved from an analysis of the throw distance of the pedestrian victim. An equation derived by Searle in the early 1980s provides a good approximation of vehicle speed from total distance covered by the pedestrian following impact.

The total throw distance includes the distance the victim is thrown through the air and the distance covered whilst sliding, bouncing, or rolling over the surface of the road, grass, ground, or concrete. This distance may well be complicated by the victim being carried forward on the hood of a conventional passenger car for some distance before being ejected.

A preliminary study by Ademac using a computer simulation model showed that "a relatively small alteration of the initial pedestrian position and/or car braking onset can result in a significant difference in pedestrian kinematics and thus a different injury pattern." The throw distance varied some 5 meters depending on whether or not the car braked before impact with the pedestrian. The longer "throw distance" was achieved by the car braking after impact as the pedestrian was then carried a significant distance from the vehicle's hood. A study by Simms showed that the distribution of predicted collision speeds could be large when a high degree of confidence was required.[2]

References

1. Neptune JA, Blair GY, Flynn JE. *A method for quantifying vehicle crush stiffness coefficients.* SAE Paper 920607, International Congress and Exposition; Detroit, MI; February 1994.

2. Simms CK, Wood DP, Walsh DG. Confidence limits for impact speed estimation from pedestrian projection distance. *International Journal of Crashworthiness* 2004; 9:219–230.

Additional Reading

Adamec J, Schonpflug M. *The pedestrian kinematics variation due to different initial pedestrian positions and braking conditions.* University of Munich, Germany: Institute for Legal Medicine; 2003.

Noon RK. *Engineering analysis of vehicular accidents.* Boca Raton, FL: CRC Press; 1994.

Sergeant BP. Project Y.A.M. *Yaw analysis methodology.* Victoria, Australia: Victoria Police. Accident Investigation Section, SAE Paper 970995.

Index

X

X-rays, *see* Radiographic imaging

Y

Yawmarks
 precollision evaluation, 198
 roadway evidence, 176–177
 and tire damage, 190

Yellow signal lights, short, 25
Young classification of pelvic fractures,
 94
Younger drivers, 28
Young male drivers, 25, 26

Z

Zygomaticomaxillary fractures,
 78